SISTERS

SISTERS

Jackie Callas

St. Martin's Press
New York

Library of Congress Cataloging-in-Publication Data

Callas, Jackie.
     Sisters : a revealing portrait of the world's most famous diva /
    Jackie Callas.
          p.   cm.
     ISBN 0-312-03934-4
     1. Callas, Maria, 1923-1977. 2. Singers—Biography. I. Title.
ML420.C18C32   1990
782.1'092—dc20
   [B]   89-27042
                                               CIP
                                             MN

First published in Great Britain by Macmillan London Limited.

First U.S. Edition

10 9 8 7 6 5 4 3 2 1

CONTENTS

PART ONE   Sisters   1

PART TWO   The Sister   133

PART THREE   Myself   219

Appendix   241

Picture Acknowledgments   249

PART ONE
Sisters

CHAPTER ONE
September 1977

'Your sister,' the man said, pushing open the heavy door to the darkened room. He half bowed so that I would have to pass in front of him.

He had told me his name but in the rush of images – the grandeur of the entrance with its arched portico and heavy brass lantern, the *fer-forgé* lift and the polished double doors – I had instantly forgotten it. I had been told that he was something between a butler and a chauffeur and, being unused to such grand servants, I kept my eyes on his respectful expression as I squeezed past him. It was only when he repeated the words that I turned and saw her.

'Your sister,' he said again in a hushed, reverential tone. I instinctively thanked him and, with the same force of habit, raised the index and second finger of my right hand to my forehead to commence the triple cross of the Orthodox faith. Only when I had made this sign did I turn to look at her. My mind echoed the words 'your sister' as if to reassure myself that the figure laid on the bed really had some connection with me. How beautiful she looked, too beautiful to be part of my memories – death plays such tricks. Some age or look pained but in death she had lost all sign of suffering. She was the sister who had never been; the face and the body were self-created, were never like that in youth. Now they had become young, she was the Mary Callas she had always wanted to be.

'Mary,' I said and stopped. She could not hear and no one there would ever have used that name. And then I realised that there was someone sitting beside the bed. She must have had her head down before but now she sat upright and stared searchingly at me, her face puffy and red with crying. I guessed that she must be Bruna the maid and I knew with a shudder of discomfort that whereas I felt the dull

3

ache of one who has lost someone no longer close, she was mourning deeply. She rose, came round the bed, bobbed a curtsy and held out her hand for me to shake.

'Madame Callas,' she said, staring long and hard. '*Votre pauvre soeur.*' And then she turned away and began crying again.

I knew why she had stared so hard. Did I look like her mistress? What of the dead Callas remained in the living? I too went over to see and knew again that there was little. No, we were not alike. Not now, not then.

'A chair, madame?'

The man was placing one behind me and I obediently sat on it.

'Coffee, madame?'

I shook my head. I didn't want to take anything. Mary had never invited me to her home, to this beautiful apartment, why should I take her coffee now?

I looked at her again. It still seemed impossible that she was my sister. Even after all the photographs, even after our last meeting in Athens, it still seemed impossible that that slim figure, that beautiful angular face could really be Mary Callas, dumpy Mary Callas, spotty Mary Callas stuffing her face with food before hurrying off to high school in Washington Heights. Now her hair was beautiful, her hands so long and fine – they were crossed, palms uppermost, the same gesture she used when receiving applause and I wondered if they had fallen naturally into that position or whether the person who had arranged her body had done it intentionally. Oh yes, she was very beautiful. She had had everything in the end. I had been the beautiful one, I was the sister who would marry. Mary, dumpy, fat-legged Mary, would sing. Now there I was, sixty and unmarried and there was Mary, one of the most famous women in the world, married, divorced, the victim of one of the most famous affairs of all time. It was unfair. Then I told myself I was being ridiculous, how could I feel like that? Had she been happy? What did it mean, this apartment with its high windows looking out on to the Avenue, the heavy drapes, the antique furniture? I knew what it meant: she told me whenever she telephoned it was a gilded prison. No, I was right: Maria Callas was not Mary Callas. Mary Callas had died years before. What I was looking at was *La Traviata* – she looked like the dead Violetta, that same ethereal, consumptive beauty. *La Traviata*, the first opera we ever saw. Who can believe it after all that happened, after she became *the Traviata*? Athens 1938, the Lyric

4

Theatre and Milton got tickets for Mother, Mary and me. Mireille Fleurie was Violetta, the first diva for Mary to model herself on. Fleurie was typical of her time, a little overweight for the part but with a good rich voice. At that time singing was more important than acting and that performance was everything that opera had been before my sister. My sister. My dead sister. I swallowed as I felt the tears rising. That memory of our young days had brought back the real Mary so that I knew at last that the Maria lying there was after all my sister. They had put on her make-up, her hair was spread out, there was no crucifix, no flowers or candles, nothing to distract from her performance. She was Violetta, she was *playing* dead. Even dead she performed the rôle better than anyone could. I lowered my head and said a prayer for her soul. I asked God to forgive what she had done to me.

When I opened my eyes I half expected to find myself back in Athens, back in my room, awakening from my siesta. The phone had rung. I had heard it ringing from a long way away, ringing in my sleep so that I was sure it was part of a dream. What dream is this? I asked myself, anticipating something interesting and I examined the dream for any signs of familiar territory, but there were none. I was nowhere and the phone was ringing. Half awake I reached for it and something told me it was Mary calling again. Last week she had talked for an hour, rambling lonely talk. Was this to be another sad session? I was not prepared for a man's voice speaking in French, even though he spoke with forced slowness so that I could follow. He said his name was Jean Roire and then he came straight to the point. '*Votre soeur est morte.*'

I tried to grasp at the words '*soeur*' and '*morte*'. Tossing them around between French, English and Greek. *Sister. Dead.*

'*Que dites-vous? Elle est morte?*'

He said it again with every word pronounced as if in capitals. 'YOUR SISTER IS DEAD.'

My sister. What sister? Mary Callas, little Mary Callas. No. My sister Maria, my beautiful, successful sister Maria Callas, the most famous diva of all time. Is that the sister he means?

'At half past one,' he said. 'I regret . . .'

Hearing the conversation the canaries in their room next to mine joined in with a song. We had always had canaries. Mary loved them; she said she learned more about singing from them than from anything else. They sang a song for her now.

5

M. Roire was asking if I was still there, was I still on the line, had I understood what he had said? I told him I had, though that was hardly the case. I had understood the words, the sense was another matter. He explained that he was a friend of Vasso's, though that meant even less to me.

'Vasso is in Athens,' he said, 'otherwise she would be speaking to you herself.'

This was nonsense, I was in Athens so why couldn't she speak to me? In any case, who was she and why did he assume I would know her?

'Vasso wants you to be at the funeral. Sunday. You must come.'

'Paris? Oh I don't think . . .'

'But you are the sister. You must be here. I have arranged everything. You must come.'

I was the sister of Maria Callas and they wanted me there? I turned that information over in my mind. Mary had never invited me, never wanted me with her, never asked me to stay in the apartment that the world's press had so lovingly described in all its splendour. Now I was to go at the behest of the dead Maria, for I was the sister.

M. Roire clearly assumed that he had convinced me. He asked me to get a pen and paper and I meekly obeyed. He gave me the time of a flight the following morning and told me I would be met.

'I will have the pleasure of seeing you tomorrow even though the circumstances . . .' he sighed. 'A demain.'

And I weakly agreed that I would see him demain.

As soon as I put the phone down panic struck – a jumble of terrible difficulties and dangers swirled into a tight knot: there was Mother, Mother to be told, Mother to be taken care of. All she ever thought of was Mary, Mary the beloved daughter she was never allowed to see. It was impossible. How could I tell her? I looked at the bedside clock: it was just after four. Mother would sleep till six then take a coffee. I could delay telling her till then. But other terrors added to my distress: I had no passport, it was being renewed; I had no money and it was Friday and the banks were closed till Monday; I had never been to Paris before; I had no clothes for a funeral. But my sister was dead and I was the sister. I had a little weep for us both.

The canaries were singing loudly again. I got up and opened the door to their room and went over to their cages. How beautiful they were, how well they sang, such force. I remembered a passage from

Un Ballo in Maschera, my favourite piece, the one I had sung at my last concert:

Deh mi reggi, m'aita, o Signor . . .

What was I going to do? How was I going to get to Paris? I was alone and I had to make my own decisions. If Milton had been alive he would have dealt with it all but I was as alone as I had been before Mary was born, the only child: Yacinthy, Hyacinth, Jackie . . .

Even in September it was warm. I went out on to my terrace, my secret garden with its pine tree and flowers in tubs, my private heaven. I looked over to Mount Parnis, at its distant church, at the Greek flag trying to flutter in the limp afternoon air. Dr Lanzounis, Maria's American godfather, had loved my terrace when he came to visit. He told Mary about it.

'Godfather told me you have a beautiful garden,' she said when she phoned.

I was going to say that she should come and see it for herself but I knew there was no point.

'I can't sleep,' she said, her usual complaint. 'You'll send me some more of the pills, yes?'

I said I would. She couldn't get Mandrax in France, they were illegal. She asked me to get them from Bekas the chemist but only after I'd checked there would be no problem because of her eyes.

And then I saw what I could do. Maybe Mr Bekas could help me again. I quickly dressed and went down to his shop.

'Miss Calogeropoulou,' he said. 'And how are you, and your sister's glaucoma? Better?'

For a moment I was lost for words. How to say it? How to tell him that Maria Callas, the most famous Greek since classical antiquity, had just died? No, there was no way to say it reasonably. No way at all.

'What is the matter?' he asked, coming up and getting hold of my arms. 'Are you unwell? Here, come and sit down.'

I let him guide me to a chair, suddenly too weak to resist. I sipped the water he gave me.

'Mary – Maria – is dead.'

He crossed himself and said something sympathetic but I only wanted practical advice.

'I have to go to Paris,' I said in a rush. 'And my passport has been

sent to be renewed and I don't know what to do and then there's
Mother and . . .'

He said soothing things to ease the rush of words. 'Money? Don't
worry, I'll lend you what you need and tomorrow we'll go round to
the passport office as early as we can. Bring your case with you, then
you can go straight to the airport.'

It was as if Milton were back. Everything done for me, someone to
work it all out so that I just had to do as I was told. I gave him my
thank-you look. Now I would have to go and tell Mother.

Out in the street I could barely force myself to walk the few blocks
from Kallinikou to her apartment. I had been less afraid when the
Germans had patrolled these streets, less frightened of what was to
come when the communists had fought their way across these same
crossroads in the civil war. She had never disguised her adoration of
Mary: Mary the beloved daughter at whose side she would know
glory, Mary who would free her from the trap of her bourgeois
marriage, Mary who would let the world know that it was her
mother, the still beautiful Evangelia, who had made all these
wonderful things possible. Mary and Mother. And Jackie? Ah
well . . .

Even when Mary threw her aside nothing changed. Mary would
one day return. Inevitably the letter, the call, the knock on the door
would reverse the nightmare of exclusion. Now I would knock on the
door, now I, Jackie, the other sister, would finally shatter the dream.
How could I do it?

I had dawdled so much it was just past six o'clock. The city was
coming to after its siesta, there was movement in the shops, people
settling down to little cups of strong coffee at the pavement tables, a
noise of traffic from the main streets. I went up to her apartment,
knocked and let myself in. I had imagined her seated with her coffee
enjoying a cigarette. I had tried to work out how I would break my
news and had decided to just let it happen. I had forgotten about the
television. She had recently taken to watching the six o'clock news
when she woke up and I found her slumped in her chair staring at the
screen. When she heard me walk up she turned and her face
contorted into a mask of grief.

'They said . . . they said . . .'

I realised at once what had happened. Of course they would have
begun the news with the stupendous announcement of Mary's
death. Even then, a good five minutes into the programme, there

8

were still people on the screen talking about her. A professor of music was recounting what she meant in the history of opera.

Mother was shaking hysterically. 'They said she was dead . . . our girl is dead.'

I got a hold of her. 'They phoned me,' I said. 'They told me she died about half past one. They want me to go to Paris. For the funeral.'

Mother waved this away. It was irrelevant. *I* was irrelevant. The only reality was her own sense of deprivation. She had been cheated of all she had yearned for since Maria was a child. She slumped back in the chair again. There was a knock at the door and her sisters, my Aunts Kakia and Pepitsa, came hurrying in, urgent with pity. The three were soon hugging and sobbing and I withdrew to one side and tried to see what was happening on the television – an extract of Maria in *Tosca*; eyes blazing, she advances, the knife concealed behind her back, she raises it and stabs Tito Gobbi. The kiss of Tosca. Catching sight of her, Mother let out a terrible moan as if she and not Scarpia had been assassinated. 'Maria, Maria, Maria.'

I went to the kitchen. The shutters were drawn and I sat in quiet solitude. I like to be alone, not that I've had much choice, but at least it hasn't bothered me. In the fourteen years since Milton had died I had got very accustomed to being alone with my thoughts. Happily I have music in my head, I can remember whole operas to while away the hours.

Pace, pace mio Dio; pace mio Dio!

Father, Father, Father in Heaven, grant me peace of mind!
Cruel misfortune
Has doomed my life to grief.
Every day I suffer
And never find relief . . .

Che l'amo ancor, ne togliermi dal core
I love him still, ah how could I forget him . . .

Aunt Pepitsa came in to see if there was any brandy. 'It will do her good. And you too, eh?'

I shook my head. I was all right really. What did it mean to me after all? A stranger had died. Oh, yes, we'd spoken recently but then I'd spoken to Bekas as often when I went to get her tablets. It was odd to think that when Milton died I hadn't been allowed to go to the funeral; it wouldn't have been appropriate for me to be there with his family and yet he had loved me. Now I was to be whisked to Paris to be there when they buried a sister who had ceased to love me uncountable years ago.

'Life is not just,' I said.

Pepitsa stopped her riffling through the cupboards and gave me a quizzical look. 'Are you sure you won't have a brandy if I find some?'

'No,' I said. 'There's some in the cupboard up there on the left.'

She thanked me. 'You'll have to stay with her tonight,' she announced.

I nodded. It was always my task to take care of her when everyone else had gone. I dreaded the thought of it. I doubted she would sleep. She would turn it all over in her mind, dredging up every grievance, every wasted year away from her precious daughter and I knew with a sickening certainty that she would gradually transform the whole matter until it somehow became my fault. I, Jackie, would, by morning, be to blame for my sister's death, would be guilty of being alive when the beloved was no more.

I stayed in the kitchen, even when the light went and darkness engulfed me, stayed quite still until my aunts announced they were going.

'Sitting in the dark?' Kakia said. 'Not upset are we? Well, I suppose you must be. You were very close, weren't you? I remember she used to worship you. The beautiful Jackie. Always wanted to be like you, no?'

I followed them into the living-room and saw them out.

'Why didn't you phone me as soon as you heard?' Mother's litany began. 'Leaving me to find out from the television, to hear about your own daughter's death like that. But then nobody cares, do they? I might as well have no children.'

I sat down opposite her and let her work the venom out of her system. She was so hysterical there was no question of her accompanying me to Paris.

Early the next morning, I hurried back to my own apartment, impatient as the lift crawled slowly to the fifth floor. I hastily searched through my clothes though I had had ample time to work out just what of my very limited wardrobe I would need to take. Having something practical to do helped divorce my mind from the memory of Mother's tearful barrage, the stream of misery that had continued until three that morning. Listening to it with half an ear I had already calculated that all I had was a black skirt and white blouse, the only things suitable for a funeral. I folded them into a small case, gathered up my make-up and cleaning things and finished my little packing. Then, carefully folding a raincoat over my arm, I set off for Bekas' shop. He was waiting for me and we went straight to Kolliatzou Square and took a taxi to the passport office near Ommonia. Normally the bored official at the desk would have made us wait an age but Bekas had a friend in the organisation and he had grandly announced just who was coming.

The man came over and clasped both my hands. 'The sister of Callas,' he said, clearly awestruck. 'My profound condolences on this sad occasion. Permit me to convey the respects of everyone here. We have prepared everything for you.'

He reached out his hand and another man placed a passport in it which was then handed to me with a flourish. I wanted to laugh but didn't dare.

Other people had come into the room and were unashamedly gawping at me as if I was someone important. I had seen this happen to famous people, had experienced a little of what it was like when I had met Onassis, but had never felt the full force of it. Staring. People staring right at me, examining me, asking themselves questions about me, judging me by standards they have created. My hand went up to my hair to reassure myself it was in order. If only I had been able to get it done.

I thanked the man. He received these simple words as if I had made a speech. People half bowed as I left and still they stared. So this was what it was like. All my life I had thought I was a Callas but it was then that I knew I had been deceived, only then did I know what it meant. I raised a hand in a tiny wave and let Mr Bekas lead me out.

He saw me to a taxi, gave instructions to the driver to take me to the airport and handed me an envelope. 'Ten thousand drachmas,' he said.

'Shall I give you a receipt?'

He laughed. 'The sister of Callas, of course not, of course not, dear lady.'

I gave him my thank-you look and the taxi pulled away.

A lady from Olympic Airways met me at Orly airport. I was utterly bewildered but she quickly spotted me and came over to take charge.

'Vasso asked me to come,' she explained.

It was no use. I had to end this mystery. 'I am sorry but who is Vasso?'

'Your sister's best friend, Vasso Devetzi. She's taken care of everything but can't get back till Tuesday for the funeral.'

I said I thought it was to be Sunday but the young lady couldn't explain the discrepancy.

We took a taxi from the airport, driving along, mostly in silence, though every time I looked her way I could see that she was studying me, no doubt examining me for signs of sisterhood with the immortal diva. I tried to ignore it, realising that it was something I was going to have to get used to.

Fields gave way to sparse housing estates, to denser suburbs and on to a wide motorway that seemed to curve round the city. I was excited, I had never been to Paris. I wanted to see the sights and longed to ask that woman in her smart airline uniform just what it was that was flashing past the windows of the car. Yet at the same time I felt that any such request would be somehow out of place. I wanted above all to see the Eiffel Tower but there were only the backs of rows and rows of high apartment houses. It was a grey day, depressing after the autumn sunlight of Athens. I pulled my raincoat closer, it was going to be cold.

'What does Madame Devetzi do?' I asked, my curiosity overcoming my more usual desire for solitude. 'And M. Roire?'

'M. Roire is a music critic, I believe.'

'And Vasso?' I presumed to use her first name as everyone else seemed to.

'Why, she's a pianist of course.' She was evidently surprised that I was not aware of the woman's talent and fame. 'That's why she can't get from Athens. She has a recital. I would have thought that you would have known.'

'I seldom go out,' I said.

'Ah, like your sister. Vasso said that she preferred to stay in her apartment. So sad.'

I thought of us both, alone in our apartments at either side of Europe. Perhaps we hadn't been so different after all.

The driver turned up a side road which rose steeply then turned sharply into a wide boulevard lined with trees that fringed handsome blocks with imposing entrances. At the end I recognised the Arc de Triomphe and felt suddenly light-hearted like a schoolgirl on an outing.

12

Still staring at me, my companion was instantly aware of my reactions. 'Beautiful?'

I smiled agreement. The car turned off the main avenue, crossed several streets and drove across another wide street to stop at an entrance guarded by two stone caryatids.

'Georges Mandel,' the woman announced. 'Your sister's apartment.'

It was even more sumptuous than I had imagined and it frightened me. The wide stairway, the highly polished brass and wood of the ancient lift, the bronze sconces and the thick carpet and all this only the public entrance. The lift shuddered up to the second floor where the butler figure was waiting for me, then there were too many sensations for me to get them straight. The woman must have said goodbye, I was ushered through rooms more elegant than any I had ever seen and suddenly there I was with Mary. You never asked me here, I thought, yet here I am now. How stupid it had all been, two lonely sisters at either side of Europe and here was this enormous apartment.

I have no idea how long I sat there. Time was suspended. They had given us something to eat on the aeroplane so I was not hungry. Perhaps I dozed off a little; the time passed slowly; sometimes I was aware of Bruna quietly sobbing or gently stroking Mary's hair. Gradually I became aware that there was the distant sound of singing: it was the voice of Mary, Mary as Tosca. It was unnerving, as if the figure lying there was projecting the voice like a ventriloquist:

Vissi d'Arte . . .

I knew the part, every word.

Vissi d'Arte . . .

What a pity that we had not realised our loneliness, had not decided to be together again. We could have sung together. I would have accompanied her just as I had done when we were children – the Callas sisters going in for talent shows. Little Mary Callas sings 'La Paloma' with her big sister Jackie at the piano.

And suddenly the butler was there beside me, telling me that M. Roire had arrived. I was clearly expected to go and see him and obediently I got up and followed. In the next room a tall, well-built

13

man with a shock of white hair was standing watching a television tribute to Mary; Mary in the mad scene from *Lucia*. As soon as I entered he reached to turn down the set and moved round to greet me. He was in his late sixties but still handsome. Again the clasped hands and the long stare, the mumbled condolences.

'I trust your flight was satisfactory? Vasso is so sorry not to be here but she has arranged everything.'

'She sounds a very good person.'

He rolled his eyes. 'Good! The best person God has made.'

I wondered just what this saint could be like. She seemed to fill this place now that Mary was merely a corpse lying there in the next room. She alone knew what had to be done. Unable to be there, the 'best person God has made' now worked through her admirers like M. Roire, who was clearly in thrall to her.

'We couldn't arrange the funeral for Sunday,' he said. 'Because of the cremation.'

I turned sharply towards him; that was the most extraordinary thing he could have said. Cremation? Mary was Orthodox, we do not burn our dead. She would have been horrified. But before I could speak he anticipated my concern.

'Vasso says it is what your sister wished. I have approached Archbishop Meletios for special permission . . . his secretary is hopeful. They are less strict today . . .'

I shook my head. I couldn't believe that Mary had ever wanted such a thing.

'Vasso said,' he insisted.

It was not for me to argue with a saint but for the first time doubt about what was going on began to creep in.

Perhaps sensing my displeasure, M. Roire suggested a diversion. 'Would you care to see the blue room? Maria always called it her "museum".'

He was already guiding me towards another door. As with all the rooms the shutters had been pulled to in mourning and he was obliged to fumble around in the half-light trying to find the switches to the tall table lamps on the draped tables before we could see the collection properly. This had been where she kept all her awards; there were medals in plush lined boxes, statuettes, scrolls of honour. It was also a kind of office with a desk on which were silver framed photographs signed by the illustrious persons themselves. Who were they? I couldn't tell. I looked in vain for any member of our family,

14

for any homely snapshot of us all when young. Nothing. Not even our father. This was her real life. This was the room of Maria from which Mary had been excluded. The most touching things were the souvenirs, engravings and mementoes of Maria Malibran, the greatest diva of the nineteenth century whose career so resembled that of Callas. Malibran, too, had been famous for her dramatic interpretations rather than for merely having a good voice and Malibran, too, had been forced to terminate her stage life after only a limited span. I wondered what it could be like to feel yourself on a par with such a figure from musical history, not to feel that it was pretentious or false to hang up her portrait and to say to the world, 'she and I are as one'. To do such a thing meant that you felt confident that you yourself were part of history, as indeed Maria now was. For those whose lives have been led far away from fame it is impossible to comprehend fully what such an awareness means.

. 'She loved this room. She often sat here. I imagine it pleased her to see so many signs of appreciation. She was the very greatest. So sad . . .'

He meant well but I was suddenly exhausted by all that had happened. I felt swamped by Maria, by her blue room, by the medals, by the presence of Malibran, by these solicitous people who had no notion of what my own reactions really were.

'You must be tired,' he said. 'I've arranged a hotel, would you like me to drive you there?'

I was aware of little on the journey from Georges Mandel. M. Roire tried to keep up a conversation, much of it about Madame Devetzi, but I was not concentrating. Paris sped by. I recognised nothing except a conventional montage of café awnings, posters for art galleries, smart women exercising their dogs. He arranged everything at the hotel reception, proposed coming for me the next day, kissed my hand and left me with a porter who would show me to my room.

Finally alone, I sank into a deep armchair and tried to shut out the world. The room was quietly elegant with space for a large bed and a round table on which someone had placed a gift of fruit. The heavily draped windows looked out on to an inner light-well which increased my sense of being absolutely nowhere. There was an impressionistic scene of a Paris square on the wall executed entirely in blues and reds. It was the only indication that I was anywhere other than in my own apartment back in Athens. I knew I would not go out; I knew no one, had nowhere to go and barely enough money to get by till Tuesday. Later I would eat a little fruit and when my strength returned I would call Mother, but not yet. It would be a terrible strain, she would be hysterical, full of grieving and complaining, rambling with sorrow and accusations. No, that would have to be later. For the moment I took off my clothes and carefully hung them up, then I stretched out on the bed and tried to relax. I stared at the tassel-shaded lamp suspended from the ceiling. There was a low rumble somewhere in the heating system. I kept perfectly still, hoping to induce a little sleep and my mind suddenly filled with the image of Mary, lying there on her bed not far away – we two sisters lying immobile, the only difference being that one could imagine the other and one was merely a shell. How beautiful she had looked. No wrinkles, no marks of age. All over the world countless people were being told of her death, were experiencing loss, grief, a sorrow that there in that elegant apartment lay the body of the great diva, while I, alive, the living Callas, had only one person who knew where I was, a French music critic whom I had met only a few hours ago and who was simply doing a favour for someone called Vasso who was, he believed, the best person God had made. God? How could He let someone be so alone, so lonely? I felt sorry – sorry for myself, sorry for Mary, sorry for both of us. We were as one again. I slept a little.

That room became my life as it usually was. It was as if I were in Athens. Living alone, going out only for certain essentials, obliged to contact my mother every day and to listen to her complaints. It was a life I was perfectly attuned to. But there was also another life, a life for which I had no preparation. M. Roire would come in the mornings to drive me to Georges Mandel where I would sit in a chair near my sister's bed and be – what? The chief mourner, someone who could be a focus for the people allowed in to see her? I quickly realised that there was strict selection with regard to this privilege. I could overhear Bruna and Ferruccio, as I learned he was called, consulting with M. Roire over what Vasso had ordained regarding this or that supplicant.

It meant nothing to me. I had no idea who these famous people were who came to clasp my hands and stare at me and express their sorrow. On the day after my arrival, the Sunday, there was a maestro, very famous judging by the deference shown to him, who was ushered up to me. He walked like a god, his gestures were expansive, his phrases of condolence rich, yet oddly enough his little wife, crouched beside him, was almost helpless with grief. She cried uncontrollably with great racking sobs. It was an uncomfortable sight; she was so out of control, it bordered on my mother's hysteria. Though less audible, her husband was also visibly distressed and he looked away abstractedly while she sobbed out her words of comfort to me. I made my excuses and left the room only to find that I had no idea where I was. Room led into room until finally there was a plain white corridor lined with china cabinets which I guessed must be the connecting link to the service rooms. Sure enough the next door opened into the kitchen where Bruna and Ferruccio were seated at a large scrubbed table drinking coffee.

I must have looked distraught because Bruna dashed up to lead me to the chair which Ferruccio was pulling round.

I accepted the coffee they offered me. There, in the kitchen, it was theirs to offer. It was not as if I was taking anything from my sister who had never invited me to her home, who had never wanted to see me there and who had never herself offered me as much as a glass of water.

I calmed down as I sipped my coffee. I liked the spare white kitchen, it had echoes of home, of Greece, after the plush drawing-rooms of the main apartment.

Bruna looked at Ferruccio for encouragement then broached something that she had obviously been longing to say. 'Madame told me she had no family,' she said. 'We had no idea about you and your mother.'

I shook my head.

She went on, 'A shame that she and Madame . . .' She left the sentence unfinished.

'Terrible,' I agreed. 'But then . . .'

'She is sad at the news?'

I explained my mother's abject grief, told them how much Mary had meant to her. There was much sideways eye-catching; they had obviously suspected as much.

'It was a great shock,' Ferruccio said. 'We hadn't expected it.'

Bruna reached for a handkerchief and blew her nose, fighting back tears. 'Madame got up on Friday morning as usual,' she said, obviously keen to tell me the story. 'She went to the bathroom and washed herself. I was in her room arranging the bed when she came back and suddenly knelt down on the floor – it was terrible, she said she didn't know how that had happened. She said she needed help. I got her on to the bed and she asked for the coffee I had brought. She took one sip and then she died.'

'What did you do?'

'I started calling out for Ferruccio. He came and when he realised what was happening he phoned M. Roire who called a doctor – but it was too late.'

'She was tired,' Ferruccio said. 'She seldom went out and she couldn't sleep so she took tablets. It was the tablets that weakened her, she took so many, they were so strong. She had many people send them to her. I told Madame Devetzi once but she just shrugged. "If she wants them, let her have them," she would say, so what could I do?'

I thought of Bekas handing me the packets of Mandrax and I wondered who else had joined in this bizarre network of death. Only later did I learn that she had been taking pills to sleep and pills to revive herself the next day and, worst of all, virtually no exercise in her final days. She had taken to sitting around, never going out, watching old movies on television. She was also gaining weight again and all that, combined with low blood pressure, must have caused a pulmonary thrombosis. She had, in a very real sense, died of the depression which had made her a recluse in her own apartment.

Was that why these people who seemed to be in charge of her affairs were rushing things and insisting on having a cremation? Were they frightened a post-mortem might reveal Maria's addiction to all those pills? Were they trying to avoid a scandal? If so, then perhaps it was for the best, though I found it hard to accept the idea of my sister being burned. But who was I to argue? I assumed these people were her closest friends, that she would want them here running things now that she was gone. If not, what on earth could I do? I knew nothing, no one, better to let them do as they thought best.

'She was dead when the doctor got here,' Bruna said. 'It was very quick.'

We all crossed ourselves, me three times in the Greek way which started Bruna snivelling again.

'La Signora always did like that,' she said. 'All the time, especially just before she went on stage. It was her comfort and her luck. Some luck at the end, eh?'

Luck. The thought made us silent for a while. Then M. Roire came to drive me 'home', as I now thought of it.

Back in my room I lay with the curtains drawn and tried not to think too much. Mother would be waiting for my call. She would want to know everything I had done, what I had seen, who had been there. When I had spoken to her the night before I realised that such details had to be recounted because they fascinated her, kept back the hysteria. I tried to marshal all my memories of the day: the maestro and his wife, what Bruna and Ferruccio had told me, so that I could pass them on. For Mother it was as if she was at last participating in the life that Mary had refused her. Mary, who in life had shut out her mother and never permitted her to be with her as she had so dearly wished, was now offering her a few crumbs from that rich banquet. I reached for the telephone . . .

The following day M. Roire told me that Archbishop Meletios had agreed to the cremation and that everything was arranged for the next morning. I wanted to tell him that I did not believe in this burning business but I knew I was up against the unseen will of Devetzi, the best person God ever made, so I bit my lip.

At the apartment the stream of visitors was still under way but I think he must have realised that after my escape the day before I was no longer content just to sit like a receptionist by my sister's side. When we arrived he handed me over to Bruna who took me into the drawing-room away from the visitors. I noted everything for Mother, the side tables set out with silver ashtrays, the towering mirrors, the prints.

'So much,' I said.

Bruna smiled and beckoned me across the corridor to another room lined with closets, a dressing-room. She opened the doors and showed me Mary's clothes, rack upon rack of dresses, jackets, coats. Drawer upon drawer of underwear, blouses, sweaters, many of them still wrapped in the cellophane in which they had been bought. It was like a warehouse, I had never seen so many clothes. I suddenly thought of my one, now crumpled outfit. There was only one thing I could do to restore my pride a little.

'I would like to get my hair done.'

Bruna said she would arrange it.

While we were talking one of Maria's two elderly dogs, a poodle called Jeda, had come into the room. Bruna led her to the bedroom to see her mistress but the poor creature only wandered about, refusing to look at the corpse lying there. It was terribly moving to watch.

We went to the kitchen for a coffee. Ferruccio's newspaper was

19

lying on the table and on the cover was a photograph of Mary with Onassis. Bruna looked at it and smiled grimly, then raised a finger and tapped the side of her head.

'Crazy for him,' she said. 'When he died . . .'

I had been with them once, years before when she sang at Epidaurus and he had berthed his yacht at Glyfada. Onassis was a powerful man who loved owning things, and he had owned my sister. To him she was like all those clothes stacked in that room. He had so much but she had brought him a prestige he could never have had otherwise. I remembered he had kissed my hand and held it just a little too long. He had frightened me.

Later, M. Roire left me at a hairdresser and the sensation of being both out of that hotel room yet still alone was wonderful. No one knew who I was, no one stared and said solicitous things, everything was businesslike. I dozed under the dryer and when I woke I could think of nothing but all those clothes. What must it be like to have so much? It was only then that I truly accepted just how rich Mary had been. The occasional gift of a hundred dollars had been nothing to her, hundreds of dollars were stacked in those drawers, thousands hung on those rails, yet she had always made such a scene about giving anything to us. She had treated Mother like an importunate beggar. A hundred dollars was nothing when I had wrecked my life to see that she had food in her stomach in the days when people in Athens were dying of starvation in the streets below our windows. I stopped myself. Such thoughts did no good. Bitter memories had driven Mother to the state she was in and I had no wish to join her in her misery. I told myself to think of what Mary must have been through. I had glimpsed some of what it meant to have the world possess you, yet that was nothing to what she had known. *Maria* Callas not *Mary* Callas had owned all those dresses and stockings and shoes.

That night I carefully broke the news to Mother that they were going to cremate Mary, but to my surprise she barely lingered over the information.

'So who was there today?'

'I didn't see. I had my hair done.'

She was furious. All those famous, important people coming to see her daughter and I had missed them. To calm her down I described the dressing-room and its contents. No child listening to the tale of

Aladdin could have been happier. She was hungry for details and I racked my memory to recall what individual robes had looked like.

'You could have had something to wear for tomorrow,' she said.

I was suddenly angry. 'I touched nothing. I didn't take even a coffee. She never asked me to her beautiful home which means she didn't want me to have anything.'

'And what do you think will happen to all those things – those clothes, that apartment? She had jewels, she had money. Just think about it.'

I didn't want to think about it. I now knew that what I really wanted was to go home, to get away from all the fuss of the next day, to avoid thinking about the things Mother was proposing. I wanted the solitude of my own apartment, my private world with all this shut out.

'Think about it,' Mother said. 'Just think about it.'

I tried not to think about it.

Looking at myself in the long mirror inside the wardrobe door next morning, I felt shabby. My things were clean, I'd washed out my blouse and borrowed an iron to press it and the skirt but there was no avoiding the feeling that I had been wearing the same things for too long. I felt even shabbier when M. Roire arrived in an immaculate black suit. The day was beginning badly.

'Vasso has arrived,' he explained as we drove off. 'She has arranged everything. A few people will come back afterwards. A few close friends.'

I wondered just whose friends they were.

She was waiting in the room that preceded the bedroom, elegant in a fitted white suit. Others had stared at me but none with the lingering studiousness of Vasso Devetzi. She seemed to penetrate right inside me, she even turned her head the better to see my profile. Satisfied, she nodded as if coming to a conclusion. 'I will take care of you,' she said in Greek, excluding M. Roire from her conversation. 'We have many things to discuss but later. Come.'

She led me into the bedroom. The undertakers were there and Mary was laid in her coffin. Vasso stepped back to allow me to make my goodbyes. I crossed myself and asked God for some of Maria's courage when she had gone out to face an audience. The nature of the ordeal ahead had begun to dawn on me. We returned to the drawing-room while they sealed the coffin. Vasso questioned me

21

closely about my life. I was not married? What other members of the family were there? She explained that Maria had seldom spoken about the family.

'Do you like this apartment?' she suddenly asked.

'Yes.'

'Trust me,' she said. 'And you will see.'

We followed the coffin to a line of waiting cars. A crowd had gathered at the entrance, first sign of what was to come. Outside the Orthodox cathedral a vast mob heaved and pushed to get a glimpse of the great diva's last appearance. I stepped on to the pavement to a bewildering experience – flashlights, television cameras, journalists hurling questions. Gendarmes held them at bay and Vasso and M. Roire guided me through into the great domed church. A vast congregation was standing as we processed down the aisle; no concert could have prepared me for the sensation of being swallowed alive in that way. I was centre stage sharing the limelight with the coffin bobbing ahead of me. I could see out of the corner of my eye that people were whispering to each other as I approached. Who's that? they must have wondered. The sister, came the reply.

As we approached the catafalque Vasso whispered that Princess Grace was there and that I should curtsy. As soon as I saw her bob I followed, then obediently went to the place indicated.

I have little recollection of the ceremony except for the beauty of the Greek psalms intoned beneath the glittering mosaics. It reminded me of the church for the Greek-Americans in Washington Heights, correct but somehow foreign.

When the ceremony ended, people came forward to lay roses on the coffin. Someone presented me to Princess Grace and one of her daughters but that was all. I was soon standing alone watching the crowd disperse. Vasso was talking to some of the other principal guests and seemed to have forgotten me. I tried desperately to register it all, faces, names, so that I could relate it all to Mother later. One man must have asked who I was because he came up to speak: 'Your sister this . . . your sister that . . . great star . . . tragedy.' I only had to nod and look sad. It was a performance; I had asked for the courage of a performer and there I was doing it. Vasso returned to place me at the head of the procession that would follow the coffin out. She was like a stage director, or perhaps a manager making sure her client was never upstaged. I blinked as we stepped outside and then the noise began. The great crowd was clapping furiously, voices were calling out Callas, Callas, Brava, Brava. I was so close to the coffin they seemed to be looking at me as they yelled their congratulations. Callas, Brava, Brava, La Divina, Brava. I looked out of the window of the hired car and gave them my thank-you smile.

'Well done,' said Vasso. 'You did all that very well indeed. Don't worry about anything now, there's just the crematorium then we go back to the apartment.'

But in this she was wrong. The crematorium was not a passing moment, it was an ordeal. A gaunt stone building like an abandoned, undecorated chapel where we waited while Maria was taken away to be incinerated. There was Vasso, M. Roire, Bruna, Ferruccio and a man introduced to me as Mr Pylarinos, a cousin of Vasso, a lawyer working in exile in Paris with Karamanlis. He was very pleasant and tried to keep me in good spirits during the long wait in that cold, cold hall. I don't think I have ever been so cold: it was like a tomb. It seemed hideously ironical that somewhere nearby they were burning my sister while I froze to death in that barren ante-chamber. Eventually, even Mr Pylarinos, who had been trying to keep our spirits up, fell silent; there was just nothing more to be said. I pulled my flimsy raincoat closer round me and prayed that the ordeal would end soon.

When it did, I cursed my impatience for when the doors creaked open they revealed an official coming forward with a plain metal box. It was so small and Mary had been such a tall woman. Whatever that little box contained was all that was left of her. He held it out towards me. I had never had anything to do with a cremation before and the object in front of me looked like nothing so much as a dull metal cash-box, no handles, no inscription, anonymous.

The very idea of a cremation nauseated me but the reality was ten times worse. I felt uncontrollably faint. Pylarinos and Roire were quickly beside me.

'She'll be all right,' Vasso said firmly. 'It's nothing. It will pass.' She transfixed me with a set smile. 'That's better, isn't it?'

I nodded, trying to please her.

'Then take the ashes,' she said. 'On behalf of the family.'

I forced myself to hold out my hands like a child waiting for a gift.

The man gently laid the casket on to my palms though it was far from heavy, and then Vasso took my arm and led me out to the waiting cars.

I felt a little better as we rode the lift up to the apartment, though I knew there would be more new people to be spoken with. After the horror of that stone vault I knew that nothing could ever bother me as much again. When she saw the look on my face Bruna took me straight to Mary's bathroom to freshen up, and as I sat before her dressing mirror I felt suddenly at ease, almost as if I were in my own bathroom. Bruna flounced my hair as she must have done for Mary.

'You could stay here a moment if you wish,' she suggested.

But I didn't need to. I was intrigued to know who was out there, who these close friends could be.

It was of course meaningless. Clusters of strange people gripped by almost secretive conversations in which I had no part, though they all stopped when I was presented and indulged in the hand-grip and long stare that I was beginning to accept as normal. Vasso introduced me to several such groups but after each set of introductions and the following muttered condolences it was obvious that there was nothing else to be said and I was shuffled off to start all over again with another cluster of strangers. After I had been guided round four such groups I noticed a man staring at me more intently than the others and I watched as he came between me and Vasso as she manoeuvred me to her next little enclave. He introduced himself as Sandor Gorlinski, an impresario who had worked with Mary. Surprisingly, he side-stepped all the usual phrases everyone else had forced on me.

'This apartment is beautiful,' he said. I wasn't sure whether it was a question or not.

'I can see that my sister tried very hard to make her home beautiful,' I said, then something made me go on: 'It makes me even sorrier that she died. I don't know what she wanted to happen to it but I would like everything to remain as it is, her clothes, her furniture, her pictures, everything. I don't know if I have anything to do with it or not but I would like it to be a museum. I'd like people to see just how my sister lived.'

To my surprise he laughed. 'That is a very revealing wish,' he said. 'So you would like the world to know that your sister hoarded a great many things here. Yes, you are right, it says a great deal about her. Did she ever give you anything? Presents? Gifts for you and your mother?' He laughed again. 'No, but excuse me I shouldn't ask. Perhaps you wish such a thing but I can tell you that this place doesn't belong to you and that it will never belong to you.'

As he was saying this I felt Vasso's hand closing round my arm to pull me away.

'I didn't mean that the house was mine . . . it was just a wish . . .'

'I know,' he said, not unkindly. 'You just don't know the circumstances. The house probably belongs to no one.'

I had no idea what all that meant and in any case Vasso was yanking my arm so hard I had to turn away.

'Time to go,' she said. 'It has been an exhausting day and you'd better get some rest. I'll see you here tomorrow. I'll have something for you, wait and see.'

She must have told M. Roire to wait for me as he was standing by the door with my coat. I didn't want to go. I was fascinated by that strange crowd but it was useless to protest. I had had my orders.

Mother tried to clutch at every nuance. 'Why won't the apartment be ours? What did he mean about it belonging to no one? What is that woman going to give you tomorrow?'

I could barely force out some sort of response. I was so cold. Away from the people in Mary's apartment the terrible chill of the crematorium had crept up on me again. I have never been so cold. It was like a winter fog seeping into the room. There were two blankets in the cupboard. I threw them over the bed but they were not enough to warm me. For the first time during my stay I rang room service and asked for another blanket. Even with three, I lay shivering all night, my thoughts filled with images of that dank stone room and the tiny metal box with Mary's ashes inside. I had completely forgotten it when I left the apartment that afternoon. I told myself that I must remember to collect it the next day, but then what would I do with it?

Vasso's 'gift' was a cheque for my expenses in Paris. There was a man waiting with it when I arrived at the apartment. He had a number of papers that Vasso said I should sign so that she would be able to handle matters for Mother and me as we weren't in Paris and then the man – from Maria's bank as it turned out – would be able to release a little money from her account. I had expected to pay everything myself. I signed and told her how grateful I was for all she was doing. How on earth would we have managed without her? She

25

told me not to think of it, it was just what friends are for, and now M. Roire would take me to the airport.

'Don't worry,' she said. 'Everything will be fine here, I'll see to it. Tell your mother Maria's things will be hers, I promise.'

I felt quite giddy. It was just the sort of thing Mother would want to hear; it might even silence her grievances for a time. I felt grateful to Vasso, as I realised I must call her. I asked her about Maria's ashes and again she told me not to bother with such things, she would see to everything. I said goodbye to Bruna and Ferruccio; they were so good I almost wanted to cry when they stood at the door to see me off. It was as if all my loneliness was being stripped away. Perhaps it was possible to have friends, to share problems with other people, to feel happy to be with them and sorry when you have to leave. Vasso and M. Roire went on ahead. They ignored the lift and set off down the wide carpeted stairway. It was the first time I had gone that way. They were soon below me, deep in conversation about lawyers and company shares and something to do with probate.

'The Moral Right,' said Vasso. 'That's what really counts.'

I was so grateful she was worrying about things I could barely understand.

They were now far ahead of me so I hurried up, taking each wide, oversized step at a jump – a sort of skip and a jump. Jump, skip, skip, jump; it was as if the years were slipping away – jump, skip, skip, jump – and I was six again, the only daughter, myself alone, little Hyacinth, the only daughter . . .

CHAPTER TWO
1920–1936

. . . a sort of skip then a jump and another jump. The staircase curved down from the first floor where we lived to the entrance hall with a door that led through to the place where my father worked. Whenever I escaped from the cook and the housemaid, whose most difficult task was to take care of me, I would run to the top of the beautiful curved staircase and skip and jump up and down its long length. I was not naughty. My father always said I was a patient child, but it was nice to be free, to leave the stuffy salon and wander in the cooler stairwell. Sometimes I even ventured into the sweet-smelling room where my father passed his days. To me then, it was a magic shop full of beautiful jars and bottles, of glass cabinets cluttered with packets and tubes. Now I know it was a pharmacy. My father was the local chemist, the only one for miles and his was one of a row of shops on the main street of our town, Meligala. It led down to the central clock tower but only now do I see how beautiful it was – the intense white light of the Greek summer reflected on the white buildings, the sharp black shadows thrown at an angle into the street. Then the world was often limited to the shady interior of our house, the darkened rooms and the chatter of the servants. The staircase was my world – a skip then a jump – I was free, I was absolutely alone, I was the only one, the only sister. Of course there was Vassily but he was only three. Vassily was beautiful, such big blue eyes and blond as all my mother's family were. But Vassily didn't count, he was too little. I was the only one, the first child. I loved Vassily. In any case he was very useful; when the heat of the afternoon subsided the maid would take him for an outing in his pram and when the cook dozed in her chair in the kitchen I was free. I would dash into the sweet-smelling room to see my father. I loved

27

to watch him graciously serving the ladies who came to the shop, carefully wrapping their parcels, passing them over with a bow and a murmured comment, twirling the end of his black moustache with a little smile. The ladies seemed to like it, they would look shy and thank him before hurrying away. They seemed to like coming to our shop very much. There can't have been much to do in such an out of the way place as Meligala – though I thought then that it was full of wonders. Everyone was nice to me. We had a young servant who went on living with us when he did his military service and he would come into the kitchen in his khaki uniform, sit me on his knee and tell me stories about the war. If she overheard him Mother would come and listen and sometimes join in.

'My family have always been at the front of things,' she would say. 'Your grandfather, my father, was a general, God rest him, as was your great grandfather Dimitrios Dimitriadis. Your Great-Uncle Kostas Louros was the king's physician and I . . .' She paused. '. . . I married a pharmacist.'

Christos, the soldier, would smile and look away until she had finished and when she had left us he would go on with his tales. My mother always seemed to be upset by something so that at that time I preferred my father with his smile and his moustache twirling and the way the young ladies giggled when he held on to their hands as he gave them their change. But most of all I loved being alone.

In Meligala that was not too difficult. It was a small place, though its centre had some fine houses for the professional people: the doctor and the teacher, who made up such society as the town could boast of and among whom we were counted. In fact Father's business was successful enough to make us people of note. I of course did not know this then and had I done so would not have cared less, but as I was later to discover it was a fact of considerable importance to my mother. She adored doing the right thing, and the only serious limits on my activities were those rules that were meant to ensure that I did not bring us into public disgrace in any way. There were those I must not play with and houses into which I must not go. Provided I kept to the fields and lanes on the nearby outskirts of the town there was no problem. In one especial activity did Mother manage to combine social cachet with personal pleasure – the theatre. Going to a play was considered smart and I learned even at that age that Mother was fanatical for anything to do with the stage. She and Father would go to Kalamata on the coast, the nearest town of any size and the proud possessor of a real theatre where they could see the travelling companies touring the plays from the previous season in Athens. Only when she returned from such an outing did Mother ever look completely satisfied with life. For once the endless fault-finding with each and every one would be suspended. I do not know whether it was she or Christos who told me that she harboured ambitions to go on the stage herself, a fact that was to have a devastating effect on the lives of her children.

One learned quickly as a child to keep out of Mother's way, for there was always something she could find in my behaviour that she felt could be improved on.

The thing I hated most was being made to eat because then company was forced upon me. I ate so little, Mother would organise impromptu parties with other children brought in so that I might learn from the example of their greed.

'See how they eat,' she would say as they scoffed whatever was put before them. 'Eat up, Yacinthy.'

But the spectacle revolted me and I ate less. These children were all from the neighbouring shops and I knew they had no need of our food. Why did she never invite the ragged children who played at the end of our street and who always looked so hungry? I ran into the pharmacy expecting to see Father but the place was empty, the door to his cellar ajar, but I was absolutely forbidden to go in. Thinking of the poor children gave me an idea. I carried over a stool from near the door and put it near the place at the counter where Father usually stood. I climbed up and pressed the keys on the cash register just as he did and was nearly knocked over by the sudden burst of the money drawer. I reached inside and scooped up a handful of coins.

At the end of the street, just before the clock tower, I collected half a dozen of the children who were never invited to my exemplary banquets. These were the children of the poor. They followed me with puzzled docility. I led them into the confectionery shop and told our neighbour to serve ice-creams and to give out caramels. For once I really felt like joining in and took a cone with two scoops.

'Are you sure . . .' the confectioner began, looking at the ragged army I had brought. 'Does your mother . . .?'

I smiled and followed the others into the street to enjoy our sweets.

The children ate their ices then went off without a word. It seemed much better than the noisy polite thank-yous of our well-brought-up neighbours. They always said thank you just as they had been taught to do; it didn't really mean anything anyway.

When I got back there was a terrible scene. Mother was walking up and down, Father was sitting in a chair with his head in his hands, the cook was crying, the maid was crying, Vassily in her arms was crying. Christos came and took me away. I asked him what had happened.

'Someone stole some money from the shop while your father was . . . occupied. Your mother's trying to find out who did it.'

'I did,' I said, and told him all about it.

He led me by the hand back into the salon but the story was already out, the confectioner was standing by the sofa describing my visit to his shop. My father burst out laughing and Christos quickly joined in but my mother looked furious and the confectioner gave the sort of loud sniff that indicates that he had expected such terrible news to be treated with more gravity. I think my mother wanted to punish me but my father wouldn't let her. When we were alone he told me I was a good-hearted girl.

About that time two things happened that I will never forget – they were not of the same importance, far from it, but I remember them as if they were. I had my photograph taken with Christos, I cannot imagine why. He wore his khaki field uniform with tight puttees. I was dressed with the sort of cuteness thought appropriate at that time, bows in my hair. The photographer's studio had a painted backdrop with trees. I stood beside Christos and he put his arm round me. He always took good care of me. In my other memory he is also holding me tight but this time he is telling me that everything will be all right. The maid had returned from the afternoon walk crying and stammering; she held Vassily close to her, his head lolling on one side. She was calling out to anyone who would listen that something had happened to Vassily. She wanted someone to come and help her. I was skipping down the stairs when she ran into the hall begging for help. My mother stumbled out of her siesta, Father appeared from the shop. They both ran to take the boy and Christos came up behind me, lifted me up and took me away to the salon. He tried to take my mind off it with his stories. But I could hear the bustling about, the coming and going, the howling of the maid and Mother shouting at her to be quiet and help.

Later that evening Father came and took me into his bedroom, usually a forbidden place. I was surprised to see Vassily in the big bed, the sheets pulled up to his chin, his head propped on the large fluffy pillows.

'Your brother is sick,' Father said. 'You must come and speak to him.'

I stood by the bed, my mind a blank. Vassily stared at me but his big blue eyes did not seem to see me.

After a while they led me away and Christos played with me until it was time for bed.

It seemed like for ever, the coming and going in the room with Vassily. Two days? Three days? No one except Christos noticed me. It was wonderful not to have the horrible eating parties. Then suddenly there was a loud screaming and people scurrying about. It was terrible. Christos hurried me out for a walk. We strolled along the main street for an eternity and when we got back the house had been shuttered as if we were expecting a storm. Inside, my father was sitting on the sofa. He had not shaved for days, his shirt had no collar. He motioned me to come up to him and he gave me a tight hug.

Meningitis. The word meant nothing to me then. Years later Mother told me the story but even then she could hardly speak from the grief of it. At the time, it was all a mystery shrouded in gloom and whispers.

The next day Christos kept me in the kitchen but I saw my mother veiled in black and heard the crowd gathered in the street below. When they had left Christos said I could play in the house. I went to the staircase and skipped and jumped for a while. Somehow I had realised that Vassily was dead, though I was unsure exactly what that meant other than that he had gone and I was alone again. I was no longer a sister.

I was still running and skipping when they returned. Mother was helped in by Father and the maid. She saw me coming down the curving flight of stairs, my little shoes clacking on the polished marble.

'Tell her not to play on the stairs,' she barked.

'Yes, yes,' my father said. 'Better not just now, Yacinthy, not the time to be playing.'

I ran back to the kitchen and Christos and cried my heart out. He did his best to comfort me but there was something distracted about him that upset me even more. For the next months he, the cook and the maid had to look after me completely. Mother had always relied on them to be with me for part of the day but now she gave me over to them completely and they had to take it in turns to see that I was amused. I had to sit silently on the heavy classical chairs, trying to be good. They did their best but I was well aware that all was not right – Mother kept to her room and on the rare occasions when she appeared she was still covered in black and crying into her little handkerchief. Sometimes she would go into the shop and we could all hear her quarrelling with Father. He stayed in the house less and less and didn't smile as he had before.

I suppose I must have got used to this gloomy atmosphere. Eventually, the servants let me run out and play with the other children so that I could be happy in the street but I have always been better at amusing myself. Then one day, only a few months later, everything changed again. I came back one day to find the maid and the cook all smiles, and eager to tell me their news.

'You're going to have a new brother,' one of them announced. 'You should go and see your mother.'

I had seen so little of her that when I went into her room it was the first time that I was able to observe in detail just how much she had changed. There was a distinct swelling of the stomach and she seemed calm at last.

She also said that I was going to have another brother and added that he would be just like Vassily. I assumed she must know for sure that that was the case and I accepted it as absolutely certain.

The house was now transformed, everything was going to be as before. Father smiled and I ran and skipped on the stairs. But not for long!

One morning I heard Mother shouting hysterically, then my father began slamming doors and the servants hid away. No one would tell me what was happening and for several days I was only aware that something terrible was about to happen. Gradually the word America crept into my consciousness and then suddenly there were boxes and cases everywhere and Christos was helping me pack my things.

'You'll like America,' he said without much conviction. 'It's very big.'

It had all happened so quickly; in an instant there was no longer the home I had always known. People came to take away all our things, everyone I had ever known, apart from my mother and father, was saying goodbye. The maid and the cook were crying and Christos could hardly speak. Of course for me it was a great adventure, though now most of it is a blur – the train, the waiting boat, sitting for long periods while things were sorted out and listening to my mother complaining without pause about my father's crazy behaviour in selling his business and emigrating to America, telling him over and over again that only the uneducated, the peasants, did such a thing.

Why did he do it? I asked him in later life and he was never able to say. It was not as if he and my mother were going through one of their bad periods – she was pregnant again, and both were convinced they would have another Vassily to make their lives as it had been before. His business was good, ours was the only pharmacy for miles and he made a good profit. In any case if he had wanted adventure one of my mother's relatives had made him an irresistible offer. The Louros family were closely linked to medicine, my mother's uncle had been physician to the king and a cousin had proposed setting up my father in a pharmacy in central Athens. If my father had gone ahead there is no doubt that today we would be rich. Similar businesses were gradually transformed into large-scale department stores as the city expanded and there is no reason to suppose that ours would not have done the same. But my father found it all very resistible. I can only suppose that he wanted no further obligation to his wife, who never ceased to tell him how much she had given up to marry him. He was the village pharmacist, she was from a leading military and medical family. She had fallen for a handsome man and had met resistance from the General, her father. It was only when he died unexpectedly that my grandmother had encouraged her daughter to follow her heart. They had married within six weeks of the funeral with my mother in the plain white of mourning. Only then, as she also never tired of telling anyone who would listen, did she discover that George Calogeropoulou was a womaniser. Father, so she said, could never resist a pretty face and his position in the pharmacy gave him plenty of opportunity to follow his bent. Today, I sometimes wonder if his decision to throw up a successful business and risk everything on that hasty trip to America wasn't in large part because he wished to punish his wife for her endless whining about what he clearly believed to be his masculine rights. Certainly many men at that time truly believed that such extra-marital adventures were no business of their wives. It was equally true that my mother was unusual at that time in having an extremely liberated view of herself and her own rights – for their marriage and for me, it was a fatal combination.

For me at the time there was simply the boat, the vast sea, the sense of wonder at the unknown. My mother often kept to her cabin, being tired with pregnancy. We would meet at meals, and one of my clearest memories is of other passengers praising my table manners and my mother acknowledging their remarks. Given the strains of that year other children might have let off steam by behaving badly, but it seems that I withdrew into exaggerated politeness. I did what I had been told to perfection, as if that would keep the chaos of the world at bay.

New York. If I had known anything about it I would have been surprised at the lack of jollity that greeted the arrival of our boat. The harbour was sombre, no one smiled and waved. When the newspapers came on board they were bordered with black. My parents spoke no English but this evidence of death enveloped them. Mother started to cry. It was August 2nd, 1923. President Harding had died.

It must all have been so strange yet I remember little. Perhaps the sensations crowded in so fast they forced each other out as quickly. Later, Mother told me of our first apartment in Astoria, Queens, across the East River from Manhattan but I could only recall rows of two-storey blocks near the river and going upstairs to a room on the first floor. Some things hardly changed: we spoke Greek and lived among Greek immigrants so the sensation of being in a foreign place was much lessened. Until he had acquired a licence to practise pharmacy Father was forced to teach Greek in a local school. Mother sulked and waited for her son to be born. She was taken away at the beginning of December and a few nights later Father returned from the hospital with a resigned look on his face to tell me that I had a sister. I was naturally confused at this change, having been as convinced as anyone of the certainty of my mother's prediction, but I tried to absorb the disturbing news. A little brother would have been nothing, merely a return to the acceptable days of Vassily; I had barely considered myself a sister, so apart was his existence from mine. But now I had a sister and I was a sister. Three days later

34

Father took me to the Flower Hospital on Fifth Avenue. Mother lay in bed looking at the snow falling beyond the window, paying no attention at all to the bundle swathed beside her. Father turned back the swaddling bands and chucked his new daughter under the chin and made baby noises.

'This is little Cecilia,' he said.

Without turning her head my mother said, 'Sophia. This is your sister Sophia. Say hello to Sophia.'

I looked up to my father for help in this first dilemma of life with my new sister but he merely shrugged. I stood on tiptoe to look at her. She was big for a new-born child and had a wispy corona of jet-black hair so unlike the rest of us. She looked very nice sleeping peacefully and I felt suddenly happy to have a sister. My father was saying something to Mother about how happy I was and why didn't she try to look at the child but she just went on staring at the snow and taking no notice. Clearly angry, my father gripped my wrist and hurried out.

A few days later he announced that 'Maria' would soon be coming home. The new name indicated that a compromise had been reached over the issue; it was to be the last time that diplomacy would prevail in the war that was to break out between husband and wife.

When she brought Maria home my mother was completely changed. Now she adored the girl and happily sat breast-feeding her and cooing over her before she slept. I was delighted too. Anything that occupied her distracted her from me. I much preferred my solitude.

Shortly afterwards Father announced that we were no longer to be called Calogeropoulou. Americans could not say the name so he had changed it to Callas, though our Greek neighbours persisted with the old one, their only concession to America being to call us Mary and Jackie as if some gesture to the new nation was needed.

When Father's licence came through we moved across to Manhattan where he opened a drugstore on 39th and 8th Avenue. It was a scruffy neighbourhood not far from 42nd Street but it was the only place where an immigrant with little capital could set up shop. My father was an industrious man when he wanted to be. In those days pharmacists didn't just sell ready-made medicines as they do now, they made their own, mixing fluids and grinding powders in their work-rooms. Father was good at this and his business did quite well but this mattered little to Mother who only noted the run-down neighbourhood and spent her days longing to be a big fish in the little pond of Meligala. Even when Father had made a little money and we had moved further uptown to Riverside Drive she continued to see New York through a haze of loathing.

For me New York was fun. I had picked up English in Astoria with the facility a young child has and I adored my junior school in Manhattan – at least it got me away from all the complaining. My only regret was that I was not allowed out after school as other children were. Mother exercised even greater discrimination than she had in Meligala – to her no one came up to what she saw as our social standards. Until Mary grew up a little my life was terribly limited. I was fascinated by the new arrival and longed for her to be able to play with me. Back from school I was always with her. She was a plump, happy child and I adored her. I was so determined that we should be able to enjoy ourselves together I taught her to walk ahead of time, holding her up and letting her toddle away, catching her as she fell. And I can well remember our delight when she first staggered right across our living-room to the far wall on her own. We shared a room and at eight o'clock we were obliged to go to bed, tired or not. We were never afraid of the dark but Mary longed for entertainment and I would read her *Little Red Riding Hood*, the *Three Bears* and other children's stories. But by far our biggest source of fun was the pianola Mother bought. She would get cylinders with punctured holes to strike the notes and would sit pumping away with her feet while Mary and I sat entranced. Mother would only permit 'good' music, usually piano versions of operatic tunes and it was on these that Mary and I were raised. We took it as absolutely natural that the only music worth spending time on was Bellini and Verdi. Eventually I was able to reach the pedals and could make the tunes for Mary and very quickly she learned to crawl over to the machine and operate it with her hands. We were raised to the sounds of grand opera and my mother's incessant nagging.

Father could avoid most of it as he was preoccupied with the problems of running his new business in a strange land. Mary was too little to be aware of what was going on but I could see quite clearly that my parents' marriage had gone very wrong. The failure to achieve a son had removed all hope of reconciliation. For Mother there was only the memory of having been, as she saw it, brutally transported to a foreign land. Her every remark made it clear that she would never forgive him for having thrown away the opportunity to better himself in Athens. Her father had been right to forbid her to marry him. Chagrin at her own foolishness drove her into paroxysms of recrimination and regret.

I could hardly understand what she found so distressing. Life had hardly changed so badly. We lived among other professional Greek-Americans. I remember a Mr Takideli, a family friend, and of course there was Dr Lanzounis, an orthopaedic surgeon, who became Maria's godfather when at the age of three she was christened at the Orthodox cathedral. By then I was nine, a little American girl, happy at school, desperately unhappy at home. Mary and I were serious children. We never played with dolls although we had them. How could we when the only example of motherhood we knew was a woman for ever bemoaning the fact that she had married our father? Yet at the same time who else was there but our mother, the most important figure in our lives? I remember a silly incident on the way home from school: one of the other girls shouted out that she knew my father was a garbage collector. Why do children get so irate about such petty insults? What would it have mattered if my father had been a garbage collector? But of course it did, so across the road I went to point out that Father was a druggist and inevitably a fight broke out. Ever watchful from her window, my mother rushed out to save me. Of course she scolded me but I could sense that she was pleased that I had taken prompt action to defend our social status, such as it was.

Had I been free to be so, I would have become quite a tomboy in New York. As it was, whenever I was out of Mother's watchful gaze for a moment, I would be for ever hurting myself in little ways, falling over and grazing my knees while roller skating or just bumping into things as I charged about. But if I did, I could be sure that there was Mother with a handkerchief to be spat on so that she could wipe me clean while lecturing me on my stupidity, my lack of ladylike qualities, my failure to live up to her standards. She never knew when to stop and there were entire days passed in listening to her upbraid me for some slight misdemeanour. She demanded absolute obedience, without question, and for a lively child it was terrible torture to be treated in this way. Sometimes she would go on and on, building up to a crescendo, so that I would run weeping to my room. I was only happy alone with Mary.

Only later did I realise that it was not just a sort of madness that made her behave like that, she had some sort of half-realised plan to gain control of her daughters, to alienate them from their father and to take them away from him. In both of these she succeeded completely. Her incessant complaints about our father's stupidity, laziness, and lack of anything that she told us was correct in life, became a matter of truth to us. She hammered it home and we accepted it. When Father wanted to play his Greek folk songs on the wind-up phonograph and she poured scorn on Bouzouki music until he gave up and let her put on Puccini, it seemed to us that he was both tasteless and weak. In this she had won. As far as control went, with me she was entirely successful. I stopped being a happy tomboy and became quiet and secretive. I took to dawdling home from school, often taking a book to the park by the East River where I would sit alone and read. No ten-year-old child should be like that but I was. It gradually became clear to me that she was at her worst at regular intervals and it was explained during one of her rows with Father when he suddenly asked if the moon was full.

She had periods of deep melancholia affected by the phases of the moon so that I would watch the night sky from our bedroom window and dread the diminishing crescent as a herald of bad days to come. On one such she nagged me to tears and when her back was turned I ran out and down to the river. I clambered up on to the stone parapet and looked into the murky waters and longed to jump in. Ten years old! Even now I can cry with distress at the misery I was put through.

The only time I can remember her letting me do something on my own was the winter when she had flu and I cooked for everyone. After I had served Mother in bed upstairs, Father, Mary and I ate together at the dining-room table. It was wonderfully peaceful. Of course Father was almost a stranger to us. Seeing so little of him we were bound to accept what our mother said about him, but that evening was so pleasant that I must have begun to wonder if the man opposite me was quite the monster he was made out to be. He still had an appealing smile, still twirled the corners of his moustache, and he treated Mary and me as if we were quite grown-up. How different from Mother with her unending discipline: pepper on the lips if she suspected you of an untruth, all your clothes dumped in the corridor if you had omitted to make your bed. One day she had insisted I wear a hat when I went out even though she knew I hated

38

it. I was no sooner in the downstairs foyer than I pulled it off and ran out bareheaded. Untrusting as ever, she was watching from an upstairs window and yelled out that I should come back. I had no sooner walked through the door than there was a terrific crash and a sharp pain – she had hit me over the head with an umbrella. Father was watching from the living-room and he leaped up, flushed with rage.

'Not the head!' he shouted. 'If you have to hit her then do it over her behind.'

For once Mother was put out. He never normally interfered between us and I suppose she must have realised that she was in the wrong. Not that it stopped her for long; within an hour the orders were pouring forth as ever.

Without Mary it would have been totally unbearable. As she was only six she had little idea what I was suffering but in her childish way she would try to comfort me when she saw I was unhappy. When neither parent was around Mary would come to me for company. She would cuddle up to me and I would try to give her the love we never seemed to get. Perhaps it was harder for her at first; at least I escaped to school for part of the day. She would be dressed up to accompany us to church, a ritual I quickly learned was as much social as religious, the occasion for the Greek community to get together – a classic opportunity for Mother to recharge the batteries of her fury at our low social status in comparison with other more prosperous immigrants. In Meligala we had been something, here we were nothing – and so it went on and on.

This deep attachment Mary had for me nearly caused her death. We were both short-sighted and when Mary was five and I was eleven we began to wear glasses some of the time. One day that summer, Mother had brought Mary out of the apartment to meet me back from school and see I got across the busy street safely. As soon as she saw me, Mary ran into the road to join me, oblivious of the traffic. One car was unable to swerve and struck the running child, dragging her some way down the street. It was all so quick and so terrible it seemed ages before anyone did anything. Mother was never rational about this incident. Over the years Mary's accident worsened and worsened in the telling, the distance she was dragged lengthened and lengthened, the suspense at the hospital over whether she would live deepened and deepened. I recall we were terrified at first but that as soon as we arrived at St Elizabeth hospital on Fort Washington Avenue we were reassured that she had only had a nasty bump and a bad shock and that she would be all right. Later, Mother also exaggerated the length of Mary's convalescence though I recall she was soon back home and begging me to sit by her and retell her favourite stories again.

The old pianola in the living-room continued to be our greatest pleasure and we were both happy pretending to be pianists. But it was only pretence. I don't think we showed much musical inclination or at least no more than any other child. In fact, given what was to happen, it is more significant that we, or in this case more importantly Mary, should have been so keen on acting the part. Away from our mother's commanding gaze we were constant pretenders: seated at the pianola we were concert pianists, there was a vast audience to be satisfied, applause to be acknowledged. What we did not know was that in her own way, quite separate from us, Mother shared these charades. She, too, was beginning to think of the theatre she had loved in Greece as a girl. Acting was one of the rare outside activities a female child in Greece could dream of entering with some hope that one day the dream might come true. At a time when almost every other profession was exclusively male, the stage was an open house for dreamers.

At first I think this can have been no more than the vaguest of passing thoughts in her mind but she took one positive step at this time by sending me to ballet lessons. Nothing unusual in that for a little girl. Many of my other school friends did similar things. For the first three months it was agony for me. My toes hurt constantly. Gradually, the pain subsided but I just couldn't get interested. For once Mother neither nagged nor commanded; it was as if she was sniffing around trying to find the right approach to some half-formed plan. She found a piano teacher, a Signorina Santrina, and the pianola was exchanged for a proper upright piano. I took to it instantly. Within weeks I was playing tunes and never needed to be forced to practise. Mary would sit happily in the sofa watching me rattle off my scales. Mother weighed all this up and was satisfied. Soon Mary was having lessons too.

After a year I was getting very proficient. It helped at home for there was less need for arguments about what sort of music should be played on the phonograph, everyone could agree that the girls should play. In many ways the early part of 1929 was the best time we would have together. Father's business seemed to be doing well, and Mother was a little better reconciled to America now that she felt we were getting somewhere.

On some occasions we behaved like a real family, going by bus for picnics in upstate New York, enjoying the open air and the trees. There was another Greek-American family called Papajohn who apparently passed my mother's stringent criteria and with whom we shared the occasional outing. Mrs Papajohn was a buxom handsome woman in love with life, a marked contrast to our slim but difficult mother. There were five girls and a young boy, all considerably older than us, but at least Mary and I had some company at last. Even so, perhaps because of the isolation Mother had kept us in, Mary was always unpredictable in her behaviour towards others, including the Papajohns. One day Mrs Papajohn was visiting when she noticed that the hem of her skirt had come unstitched. She asked Mother for a needle and thread but when she went to get it Mary ran after her and began frantically imploring her not to let the woman have any.

'Don't give her it,' she begged. 'Let her go home and use her own.'

It was one of the first signs of the almost neurotic possessiveness that was to be such a feature of her later life and which was to be the sharpest element in her relationship with Mother. On that first occasion, it was all Mother could do to calm Mary down so that Mrs Papajohn would not be aware of what had taken place.

Just occasionally Mother would permit us to attend children's parties and to give one in return, but as she always picked who could attend and the events were so ordered by her rules of protocol, they were hardly fun for us. However, in 1929 we did have our first holiday when mother's cousin Harikia invited us to Florida to stay at the home of her Greek-American husband George Kritikos. He was something in shipping and had a nice house in Tarpon Springs, Florida, not far from Jacksonville and Miami. Father had to remain behind at the shop while the three of us went down by train. We spent a month away. Clearwater Beach was only half an hour from the house and, more important, there were three boys and a girl, Heleni, for us to play with. As Mother did not dare nag us in such company we were in heaven. I think Mary was happier than I have ever known her. Her face seemed very pretty then, with wide dark eyes and deep dark hair. We were both slim children and strangers often told us we would be great beauties. But then our only thoughts were to run in the sand and splash in the water. We were not to know that that holiday marked the end of such happiness as we were to know in America. From then on, life was to get very hard indeed.

What do I truly remember of the Great Crash? Did I really see people throw themselves off high buildings? Did I witness the panic that swept Wall Street? No, of course not, but it is difficult now to disentangle real life from the endlessly repeated newsreels which brought us those images of a world gone mad. I doubt we children knew what was happening at the time. We certainly had little idea at first what the collapse of the stock market meant, though we were not to remain in ignorance for long. As the children of the rising professional classes we were soon to be made aware that all was not as it had been, that many things formerly taken for granted were no longer to be relied on. At school there began to circulate rumours of anxious parents, tales of treats postponed or cancelled, of family quarrels and slammed doors. Not that any of that was unusual for Mary and me. I suppose each child thought him- or herself untouched by these strange events until one evening on returning home from school came the realisation that financial disaster was upon us. At first Father's business staggered on, far removed from the tottering industries that first experienced the effect of the crash. But when the ripples spread outward and the problems of the stock market descended into the Depression, then it was the turn of the small businessman to feel the wash of economic disaster. Gradually, unemployment spread and money became scarce – no money, no shopping. Of course people still needed medicines, though even there they were to be more cautious from now on. But drugs were not the real source of Father's income. An American drugstore relied heavily on people buying sweets, drinks, ice-creams and a host of small goods, most of which you could describe as luxuries in that it was perfectly possible to survive without them. Now everyone was into mere survival and Father began to sink into debt.

Mother was delighted. It was the fulfilment of all her prophecies. Father's new business had momentarily eclipsed the loss of what might have been back in Meligala – no more. We were reduced to what we had been when we first arrived. The pharmacy had to be given up, the stock sold to pay debts, a smaller apartment found.

When Mother heard of the sale she dashed into the drugstore to confront Father as if he had been personally responsible for the financial instability of the Western world and when he turned his

42

back on her and walked away she rushed to the dangerous medicines cupboard, grabbed a handful of pills and swallowed them. Had she really intended to make an end of it all she could easily have crept in one night, carefully selected her poison and lain down and died. In reality she made a noisy drama out of the whole thing, her one and only personal appearance in opera. Father was well aware of what had happened. He quickly rushed her to hospital where they pumped out the drugs. After an unpleasant period of purgation she was allowed to return home, a little weak and wretched but with no lasting side-effects. Using his medical connections, Father was able to see that nothing was made of the incident, but Mother's self-indulgent coup de théâtre effectively marked the end of their marriage – from then on they would live under the same roof as irritable strangers.

Of course poor Father took the brunt of all these changes. He was forced to take a job as a travelling salesman for a drug company. Later in life he would admit to me that the attraction went way beyond the salary offered; he was able to have days away from home and escape the incessant nagging over which he had no control. At the time, of course, I had only Mother's view of the world. The entire Wall Street crash was pictured as a personal failure on the part of George Callas and indeed he did seem to be weak and uncaring about the whole thing. Only years later did I realise that there was nothing the poor man could have done: that he, like countless others, was a victim of history and that the least he could have expected of his wife would have been her loyalty, support and encouragement during the most difficult period of his life. Though he never said so, I rather suspect that if she had stood by him he might have been able to salvage something of his business or at least begin to re-establish himself as soon as the worst effects of the Depression were over. Instead he appeared to us to have accepted her view of him and to have ceased to have the energy or the courage to run things himself. Mother's predictions had become self-fulfilling, her father was vindicated, she had married a nobody.

With hindsight I can see how unjust we were to him. In fact he used his considerable skills as a pharmacist to perfect his own treatment for gingivitis and began slowly to establish himself as the sole purveyor of the ointment which he travelled round the eastern states selling to dentists and druggists. Within a year of the crash we were able to move to a small but respectable apartment in

Washington Heights where I went to the George Washington High School and Mary to the local junior school. Mother, of course, refused to recognise that Father had pulled off a small miracle given the problems he faced.

Far from having her mind directed towards helping her husband, all my mother's thoughts were on salvaging her own dreams from the wreckage. At first, Mary and I had no clear idea just what was fermenting inside her mind. We were the passive agents of her schemes. Some sort of cultural education came into the plan – we were taken to the New York City library on the corner of 42nd Street once a week to read the classics. We quite liked that, though the sight of two schoolgirls poring over Dostoevsky must have seemed more than a little bizarre. Music was central and to Mother that meant opera with its combination of high art and social acceptability. At first there had been an attempt to purchase our own record collection so that we could have gramophone concerts of our choice. Now Mother accepted that such outgoings were impossible and that we would have to borrow boxed sets from the library. This was our favourite moment in the week, Mary and I browsing through the stacks trying to decide which opera we would have. How did we start to love that strange art form? I cannot say for I cannot remember a time when we weren't listening to it. I'm not sure what notions we had about what it was really like; after all we had never been to an opera house and I'm not sure that we thought of it as anything other than beautiful noises to which somehow Mother had attached a romantic story. But then she was very good at that. To set against the idea that she was for ever complaining was the Evangelia Callas who loved to fantasise – she could transform the most everyday event into something special: our trips to mid-town Manhattan were great adventures, especially at Christmas when we would go to see the lights and visit Santa Claus in the big stores. Mother made the whole thing magical even though three years after we had lost the business there was little chance of our affording the marvellous presents on show. It didn't matter, we had Mother to turn the trip into a great adventure. To Mary aged nine and me aged fifteen, opera was a simple extension of Mother's golden world. There were dreams of princes and lovers, of castles and ballgowns, adventure, love and tragedy. We would sit round the radio and listen to Rosa Poncelle from the Met and dream it all, a romantic jumble of images conjured up by Mother.

We never thought of actually going to the opera. I can only remember Mother going once when Mary's godfather Dr Lanzounis got two tickets for *Tosca*. She returned ablaze with excitement and described the whole thing to us blow by blow, note by note. It seemed like heaven.

I doubt if at first she had any clear idea of how this might be transformed into something other than an amusement for her daughters. We were still having piano lessons with Signorina Santrina but they were no more than any other girl might do at our age, though Father was said to object to the spending of money that could have gone toward re-establishing his business. Whether he really wanted to save up and get a new shop it is impossible to say at this distance; it's probable that such complaints were now merely skirmishes in his war with his wife. Certainly he did not put up a very spirited defence of his case and the lessons continued.

At first Mother seemed to think only of our being pianists and initially she seemed to think that I was the one who would succeed. Mary had shown an interest in singing but only for fun. Back in Riverside Drive she had sung along to the piano and I had bought some music for us. Our first song, with me accompanying Mary on the piano, was 'La Paloma' and later a waltz called 'The Heart That's Free'. We played them over and over again and I thought from the first that Mary had a nice voice but no more than that. Certainly neither Mother nor I, nor indeed Mary, believed that she merited singing lessons. Father would in any case have refused to pay for them.

The effect of this incessant warfare on us girls may be imagined. One does not have to deal in profound psychological explanations to see why I have grown up with a deep-seated fear of marriage, and of what the close proximity of a man to a woman can become. For little Mary, it was a living nightmare. She clung to me in desperation.

'I want to hug you,' she would say. 'Let me cuddle up to you.' She would get beside me on the sofa and I would comfort her. 'How sweet you smell,' she said, her face pressed into my neck.

We both liked school. Mary loved the school plays and Mother and I always went to see her perform. To me, George Washington High School was perfect. I adored the handsome, neo-classical building with its imposing columned portico and the tower above the central block.

How different school was in New York then from what one hears now. We were well-mannered happy children looked after by caring teachers. We all came from apparently stable families so that I used to think that ours was the only odd one out. But as none of our indoor troubles were ever allowed to appear beyond the front door who could tell? To me school was a haven of peace and friendship. We had a spacious playing area in tree-lined grounds and there were two swimming pools for exercise in good weather, though I was never able to learn to swim – the thought of letting go, of just releasing myself into the water with no contact with the earth was beyond me, I just couldn't do it. Still, I loved to splash about in the shallow end with my friends. Above all, the neighbourhood was respectable and safe. We could walk to and from school in laughing, giggling groups without a worry. Of course our mothers would be watching for our return and if we were ever a moment late there was trouble, but on the whole we never thought that anything could harm us. Today that neighbourhood is just another run-down New York slum, a far cry from what it was before the war.

By now I had a special friend, Clare Poretz, also aged sixteen. We were together almost from the first day in high school. Her family, too, lived in Washington Heights though later they moved to Brooklyn. They were Russian Jews, her father was in insurance and when they left the neighbourhood I used to go and spend weekends with them. It was only then that I truly understood what was wrong with my own home – the Poretzes loved each other. They were such a happy family, hardly ever a quarrel, I could barely believe it. I used to love those weekends. Mary too loved Clare. She would sometimes come to us and Mary would be with us. I don't think she was ever jealous, after all we were a lot older and I think Mary accepted it, but looking back there must have been many long, boring days when she was thrown on her own resources with nothing but the piano and the opera records to amuse her.

I have read books about us that suggest that from the start I was the pretty one destined for marriage and that Mary was the fat, unattractive one who sang to comfort herself and who in her loneliness and rejection developed a burning ambition for theatrical success. Would that things were so easy to explain. In truth Mary did not start out as an unattractive child; she was very pretty, dark rather than with my paler looks and at first no one made unfavourable comparisons. Nor were any musical judgments made so early in our lives – if anything I think people still thought that I might have a

46

career as a pianist. At first Mary would simply sit near me while I practised, later we would have good-natured tussles over who should practise first but it was never thought that one was more especially gifted than the other.

Two things combined to change all this. Perhaps because I was now more often with Clare, Mary took to amusing herself with longer hours singing at the piano. Unknown to us, one of our neighbours was a singing coach and he overheard her usual repertoire of 'La Paloma' and 'The Heart That's Free' and came round to see Mother to offer to teach Mary for nothing. He was Swedish and why someone not of our community should have wanted to help a girl with only little apparent talent will never be known, but for two months he helped her work on the songs and her progress was astonishing. From being just another sweet voice there now appeared the first signs of something special.

The second factor that was to change Mary's life at this time was Mother's instant recognition that here, in her daughter's voice, and not in the piano, lay the solution she had been striving for. But how to give it practical effect? After about a month of lessons the answer suddenly appeared like a sign from heaven in the form of a newspaper advertisement calling for entries in a radio talent contest for children. That was it, Mary must be entered.

So it was that at the age of eleven my sister made her first public appearance along with a lot of other children, some of whom recited poems or told jokes or sang ditties. She was dressed in a simple straight dress with her hair cut short and bangs at her forehead. I accompanied her as she sang our two songs and we finished to strong applause. Mother was delighted. W O R was a national network and the whole thing was exactly how she had dreamed it, including the final judging when Mary was awarded the first prize, a Bulova watch.

That was it for Mother. It was now that she started to dredge up from her memories a family history that was used to point the way towards an inherited talent that we could draw on: she described to us how her father the General, Petros Dimitriadis – the stern forebear who had so wisely warned her against the feeble George Calogeropoulou – had himself been a wonderful tenor. How a visiting Italian opera singer had overheard that hero of the Balkan War singing an aria and had fled our town rather than face such competition. We, it was made clear, were of a line of Great Voices:

47

this surely was destiny. Of course Mary, who loved to sing, was perfectly willing to let Mother persuade her that she had this hidden, inherited talent waiting to be unleashed.

From now on everything was singing, singing, singing. Mary's appearance in Public School 164's production of *The Mikado* was later transformed into another milestone though I recall that Mary only had a minor rôle. Nevertheless, Mother had found *her* rôle in life, happily making a Japanese costume out of this and that. From now on we never missed an opera on the radio and Mary began to be more discriminating. Her favourite was Lily Pons and she would sing along with that great voice soaring from the radio. Mother would look over at me as if to say: 'see how similar they are'. And astonishingly they were – raw and untrained as Mary's voice was, it was nevertheless of the same kind, lyric towards coloratura, as the great diva's. But therein lay the problem. How to train that voice? Lessons cost ten dollars an hour, a fortune at that time and far beyond anything Father could afford even if he had been willing, which I doubt he was. Unknown to us, this became the new central fixation of Mother's life, how to handle The Voice. Looking back I can see that from 1934, the year Mary won that contest, Mother thought of little else.

But there was an even better source of instruction than those disembodied radio divas – Mother returned one day with a canary. Imagining it to be lonely, she soon acquired two more, thus Mary had three tutors: David, Elmina and Stephanakos, whom she could observe at close quarters. Elmina and Stephanakos were bright yellow, David was darker. He was the jealous one. If I let Elmina out of her cage I could only permit one of the males to be with her at a time. If it was Stephanakos he would go up beside her and sort of nudge her and this would send David wild in his cage. It says much that I was fascinated by them as creatures – how they behaved, what their feelings were; but Mary was only interested in their voices. She would stare into the cages watching them sing their hearts out. 'That is how it's done,' she would say. 'They know the secret.'

Given all this emphasis on singing it is strange that no one ever wondered if I might have a voice. I never wanted to sing and I never tried and Mother must have reckoned that at seventeen I was now beyond the point where I could hope to take it up. Anyway, my mind was now elsewhere. Like any other teenager, all my thoughts were of romance – I was falling in and out of love with all the frenetic energy of any girl my age. At sixteen there had been my biology teacher. He was German and stunningly handsome. Was it my imagination or was it true that he was always there to help me as I bent to the microscope? He had chestnut hair, was clean-shaven and in his late twenties. I spent hours talking to Clare about him until he was utterly displaced in my affections by a much more powerful subject. I went one day for a dental check-up, the nurse settled me in the reclining chair, attached a bib to my front and a disembodied voice asked me to open wide. I did as I was told, then suddenly *he* bent into view. It was love at first sight, real burning passion. I barely noticed the discomfort of the treatment and when I stepped out on to 48th Street near Times Square I was absolutely hooked. I now embarked on a major course of dental treatment. For some reason I always seemed to have something wrong with my teeth. Fortunately, at that time, pharmacists in America had special relationships with doctors and dentists so we got free treatment, otherwise I would have ruined my poor father all over again.

A few weeks later I announced that my ambition in life was to become a dentist. Why not? I was quite good at school and it was a not unreasonable prospect. In fact many of our Greek-American friends had chosen that career – the object of my affections was one of our community. I think Father would have liked the idea though he never got to hear of it as Mother forbade all talk of such a thing.

'A dentist, a dentist!' She was red with fury. 'Whoever heard of such a thing. No *lady* could be a dentist. Forget it!'

To Mother all thought of anything vaguely medical had been rendered repugnant by her life with Father. When I was fourteen I had come home from school complaining of chills and when the doctor arrived he had ordered me straight into hospital where my appendix was removed. Within six months Mother went down with the same thing but because of her reluctance to entangle herself with the accursed profession she delayed so long that in her case it was almost ruptured and the operation was extremely risky.

Soon, my naïve dreams of love with distant figures like the dentist began to give way to real people nearer to hand. In the sweltering New York summer I took to sitting at the entrance of our block. I'd take some knitting and enjoy the peaceful late evening away from Mother and the endless practising she obliged Mary to do. There was a very good-looking boy in the building, a little older than me, and I found myself hoping he would pass. Naturally, I dreaded the possibility that Mother would guess what I was thinking. One day I went up on to the roof to hang out some clothes when he suddenly appeared. Without any warning he came up close.

'D'you wanna be my girl?' he demanded.

'Don't say such a thing,' I protested, delighted and terrified in equal measure. 'If my parents found out . . .'

He laughed, and I admired his devil-may-care attitude in the face of such an awesome prospect as my mother's fury.

'Can I kiss you?' he asked.

That was too much. The world would end. 'Go away,' I said, looking round, convinced that his words must have summoned Mother from our apartment.

He laughed again and walked away. When I'd calmed down and got my breath back, I went home sure that guilt was written all over my face. However, I was nothing if not a risk-taker so the next day I was back on the front porch with my knitting. But if I'd imagined that Mother had entirely abandoned me in her push to advance Mary I was recklessly mistaken.

A few days later she suddenly loomed over me as I walked through our front door. 'What do you do out there?' she asked menacingly.

I told her I went out to get a little air.

'Air,' she snorted. 'Are you sure you're not hanging around to see that skinny boy, that living skeleton, who lives next door?'

I should have said nothing and just let her suspicions play out but I was so terrified I fell right into the trap. 'Oh no,' I said. 'He lives on the fourth, we're on the fifth.'

As soon as I'd said it I realised that my knowledge of his whereabouts was certain proof of my interest. 'He just says hello,' I protested.

'He doesn't just say hello, he speaks to you. What does he say?'

I told her we just talked about school, about lessons.

'You don't speak to him any more, you just say hello that's all.'

Next time he went past I quickly insisted that that was that. I told him about Mother and warned him that she was capable of coming to see his father. He got the point.

In the end there was only Clare Poretz that Mother approved of. She considered the family acceptable so that was all right. We were always happiest when Clare came round because Mother couldn't get at us. In fact it brought out the best in her, that side of her that let her turn even the most ordinary event into something theatrical. She

50

taught us our first dances, the tango and the foxtrot. The four of us, me and Clare, Mary and Mother, would jog around the living-room, with Mother transforming it into the most sumptuous ballroom. When people ask where Mary got her sense of theatre from I always say that it was from our mother. On Tuesday nights we would go to the local Chinese restaurant. All we could ever afford was chop suey but nothing mattered, we were dining at the Ritz, we were habituées of fine places, we were princesses waited on hand and foot. Yes, when people ask whence Mary got her sense of theatre, that great gift for the dramatic moment that was her greatest contribution to the lyric theatre of our day, I immediately think of we three girls seated in that restaurant with my mother creating, with a look or a gesture, an atmosphere that transported us beyond the cheap flock wallpaper and plastic lanterns of a Chinese noodle house and into the banqueting hall of a Renaissance palace. At such moments Mother was the most magical person on earth.

Poor Father was by now a mere detail in our lives. He came and went, occupied with his travels. Sometimes he tried to ask Mary and me about our lives, tried to join in whatever we were doing but it was impossible, we had been too much influenced against him and we felt embarrassed by his attentions. Later Mother would insist that it was his philandering that had led to the breakdown of their marriage but I was never aware of any such behaviour on his part aside from his solicitous behaviour with all women. I just put it down to his nature that he should behave like that.

Except where my mother was concerned he was the gentlest of men and his disgust with her led him to ignore us. When Mother began to think of Mary as a singer he flatly refused to take any notice. I think Mother wanted to blame him for not paying the ten dollars an hour but even she must have realised that such a sum was beyond him. I don't know, but I imagine it was about then that she began to realise what she needed to do to get Mary the lessons necessary to make a career out of her voice. I was far too preoccupied with my own life to care.

Having been refused a career in dentistry I had abandoned all thoughts of a college education and settled for the commercial course at high school. Clare and I were quite happy with it and imagined we would get jobs as secretaries. Most of our thoughts were about love anyway. I had already had my first proposal, from George Vanson, another neighbour's son. He was twenty-five and had been allowed to come round and dance the tango and foxtrot with Clare and me. But when I announced that he had asked me to marry him all that changed. Mind you, he did it correctly and came to see my parents to ask permission but Mother wasn't having it. She went round to see his family and told them firmly that I was far too young. George asked if we could get engaged and wait a few years till I had grown up, but that too was unacceptable – although she was concentrating most of her efforts on Mary my mother wasn't prepared to risk everything just yet. I was still considered a fine pianist and, who knows, I might make the grade if Mary didn't. Tying me down in marriage was out of the question. George was turned away.

Clare and I graduated from high school early in 1935, I was seventeen and was beginning to get a little self-confidence about my looks, though Mother still insisted on choosing all my clothes. Perhaps because of her concentration on Mary I was given some room to breathe. It was decided that I should go alone to stay with our relatives in Florida while Mary went on practising. Father came down to join me for the Orthodox Easter celebrations and to take me home afterwards. It ought to have been a marvellous opportunity for us to get to know each other but it was too late, there had been too many years of listening to him derided to be able to see him in a new light. It is hard to esteem a man after you have heard his wife insulting him for seventeen years.

Still, I felt very grown-up riding back on the train with my debonair father – he still had an eye for the ladies and still twirled the end of his moustache as he had when I was young.

'What do you want to do with yourself?' he asked at one point. 'Do you want a career?'

I nearly told him I wanted to be a dentist but that was an old story and it was too late now.

But his question set me thinking and when we got back to New York I began to look around for things I could do. The only thing that everyone seemed agreed on was that I had looks, so when I saw an advert for a modelling school it seemed the perfect answer. As this seemed fairly practical, Father found the necessary fees and for a month I went to a school run by a charming lady who trained girls to work as demonstrators in stores and showrooms. It was a very down-to-earth course meant to find you a job, not to give you false dreams about fame and I liked the work. Best of all was the fact that our teacher inculcated the idea that we should exercise for twenty

52

minutes every day of our lives. She taught us her own régime of stretching and bending and as she was a handsome woman I paid attention.

'How old am I?' she demanded at our first lesson.

Someone ventured forty.

'I'm fifty-five,' she said proudly.

A day has not gone past when I have not followed the pattern of press-ups and arm swings she set out for us then. Today, in my seventies, my waist is the same as it was then at seventeen, I barely need a bra and I can wear a sleeveless blouse with confidence.

When I finished the course I got a job in the mid-town garment district working on the first floor of a clothes studio run by two Jewish gentlemen. A seamstress made up the garments and I modelled them to the buyers from the stores. I loved it. Any sense of theatre I might have had was satisfied by my little shows. At that age it was wonderful to be looked at and admired. At home Mary would lie on the couch and watch me rehearse my moves and I would show her how to parade and turn, open the jacket to display the skirt and so on. It was a happy interlude and I thought I had a career ahead of me. I had forgotten about Mother's ambitions.

One day in the summer she said she wanted to talk to me. Had I noticed Mr Raynes, the landlord, when he came to collect the rent? Such a nice man, young, only twenty-five. I told her that I had noticed him when he came but that was all.

'He wants to marry you,' she said. 'He says you're a nice quiet girl and he wants a good wife. He's a lawyer but he has apartment blocks.'

He could have owned Texas for all I cared. I was quite happy learning to be myself and in any case I was utterly disgusted by what I had seen of marriage and had no desire to try the institution for myself. I told Mother I wasn't interested.

'Why not?' she said sharply, which surprised me, given that she had always kept any previous suitors very much at bay. 'Didn't you hear what I told you? He's got a lot of money, you could do worse.'

'But I don't love him.'

'Love.' She gave an incredulous snort. 'Listen, Jackie, this is a chance for you to do something useful. This man could pay for your sister's lessons. Ten dollars an hour. Where am I going to find that with a useless lazy husband who never does a stroke? Tell me that if you can. And you talk about love. What's wrong with Mr Raynes?'

I was appalled. The woman would sacrifice anything including her daughter's happiness for whatever was obsessing her at that moment.

'I can't,' I said, and left her standing there.

From then on she grew silent, clearly brooding on this set-back and preparing her next moves. I tried to shut her out as I went on with my work but I knew by now that she was not to be so easily thwarted. The answer came a week later when she summoned Mary and me and announced that we were leaving New York and Father and returning to Greece. It was a devastating piece of theatre delivered without warning and it was made clear that she would brook no argument. My first reaction was horror at the ruin of a career I was learning to love and the loss of Clare, my best, indeed my only real, friend. But what could I say? The whole thing had been dressed up as a way of advancing us, of turning both Mary and myself into something special – I would have piano lessons, Mary would have her voice trained. In Greece we would have a family behind us whereas in America we had nothing and no one. When she left us Mary and I frantically debated this bombshell but it was clear from the start that she was delighted with the idea. Real singing lessons were what she longed for and in any case she had never seen our homeland and the whole thing seemed like the most wonderful adventure. What could I say? I began to feel more and more trapped. I suppose if I'd managed to forge a relationship with Father I could have turned to him for help. Perhaps he would have stood by me and let me stay behind with him while Mother took Mary away, but it was too late to start thinking of Father as a real parent. If I had found a way to remain much misery might have been avoided. I could already foresee the troubles to come and knew by then that Mother was quite willing to sacrifice me on the altar of Mary's success.

The first sign of Mother's disregard for me was her decision that I should precede them, travelling alone to Athens in December that year, while they would follow a couple of months after, early in 1937. Before, she would never have entertained the idea of her eighteen-year-old daughter travelling unaccompanied aboard an ocean liner. Now, she simply wanted me out of her hair.

I managed to dull the trauma of leaving by insisting to myself that this would only be a visit, a sort of extended holiday to complete our musical education after which I would be safely back in New York. Father hardly mentioned my departure, though whether this was because he too believed it was not for long or because he was glad to be seeing the back of his troublesome womenfolk I cannot say. Clare wept and begged me to come back soon and I promised I would, though without total conviction, for who could say just what Mother was plotting. She never told us her plans and she may not have worked out fully what she meant to do at that stage.

It was Mother, as usual, who chose all my clothes for the journey and Mother who, with no recollection of her attempt to marry me off when it suited her, warned me of what would befall if I so much as looked at a member of the opposite sex. She accompanied me aboard the SS *Vulcania*, an Italian liner sailing between New York and Patras. It was December and bitterly cold on deck. We were both wrapped up in long winter coats and Mother was keen to be away. She was also plainly indignant about something.

'Do you know what your father did when I told him I was leaving for Greece?'

I said I didn't.

'He knelt down, crossed himself and said: "At last, my God, you have pitied me." '

I was grateful that at just that moment the siren sounded to warn visitors to leave the vessel otherwise I think I might have burst out laughing. With a final indignant sniff she wrapped her coat tighter round her, kissed me on both cheeks and hurried off.

Despite the icy wind and the drifts of snow, I stayed on deck until the towers of Manhattan had disappeared from view.

CHAPTER THREE
1936–1940

Eventually I went below to the lounge which was completely deserted. The other passengers were either exhausted from the effort of boarding and finding their cabins or were getting ready for dinner. I sat alone at a table near a window where I could see the grey waters heaving and rolling as the boat gathered speed. A waiter, arranging glasses at a bar in the far corner of the room, came over to ask if I wanted anything, his accent heavily Italian. I shook my head, terrified that I might be expected to pay for something – I had very little money and strict orders about touching anything beyond orangeade. But I was no longer unhappy, the sense of adventure was beginning to grip me and in any case there was no Mother, even if the shadow of that stern presence still hovered somewhere nearby. Staring out of the window imagining Greece, I suddenly realised there was someone reflected in the glass, someone standing by my table staring at me.

'Excuse me,' said the stranger. 'I couldn't help noticing you standing on deck. I'm in a first class cabin and I could see you below. My name is Santini.'

I turned to see a man, possibly late thirties, whose accent was that of an Italian-American, just the sort of passenger you would expect on the *Vulcania*. He was noticeably polite despite the forwardness of his approach and I didn't feel at all reluctant to have him there until he also asked if I'd like something to drink. The request brought back all Mother's dire warnings about accepting alcohol from strangers.

I shook my head violently.

'Perhaps a martini?' he said.

More violent head-shaking.

'Whisky? Gin?'

I weighed up the situation. He was bound to think me more than a little peculiar but there was also Mother's terrible threats to be considered. She had said only orangeade but I was determined to exercise at least a fractional independence.

'Coca-Cola,' I said, looking round to see if this flaunting of the letter of the law would bring Mother screaming into the lounge.

When she failed to materialise I began to relax. Mr Santini called over the waiter and sat down beside me. It was then that I began to learn some of the basic rules of survival a girl needs in a man's world. Desperate not to be questioned I began to draw him out about himself and his journey and I was pleased to discover that this was precisely what he wanted. He told me about his moving and storage business – very successful – and how it permitted him to make a tour of the world – and how I was such an interesting person, presumably because he'd done all the talking. It was a simple conversational formula which I have used ever since and which has never failed. It has allowed me considerable peace of mind; it's like starting a snowball at the top of a hill and watching it gather momentum and size as it goes – so little effort for such a spectacular result.

Still merrily recounting his life story, Santini led me into dinner where he managed to find a table with some people of my own age. There were three Greek-American girls and some other Italians and together we passed a very jolly twelve days. The boat stopped in Lisbon for two hours and we hurried off the ship for a quick walking tour. The next day was Christmas, which seemed odd with the Italian food as I was by then used to the American feast. That afternoon there were games on deck. I won a prize for a sort of golf and felt very pleased with myself. The Italian contingent disembarked at Naples but Santini promised to come and see me in Athens on the next stage of his great voyage. By the time the boat docked at Patras I was feeling almost completely liberated from Mother's shadow and as we approached the harbour I realised that I was nervously expectant at the thought of seeing my native land again. It was all of twelve years since I had been whisked away and I had only the vaguest recollections of what I had left behind. In the intervening years Greece had taken on a sort of golden glow. Among the Greek-American community Hellas was the terrestrial paradise from which we were exiled but would one day return. It was essential to our sense of community that we should succour an image of our homeland that would help us maintain our separateness and our dignity in a land of numberless immigrants. Imagine then my surprise when the boat docked and I looked out on the dingiest place I had ever seen. Pre-war New York was a well-run, modern miracle; its public services the finest in the world, its streets were clean, its buildings sparkling new. Here before me was a run-down, filthy Greek port. I was appalled. Trying to disguise my distress I shuffled through the immigration formalities and asked about trains to Athens. I had been given precise instructions about what to do on landing, nevertheless I felt very inexperienced over the way I handled the matter in what I now realised was in many ways a completely foreign country. The journey at least restored my sense of adventure: the old wooden carriages, the slow train chugging through the then unspoiled landscape of mainland Greece; peasant women garbed in black, hauling heavy wicker panniers, men in black jodhpurs and boots herding their sheep and goats – for a young woman from New York it was entrancing.

Three of Mother's sisters and her brother, my Uncle Dukas, met me at the station. They were delighted to see me and I began to sense that there was the possibility of family relationships other than those I had so far experienced. Bursting with questions and with much good-natured clucking over my looks and my clothes these jolly aunts bore me off to my grandmother's house in Sopolia. I had no recollection of her from my infancy in Meligala though I supposed I must have met her, but I did know that everyone said she was a great beauty, always known as Helen of Troy. She was old by then but indeed very beautiful. I could see where my mother had got her dramatic looks. But Grandmother was not the haughty type; as soon as I appeared she drew me to her and gave me a loving hug. After the years of Mother's temperament, Grandmother was pure balm. She would get me to sit with her and let me talk about myself.

'What do you want to do?' she would ask, with the emphasis on the you rather than the do. It was so different from Mother's life plans. Grandmother quickly realised that all was not well with me and as quickly realised that it had everything to do with her daughter. I should have realised that if anyone understood what a difficult character my mother was it would be her own mother. Perhaps realising that there was no time to lose, Grandmother suggested I search out a career of my own choosing before Mother arrived with Mary and took over my life again. Aided by my aunts we searched the newspapers and came up with the unoriginal solution that I should take a secretarial course. It was not quite as common in those days as it is now and with my two languages I would have an advantage. Best of all it implied a degree of liberty.

It was arranged that I should go to the school of a Mr Ablonitis who taught typing and commercial correspondence. I quickly settled down, happy to have a goal to work towards and intrigued by my new life. Although I had no friends as yet, I was completely charmed by Greece. Athens in those days was a small town of mainly one- and two-storey buildings which, away from the more French-style centre, were largely rustic in character. Most roads were mere dirt lanes, there were gardens everywhere and the air was scented with lemons and oranges. After our somewhat frugal life in New York, where the weekly chop suey had been the great treat, it was amazing to be in a place where eating out was the norm. Though we were far from rich, almost every night a party of my relations would set off for a meal in a local taverna. Even in January the weather was warm by North American standards and life seemed like a perennial holiday. There was also the sheer delight of being with people who were so good-natured and relaxed. I wondered if Mother would change when she arrived. Would she become like her sisters, a jolly Greek lady freed from the driving ambition under which Mary and I had suffered? Foolish pipe-dreams!

Mother and Mary arrived in February 1937 and I, with a contingent of aunts, met them at Athens station. Mother was wearing a tailored suit and an elaborate hat with an enormous feather, clearly intended to impress her relations. Mary was introduced as a person of consequence embarking on a brilliant career. She looked embarrassed and downcast, clearly the result of her isolation with Mother whose nervous chatter seemed endless. As soon as I could I took Mary aside and tried to cheer her up with my description of the good life with Grandmother. At first that kindly lady did manage to put her at her ease despite the constant chatter of our mother about her voice and her career. But Mother no sooner set foot in Greece than her campaign to advance Mary's cause got under way in earnest. There was Uncle Efthimios to be sent for, who had contacts at the Conservatory. There were unrestrained enquiries as to who might help finance all the plans she had been brooding over. I sensed disaster. Although my relations lived fairly well and ate out constantly, that was simply the Greek style in those days. But I had already realised that they were far from rich. Most were quite elderly and lived off pensions or other small fixed incomes. Mother in her unthinking way had built up a complete fantasy about her family. Over the years of absence they had been transformed into people of considerable means. While it was true that our distant Louros relations were connected with the court, our immediate circle was basically petit-bourgeois. They listened to Mother's endless stream of ambitious plans, looked at each other and wondered.

First off, Mary was made to sing for Uncle Efthimios. It was odd to hear 'La Paloma' again so far from New York. But he only nodded and announced that there were hundreds of girls with pleasant voices and what was he supposed to do? Knowing my mother of old, the family's initial reaction was to dampen down her more manic ideas in the hope that she would abandon her schemes. I suspect that they rather wanted her to have a reasonable holiday, then pack up and go home to her husband. They were to be disappointed. Much of what Mother wanted was to get away from our father; that rather than Mary may have been the prime motivation of all this upheaval. In any case a woman like Evangelia Callas wasn't to be stopped at the first hurdle. She got Mary to sing for anyone who had even the vaguest connections with the musical life of Athens – and how poor Mary loathed it.

'I don't want to,' she wailed to me. 'Please tell her to stop.'

Me? What on earth could I do? I had only just survived Mother's fury when she discovered I had broken loose and taken up a secretarial course. She blamed Grandmother for this display of independence and I suspected there would be trouble as a result.

In only one regard did Mother's family prove useful – her brother Dukas told her about a taverna at Perama on the coast where people got up to sing operatic arias. Clutching at any straw by this time, Mother made him take us and to Mary's disgust she was ordered to take the stage and show what she could do. I went to the piano and we did our usual routine: 'La Paloma' and 'The Heart That's Free'. She sat down to ecstatic applause and I could see that my uncle was intrigued, the more so when we were joined by John Cambanis, a singer just starting his career with the Lyric Theatre but already gaining a reputation. He congratulated Mary on her performance and my mother went into top gear as she attempted to win him over to her cause. Cambanis had been trained by Maria Trivella, one of the leading names in Athens musical circles, and this was just the entrée Mother needed. Uncle Efthimios knew Trivella's brother-in-law but had so far proved unwilling to utilise this valuable connection. Now with Cambanis on her side Mother could bring out all her weapons.

While these contacts were being established we were constantly on the move – we left Grandmother's tiny home for an apartment in Terma Patission where we spent the summer. Fortunately it was furnished, as we were running out of money. At first, Father had sent us a hundred dollars a month, but eight or nine weeks after Mother left him he went down with pneumonia and was hospitalised. Without income and with all his savings going on medical bills he was unable to keep up Mother's allowance. She of course interpreted this as just another example of his perfidy and took it badly that we were now utterly dependent on the goodwill of relations who had little enough for themselves.

Mother tried desperately to re-establish contact with anyone of substance she had once known in Athens who might prove useful. One day, about two and a half months after her arrival, she took me round to the office of a Mr Polikala, a notary and family friend and the sort of solid established figure she thought might somehow help her. As the real reason behind these visits could never be openly discussed I found them rather embarrassing. In any case, people like Mr Polikala were usually busy and the arrival of Mother and me was always something of a nuisance. Inevitably we were asked to wait in an outer office as he was occupied with clients. I could see them through the glass panels in the door, a young man with his advisers deep in conversation over what looked like deeds and plans spread across a dark wooden desk.

Mother pretended to be interested in the faded magazines curling on the waiting-room table while I fought off the boredom by trying to memorise some of my secretarial lessons. Eventually Polikala came through, full of apologies, and introduced the young man as Harry Emberikos. I could tell from Mother's effusive reaction that the name meant something to her and we were soon drawn into conversation. I could see that the young man was interested in me and so could Mother who began to introduce me into the conversation, the fact that we were newly arrived, that I knew few people, that I was so talented, and so on. I hated that sort of thing but soon the young man was asking whether Mother and I would accompany Mr Polikala and himself to dinner one day and just as quickly she

61

had said yes on our behalf. This was no sooner concluded than another young man appeared and was introduced as Harry's elder brother Milton. There was more polite talk before Mother decided to leave them to their business and whisked me out into the street.

She was ecstatic. 'Do you know who they are? The Emberikos family? Ship owners. Rich.' She was irritated by my ignorance and told me I'd do better making myself attractive to one of the brothers than in wasting my time studying to be a stenographer.

Her wish was fulfilled a few days later with the arrival of a note from Harry inviting us to lunch in a restaurant that Friday. As we set off for the encounter I didn't tell Mother that I would have rather it had been the elder brother Milton who had asked us out.

In a way it didn't matter; Mother did all the talking, Polikala smiled and responded and Harry stared at me. At the end of the meal he invited me to go on a trip with him to Kiffissia which was then a rustic village in open country beyond the city and not as now a mere suburb of the metropolis. This was a little hasty by Greek standards and Mother ought to have demurred until we had had more chaperoned encounters. Not surprisingly she didn't, which can only have given the wrong impression to a man like Harry. Indeed we had no sooner left the little station and were walking across the fields than he made a lunge for me and tried to kiss me. I pulled away.

'I don't like that,' I said sharply.

'Why? Is kissing so bad? You're a pretty girl, why shouldn't I kiss you?'

But his pleas were pointless, I had already turned back.

I said nothing to Mother and just hoped that that was the end of the matter but a week later he sent a message inviting me to Zonars. This was a clever move as Zonars was then the most fashionable café in the city at the Syntagma end of Panepistimio, that broad avenue with its handsome neo-classical university buildings. In those days to sit at Zonars' pavement tables eating their famous cakes and ices was the height of Athenian sophistication. Intrigued, I decided to risk another encounter with Harry. Imagine my surprise when I found the elder brother Milton waiting for me. He apologised, explaining that Harry was unwell, and though I realised at once that they had set the whole thing up I was far from displeased. We sat for some time enjoying our coffee and watching the passing crowd and I was gratified to note that the elder was as different from the younger as it was possible to be. Milton was gentle and reserved. We talked

62

about our families and, despite the fame of his, we found much in common. His father had been well-known as a minister in the Venizelou government but they too had lost nearly everything in the American crash. What had saved them was the building that he pointed out, almost opposite Zonars. It was an office block and had been a present from his father to his mother after the birth of their first son, himself. It was the building he and Harry had been discussing that day at the notary's. Their other saving asset was a boat, named *Eleni* after their mother, which plied between the mainland and Corfu. With these two assets Milton hoped to rebuild the family fortunes. I was fascinated. He seemed so serious and dependable and I was delighted when he asked to see me again.

Mother was thrilled; this was just the sort of man from good society she approved of and would do nicely to keep me occupied while she concentrated on Mary. In fact Milton went out of his way to be pleasant to Mother who at first acquaintance could be very charming. Initially he was more than happy to include Mary and Mother in our outings to the countryside, or to take Mother, Mary being too young to go along, to nightclubs where the lessons in tango and foxtrot came in useful. The Emberikos had a beautiful home in fashionable Kolonaki but at first Milton was happy to come to our simple rented apartment and share my mother's cooking. Only gradually did he begin to see her true character.

His first glimpse was after we had gone for a walk in the mountains about three hours' drive from the city. It was a hot summer's day and we had stopped at a taverna for a drink. Without thinking I had accepted his offer of a glass of wine. I never drank alcohol at all and that one glass completely knocked me over. I tried to stand and couldn't; walking back to the station was out of the question, I was limp and giggly. The possibility of a taxi in so remote a spot was slight and even the normally unflappable Milton was beginning to panic.

'Can't you try and walk?' he begged. 'Come on, you can do it.'

By a miracle, just as he was on the point of despairing, a taxi appeared and he ran joyfully to grab it. Even after the long drive back I was still woozy and unsteady on my feet. As soon as we got in, Milton began to explain to my astonished mother that he hadn't realised I was unused to wine and that he was deeply sorry. She, however, would have none of it.

63

'How dare you get my daughter drunk. She has never been permitted alcohol. If you think . . .'

And on and on. As ever, she was unstoppable once she got under way. For Milton it was a revelation and one he was not likely to forget.

We continued to take Mother out from time to time but now he was more aware of her real character and more cautious in his dealings with her.

Soon after, we moved again, and I had to keep Milton away for a while as our new apartment in Harilaou Trikoupi was unfurnished and with no more funds from America we had no money to buy any. Quite simply we slept on the floor, though under pain of Mother's worst threats if anyone ever found out. She was by now increasingly furious with her husband's inability to support us. For his part, he must have been increasingly exasperated by her endless begging for help that he could not afford to give. Only Uncle Efthimios finally did as she requested by arranging an interview that September with Maria Trivella at the National Conservatory. We all went with Mary to give her our support. She looked both nervous and in an odd way determined, as if to say: I have to get through this ordeal in order to put an end to the misery of the past few months. She certainly sang 'La Paloma' better than ever before and Trivella was entranced. Yes, she would enroll Mary as a pupil but there was just one problem: the fees. Of course there was nothing our uncle could do but Trivella stepped in to save the situation: she could offer a scholarship. The two formidable women put their heads together. Mary, it turned out, was too young. No matter, they'd alter all the papers: at a stroke, she became a year older. Mary stood to one side watching her life being ordered about as if she didn't exist and I suddenly wondered just what she did want. What on earth was going on inside her? Was this what she really longed to do or was there some other unspoken ambition locked up behind those wide dark eyes?

Having settled the matter of Mary's future, Mother now picked a quarrel with her brother Dukas which led to a full-scale row with their mother and the severing of all relations. I was devastated. I loved my grandmother; she was an island of loving calm, of decent good sense in the restless tides of my mother's insatiable ambition. Now even she was taken from me. Well, at least I had Milton. He was in his late thirties, a reasonable age for a man to be courting a girl of nineteen in the Athens of that time. I was far from being in love with him, but I liked him a lot and it was pleasant to go out of an evening, perhaps to the cinema or just for a walk in the cooler evening air. I doubt I thought then that it would go any further. He was a charming boyfriend, and I assumed there would be others until the day came when I fell in love and got married. Life seemed as simple as that. Again I had reckoned without Mother.

'You do know we have no money at all?' she said one day, contemptuously scanning the bare living-room. 'It's all right Mary getting her fees paid but we have to live as well and this wonderful course you're doing doesn't bring anything in.'

'I'll be able to get a job soon,' I said. 'When I get my diploma.'

She gave me her most pitying look. 'We'll have starved to death by then. We need money now.'

I asked her what she imagined I could do about it. I pointed out that if she went to the American consul we were still within the six months' time limit to get repatriated to America and that Father would have to settle the bill at the other end.

'And give up Maria's training. Do you always think of yourself? Maria has to have her lessons and you're the only one who can help.' My puzzled expression made her even angrier. 'Milton,' she said, as if explaining something to a retarded child. 'Your precious boyfriend is from one of the wealthiest families in the country.'

It dawned on me what she was proposing. 'Oh Mother, I couldn't. We're just friends. I couldn't ask him for money, not now. We hardly know each other.'

She let the matter drop for the moment but I was too used to her to think that that was the end of the subject. She returned to it the next day and the day after and the day after that. Each time she played either on the need to help Mary or on my own selfishness in ignoring a mother's express wishes. I tried to resist and I was terrified she would wear me down as she usually did.

Of course she knew exactly what she was doing. The next time I met Milton I had lost weight and my eyes were red from crying. As soon as he asked me what the matter was I burst into helpless floods of tears and poured out the whole sorry story of Father's illness and the fact that we were trying to live with no money and that we were soon to be turned out of the apartment. It all came out pat, just as Mother had implanted it in my mind and Milton swallowed it all. He was horror-struck at the idea that we were in need and offered immediate help. I tried to salvage what I could of my pride and independence by converting the request into a loan but he would not hear of it and insisted on making me a gift. In any case the whole thing was soon out of my hands because Milton insisted on coming home to see Mother and as soon as he walked into the empty apartment the full scale of our problem was brought home to him. I was instantly shunted aside while he and Mother worked out what needed to be done. Within a matter of days tradesmen were delivering furniture, a maid had been hired, the larder was full – all at the expense of Milton Emberikos. Mary would have her voice; I had been offered in exchange.

To his credit Milton was in no hurry to take advantage of my predicament; it was a year before I became his mistress. Why that happened who can say? It just did. I had been delivered into a gentle trap and once in there was nothing to be done but accept it. Of course the transition had to be slow. I was still in many ways a naïve girl, looking for love, expecting marriage. Had Mother shown any sign of being opposed to my new status I would never have accepted this rôle but as she did not, rather the opposite, I let it happen. In that first year I was gradually absorbed into Milton's life, a process slow enough for me not to realise fully that it was happening and was irreversible.

In that interim period I was taught the rules of behaviour that he expected. First, I could not expect to have formal relations with his family, since his father wanted him to marry the daughter of one of the other shipping dynasties. In any case, he could not marry yet as his sisters had not found husbands and it was his duty as the elder brother to provide their dowries before considering his own marriage. This didn't bother me, it was the lesser rules of behaviour that I found difficulty in coming to terms with. I teased him once after he'd been to a party with his sisters, asking him if he'd looked at any pretty girls there. He said there had been a few. After a pause I asked him again if he'd liked any of the pretty girls, whereupon he turned and informed me that I was allowed to ask him something once but never, ever, twice. Had I got that clear? I had. As long as we were together I never again asked him where he had been without me and for most of the time he never told me.

The third rule came when I was passing his office one day and, full of high spirits, called in to see him. His secretary told me to sit in his outer office while she went to see if he was free. She returned after a while with the message that he was too busy to see me. That night I was told never to visit his office again. I promised I would not. Rule four was promulgated when I finished my secretarial course and came home proudly with my diploma: I was not to consider taking a job. It would be demeaning to a man in Milton's position if his woman did a menial task.

This was exactly what Mother wanted and it was agreed that I would resume my piano studies under Madame Tassia Filtsou at the National Conservatory. As skill at the piano could be considered useful in a singer, Mary too would have lessons. Our lives were thus laid down for us, though it must be said that Mary was delighted with the arrangements. She plunged herself into her music and in Trivella she at last found an attentive caring person. As often and for as long as possible she would be round at the Conservatory, either taking lessons or hiding in the background watching others do so. Something had unleashed a sense of rivalry in her that made her need to come out on top in whatever she was doing.

It was about now that the obsessive eating began, the careless stuffing of herself with rich food at all hours. Mother had always tried to feed us up on heavy Greek dishes, eggs and soft cheese, stewed meat and potatoes, macaroni with her own rich tomato sauce but, as children do, we had burned up all this food with our restless energy. As young women this was no longer the case. To add to the problem Mary ate at odd hours, whenever she was forced to leave practice, and she took to eating large snacks at night. All the theories to explain such behaviour have been aired: that she was without mother love, that she wanted the sort of success with boys that I had, that she was lonely. There is probably a little truth in each of them but to all these psychological explanations must be added the simple fact that she was a careless youngster in a hurry, impatient with proper meal-times and keen to eat up quickly and get on. Gradually she came to have a serious weight problem; she had always had plump ankles and now they thickened badly. She became first dumpy and then truly fat. Her skin was allergic to perfumes and deodorants and in the heat of an Athens summer this caused her serious embarrassment. Eventually, whatever it was she was reacting to became a self-fulfilling prophecy as she got more and more unattractive and consequently submerged her misery by consuming more and more platefuls of food. I tried to talk to her about it but she had found out about me and Milton and, prudishly shocked, was no longer prepared to accept my elder sister rôle as she had in the past.

That aside, there were few quarrels between us; defending ourselves from Mother still kept us pretty close. Our only battles were fairly good-natured ones over whose turn it was to practise at the piano. I can remember a very cold day in winter when I wanted to get her away from the instrument so I stood behind her waving the ends of my dressing-gown up and down to create a chilly draught until she turned and saw me and started a mock fight. Usually these tussles ended in tickling and laughter but as she got heavier and heavier I could no longer hold her at bay and I started to surrender in case she wrestled me to the ground.

Between 1937 and early 1938, Mary took her first steps in serious voice training, learning to strengthen her diaphragm and undertaking long bouts of vocalising. I've read that she plunged straight into opera, which is nonsense. If she had she would have ruined her voice before she began. No, Trivella started her on simple songs that enabled her to begin the mastery of her vocal organs at a reasonable pace. It was only about spring 1938 that she began to work on her first arias and at the same time she was sent to the Academy to work with George Karakandis, a drama coach, who began the process of turning her into an actress as well as a singer.

Astonishingly, through all this neither of us had actually seen an opera! I suppose we just imagined it would happen in God's good time. Then one day Milton announced that he had got us all tickets for the Lyric Theatre. We were to see *La Traviata*. Mother was beside herself. Her greatest joy was to be seen at the theatre and the opera house was the very pinnacle of that world. For Mary and me, it was a curiously unnerving experience: we had thought so much about opera, what if it failed to live up to the fabulous imaginary world we had invented for it as we listened to records and the radio?

It was a tired, old production of no particular merit, the sort of thing that puts many people off opera for life. I was deeply disappointed and worried, as I was sure Mary must feel the same. But no – as I turned to look at her after the final curtain I saw someone transformed with sheer pleasure. She was in another world, she had in fact entered her own world. Of course she knew that what she had seen was a poor thing but she had simultaneously experienced what it might be. I did not need to be told that while I had seen a rather overweight soprano giving a middling performance, Mary had seen

68

herself, Maria Callas, up there being brilliant. From then on I wriggled out of going to the Athens opera whenever the offer came up but Mary would see anything she could.

Not surprisingly, given this dedication, she was soon noticed at the Conservatory and was picked to take part in the first student concert after her enrolment. It was Monday, April 11th, 1938, that she made what was in effect her Athens début, though most of the pieces were choral works sung by all the students. Mother and I went along to support her. The evening began at six forty-five in the Parnassos Concert Hall. It was an almost indigestibly mixed menu: Weber's *Freischütz* aria, Gounod's *Reine de Saba* then a Greek song, 'Two Nights' by Psarouda. Presumably the pieces had been chosen to give as many students as possible a chance to shine in front of their adoring families but there was one major exception: Cambanis, the tenor who had recognised Mary's voice that evening in the taverna and who was still studying under Trivella, had agreed to end the evening by singing a duet from *Tosca* and it was Mary who was chosen to join him. Accompanied by Stefanos Valtetsiotis, the imposing figure of Cambanis and the diminutive fourteen-and-a-half-year-old Mary took centre stage. It was terrifying, and Mother and I could hardly breathe until it was over. But when they had finished and the applause was lapping all round us and Cambanis was gesturing Mary forward to take her bow, I suddenly knew that things would never be the same again.

That year marked the turning point in both our lives. At twenty-one I had been committed to a man I quite liked but no more; at fourteen Mary had taken the first step in her amazing career. In retrospect it seems like a poor bargain for me, though at the time, with all the uncertainties that lay before her, Mary must have thought that I had had the lucky break. So how did we react to each other as sisters now that our lives were taking shape? The answer is as most sisters do, with a mixture of loving support and furious antipathy. I was far from perfect – I remember a party we went to that Christmas where I noticed that Mary was interested in a boy a little older than her. Driven by who knows what demon, I suddenly decided to spoil things for her and did everything to make sure he spent the entire evening dancing with me. I was no sooner home than I deeply regretted it; it had revealed an unpleasant side to my character that I knew I would do better to suppress. But then there was so little fun for me. Committed as I was to Milton, any evening away from him was a void. All I could do was flirt and make mischief.

In many ways it was her inability to play in life the sort of feminine rôle I had been forced into that drove Mary on at the Conservatory. After that initial success in 1938 the new year brought her even greater challenges. George Karakandis, her drama tutor, was even more impressed with her than her voice teachers and he fought to have her play the lead in the student production of *Cavalleria Rusticana* planned for April 1939, even though she was the youngest and supposedly the most inexperienced student in her year. She got the rôle, her first full-length opera part. How could I ever forget the hours spent listening to her learning the part of Santuzza at our piano? The sole performance took place on Sunday, April 2nd, at six fifteen. It was a simple affair: plain backdrop, the boys in black trousers and white shirts, the girls in simple skirts and blouses, but already Mary brought something special to this basic production – she acted as if she really believed it. Everything she did, every gesture, every note proclaimed that this was not a student show but true theatre. Beside the other young people struggling to get their notes and their movements right she was already a professional.

Had the outside world not intervened, this might have been the pattern of our lives for the next few years with Mary steadily progressing towards a full career. But that April of 1939 was overshadowed by events on our borders. That month Mussolini invaded Albania and increased his threats against the Balkan nations, including Greece. It was suddenly brought home to us that we might all be in danger.

Mary was able to drown any fears she might have had in a flurry of work. The Conservatory had embarked on a programme of concerts and as their new star pupil Mary had new pieces to master every week. On Monday, May 22nd, there was another concert in the Parnassos Hall in which she sang the 'Barcarolle' from *Les Contes d'Hoffmann*, an aria from Weber's *Oberon*, 'Ritorna Vincitor' from *Aida*, another Greek song, 'I Will Not Forget You' by Psarouda and ended with the 'Addio Terra' duet from *Aida* with the tenor Zanni Campani, again with Valtetsiotis at the piano. She was still only fifteen! The following night she sang the 'Rezia' aria from *Oberon* and 'Air du Miroir' from Massenet's *Thaïs*. The following month, on June 25th, she sang extracts from Amelia's rôle in *Un Ballo in Maschera* and Santuzza's rôle in *Cavalleria Rusticana*. It was an astonishing range in so short a time, and clearly Trivella was determined to push her forward as fast as possible, or perhaps she was merely trying, as we all were, to shut out the bad news that every day grew more strident.

With all this talk of war I suddenly realised that I would have a special problem if I tried to escape: I had been born Greek and because I had not returned to America in time for my twenty-first birthday I had forfeited my right to American citizenship. Only Mary had retained that right, having been born in New York. But in any case I had no desire to leave Athens. My relationship with Milton had changed over our year together. Although I did not move in with him, he had become my lover and I was indeed now in love with him. It was inevitable, I suppose, and I believe he, too, felt the same way. At least he could be very jealous if anyone else showed any interest in me. It was the approach of Spiros Skouros the son of the famous film maker whom I'd met at a party that finally provoked Milton to action. He proposed that we should get engaged – secretly, he insisted, so as not to upset his family. What had I to lose?

That summer he took me, along with Mother and Mary, to Corfu aboard the *Eleni* to celebrate this peculiar union. I don't know what Mother felt about it at the time, she probably had other things on her mind, but I could tell that Mary, by now fifteen, was not pleased. She looked plainer than ever and the sight of me and Milton so happy together can hardly have amused her. About that time we rented an apartment at 61 Patission and we sub-let a room to a woman called Marina Papageorpoulou and Mary was for ever in her room asking her what she should do to be attractive, begging her to tell her the secret. She vowed that she would give up everything if she could find true love. Of course this was just the sort of thing any girl of her age gets preoccupied with, but it was sad that she no longer turned to me for comfort and advice; we had grown apart.

Later, our neighbour, Marina, told me that Mary often begged her to explain why I and not she was always loved. Thinking to placate her Marina reminded her that she had her voice but this only made Mary angry.

'What is a voice?' she cried. 'I'm a woman, that's what matters.'

Coming back from Corfu on the *Eleni*, Milton introduced us to a fellow passenger, Mr Dorentis the Minister of Culture. There was much talk among the men about the forthcoming war, so certain was everyone that there was going to be a massive conflagration. For me it was typical of my peculiar life with Milton that on the one hand I had to be his secret liaison and on the other I was standing on the deck of his ship making conversation with a minister.

Back in Athens all the talk was of war and the approach of the Italians. For Mary the great upheaval was the finish of her studies with Trivella and her audition at the Athens Conservatory. It is a story much told, how she stood up to sing 'Ocean! Thou mighty monster' from *Oberon* for the famous Spanish soprano Elvira de Hidalgo. She had recently arrived in Greece and was so unimpressed by Mary's appearance she had already written her off until she started to sing. For the rest of her life de Hidalgo was to speak of her sudden vision of what that voice could become. Mary was taken on as her special pupil and more even than Trivella, de Hidalgo became the central figure in Mary's life.

Shortly after, in September, the newspapers were full of a world at war but this seemed only to fuel Mary's sense of urgency, to make her redouble her practising and to spend even longer hours at the Conservatory or at de Hidalgo's home. This panic to get on before we were engulfed by some nameless horror made her increasingly impatient. She no longer maintained any pretence of obedience to Mother. When I left for my piano lessons it was: 'And *when* will you be back?' To which I would obediently reply in an hour or whatever. But Mary would just yell out that she'd be back when she chose and off she'd go, slamming the door behind her. Far from upsetting Mother this seemed to please her, as if Mary's stubbornness was all part of the master plan that would lead to fame, which I suppose in a way it was.

Aside from her devotion to de Hidalgo as a teacher, Mary still had one close contact with Mother: their mutual joy in malicious gossip. Perhaps I'm just not interested enough in other people but I could never see what it was they found so interesting in all the local scandal. It was as if Mother wanted to encourage a spiteful streak in Mary. No doubt she saw me as too sweet and ineffectual to ever achieve anything, so it was up to her to toughen the other daughter. It revolted me and I never liked listening to them at it.

Throughout the early part of 1940 we went through the same phoney war the rest of Europe experienced. We were instructed in air-raid drill and ordered to make shelters in our cellars, but apart from that the danger seemed for a time to recede and a sort of false jollity overtook us.

I hardly saw Mary now, she spent most of her time with de Hidalgo, though whenever she did stay at home to practise I could tell that her voice was getting stronger and her higher register more confident. And like Trivella before her, de Hidalgo seemed anxious to push her favourite pupil forward as fast as possible. As early as February 1940 she sang Bellini's 'Mira, o Norma' duet with Arda Mandikian in a concert at the Odeon Concert Hall and returned there in June to play the title rôle in a full production of Puccini's *Suor Angelica* where although there was no scenery they did manage to dress the cast as nuns.

All this attention was clearly having its effect. Mary was now seventeen and was showing her independence in small ways clearly designed to irritate Mother. For example, she only showed up for meals if it suited her. But in one thing Mother did maintain control, just as she did with me: she went on choosing her clothes. The problem was Mary's size. Mother never seemed to acknowledge that Mary had put on weight and that her clothes needed special thought. One day she came back with two hats, not unlike oversized baby bonnets. Mine looked fairly ridiculous though I could just about get away with it but Mary, with her plump round face, looked hilarious. Just as she was trying it on Milton arrived and burst out laughing.

'What are you trying to do?' he asked Mother. 'Make her a baby again?'

Mary was furious and started to argue with her. She was increasingly aware that her weight was making her unattractive. We were walking down Patission one day when a boy ran up behind us and started chanting, 'Laurel and Hardy, Laurel and Hardy . . .' Yet she, despite her distress at her appearance, seemed totally unable to do anything about it and just went on eating and eating. At seventeen this was a miserable state of affairs. It was the time when she should have been having her first innocent love affairs and although she pretended indifference I knew she cared deeply.

At that time we had a dentist, Dimitri Dustabanis, and as Mary's teeth were not good – she had a noticeable gap in her front teeth and needed several fillings – she was often at his surgery. He, poor man, had had an unhappy engagement, having been unable to marry the girl he loved because of a problem over her dowry and was considered by the local girls to be a figure of romantic melancholy. This must have appealed to Mary who showed as little reluctance to have her teeth fixed as I had all those years ago in New York. Then, many years later, I bumped into Dimitri's brother who told me how Mary had made the poor dentist's life even more miserable by forever trying to get him to pay attention to her. Apparently she would lie back in the operating chair and when he bent near to examine her she would suddenly say things like: 'Oh, Dimitri, you're just the sort of man I'd like to marry.' But it was no use, the poor man was preoccupied with his lost fiancée and eventually he emigrated to get away from the memory. For Mary it was just another rebuttal to cry over with Marina.

'Why does nobody love me?' she would moan. 'Why do they always love Jackie?'

Once, she brought a young man to the house and introduced him to me but then she sat between us and leant forward so that her long hair hung down like a curtain, shutting me out. It was a ludicrous performance and heaven knows what the boy thought about it. It was all part of the increasing conflict between the ambitions Mother had provoked in her and a natural desire to be a young woman enjoying a little romance.

After little more than a year with de Hidalgo Mary was ready to begin her professional life and in June 1940 was given a contract with the chorus of the Lyric Theatre. It was the humblest job going but, given the upheavals of the time, the best that could be expected. In any case, with de Hidalgo pushing her forward she had every hope of moving out of that anonymous position quite quickly. Oddly enough it was the impending war that did most to give Mary her chance. It was de Hidalgo who developed in her that extra something that distinguishes the professional from the gifted amateur, and under normal circumstances the older woman might very possibly have left Athens where she had been living only temporarily. Now, like the rest of us, she was to find herself trapped and obliged to go on promoting her talented pupil.

CHAPTER FOUR
1940–1945

For the Greeks the war really began in October 1940 when Mussolini sent his notorious ultimatum ordering us to lay down our arms and our government replied, '*Ohi*' – a resolute no! By November 22nd our small army had not only succeeded in holding back the Italians but had invaded a large part of southern Albania. In Athens we were jubilant, there was an air of festivity but by the beginning of December the euphoria in the city had begun to subside. The war had reached a stalemate, there had been one or two small victories for our side then nothing. Rumours began to circulate and people began to stock up with food. It was not a happy Christmas that year but that was nothing compared to the miserable year that lay ahead of us. In retrospect 1940 seems like a hole punctured in our lives. For the first three months nothing tangible happened except an increasing awareness that our humiliation of the Italian fascists was not to go unpunished and that the Germans were preparing to come to their aid. We were aware that a small contingent of British troops had been sent to help us and that gave us hope. We did not know then just how ineffective they were to prove against the well-organised German steam-roller.

The first that we ordinary citizens knew about the invasion was the bombing of Salonika, news of which spread quickly through the city. Milton hurried round to see us. He had been called up but allowed to take an office job. He told us that he thought we could get out if we hurried, there was a boat at Piraeus going to Egypt and he thought we could all get on it. We hastily bundled some things together, handed the poor canaries over to the maid for safe keeping and set off for the harbour. Everything was noise and confusion as we settled down uneasily to wait while Milton went off to bargain for our passage. I hoped he would succeed, not because I was afraid of the enemy, but because I knew that if we got away from Greece and his family he would marry me. It was not to be. Just as we were about to board, word came that the Greek battleship the *Elli* had been sunk and panic broke out. Mother flatly refused to consider getting on board the passenger ship. I begged her but she wouldn't listen. I suspect that having had all day waiting on the dockside to weigh the matter up she had concluded that even under enemy rule Athens was a better prospect for Mary's career than Egypt would ever be. She was glad of the excuse to turn back. We made our way home through the darkened city aware that for better or worse we were trapped.

When the enemy finally moved that April nothing could stop them. Our Prime Minister committed suicide, the army retreated, the king went into exile and Athens was occupied. As we waited in the defenceless city for the Italians with their German allies to arrive there was an air of unreality about it all. People went on last-minute shopping expeditions to stock up with what provisions were left. Women, including Mother, went to get their hair washed and set as if this gave them a little more confidence to face the uncertain future. Then when the soldiers started to appear on the streets we took part in almost childish acts of defiance: Mary and I went up on to the roof of our building and, along with countless other people that we could see on neighbouring buildings, we started spitting into the street below. Over and over – sputt, sputt, sputt – until we were dry. I doubt any of it ever as much as marked an enemy uniform but it made us feel better.

As far as possible people took to avoiding the enemy soldiers, even making the elaborate gesture of stepping off the pavement if any were passing. But there was little other than those symbolic acts to be done. There was as yet no resistance and in any case little news; the occupation had happened and that was that. Our main fear was air-raids and when the sirens went we hurried down to the cellars, usually with Milton struggling to carry the bird cages. I never liked going and would have preferred to take my chances in the open air but Mother wouldn't hear of it. Eventually we realised that it was the Acropolis that was saving us, for while Piraeus was devastated the enemy drew the line at putting the Parthenon at risk and thus central Athens was spared.

Eventually there was a ten o'clock curfew but Mary always stayed at de Hidalgo's until the last minute, driving Mother insane with worry. But of course she just refused to listen and went on insisting she would do whatever she pleased.

Despite, or perhaps because of, all the confusion and terror there was a desperate attempt to get back to something approaching normality. But the best the Lyric Theatre could manage was a solitary concert performance of Franz von Suppé's *Boccaccio* at the Palace Theatre on Tuesday, January 21st. Because of the curfew it had to begin at five o'clock. At least for Mary it marked another step forward she was picked out to sing the rôle of Beatrice. But aside from that solitary afternoon the theatre languished and her life returned to the daily round of lessons with de Hidalgo.

For a while there was still news of fighting in Crete but eventually we heard that the British had evacuated the island. And then in the late summer a Greek air force officer Mother knew came to the apartment late at night with two men. They were young British officers who had escaped after being captured during that final retreat and who were now being helped by the new Greek underground. The Greek officer asked Mother to shelter the men until some way could be found to smuggle them out. At first she protested; it was after all incredibly dangerous, but he appealed to her sense of patriotism and she reluctantly agreed. There was a Scottish boy, dark, and an English boy, blond, and we hid them in the room with the canaries. They were kept almost totally in darkness but they were full of life and didn't get down-hearted and Mary and I loved to talk with them. The problem was Milton, who Mother felt had best be kept out of the secret for his own sake. One day he came round and we hadn't time to warn the boys who were chattering away in their room. Thinking the canaries were behaving oddly Milton went to have a look whereupon Mary, with great presence of mind, started singing some aria she was learning at that time. Fortunately Milton, who loved to hear her, stopped to listen and forgot about the canaries. After about a week of being shut up, the poor boys were getting restless and wanted to listen to the BBC, a punishable offence by then. So again Mary sang every evening at nine to cover the noise. We felt very sorry for them cooped up like that and hit on the idea of dressing them as Greeks and taking them for a walk. We dyed the blond one dark and borrowed some old clothes and off we went for a stroll in the centre of town. It was thrilling as we passed enemy soldiers, not knowing if they would stop us and ask to see our papers or even if a fellow Greek might try to speak to them and unmask our secret. But in the end absolutely nothing happened except that Mother nearly died when we returned and told her what we'd done. Still, it was a relief when, after a fortnight, the Greek officer returned and took them away. A little later, a coded message on the B B C referring to 'Patission' told us they were safely out of the country. I had enjoyed the episode. Would that that had been our only contact with foreign soldiers and that events had not turned out the way they did.

As the year drew on, the situation began to get worse. The panic buying had emptied the shops and the British blockade shut off the country's food imports. By autumn things were serious and shortage turned to famine. People would pay and do anything for food. You could see people fall in the streets from malnutrition. The horror was indescribable. The only thing that could help was gold, which always works wonders, or connections in the nearby farms and villages. It was now that my meeting Milton came to seem like a miracle.

He was the only one we could turn to for help. Mary's salary from the theatre was little more than a token gesture and in any case there was only one further performance of *Boccaccio* at the Park Summer Theatre on July 3rd that year which barely brought her enough for a meal. Somehow Milton managed to arrange that his family and ours always had something to eat. He would make long treks outside Athens, often at considerable risk, to bring back olive oil, figs, nuts, anything to keep us from the starvation that surrounded us. Once on the road he was stopped by a party of young Italian conscripts, one of whom searched his bags and when he saw the food started insulting him and struck him hard across the face. For a man like Milton, from one of the best families in Greece, such things were a terrible humiliation. But still he went on. We three owed our lives to him. He found us clothes, nothing special but adequate. If there was anything he could do he did it and no one will ever fully understand what he suffered to make sure that we did not.

Those early months of the occupation were certainly the most dangerous. We had not worked out a way of existing side by side with the enemy and everyone was nervous and afraid. There was always the risk that the smallest thing would spark a violent reaction. I came home one afternoon to find Mother and Mary in a terrible state, after a party of Italian soldiers had come to search the apartment. It might have been a coincidence or someone may have tipped them off about our hiding the British soldiers. Whatever the reason, they found nothing and left. Later, Mother was to transform this into part of the Maria mythology with her daughter singing *Tosca* to entrance the opera-loving soldiers. At the time they looked like two scared females rather than heroines of the resistance, but then Mother's stories about the war always seemed to outrun the reality. In later years she spoke and wrote about trekking out to the villages to find food, she spoke of deprivation and neglect when the truth was that Milton gave us whatever could be found. I cannot deny that it was obtained on the black market. I am not proud of the fact but nor am I ashamed – it was a matter of life or death and we were fortunate, through Milton, to be in a position to survive, but I have always believed that Mother was wrong to try to claim afterwards that she was one of those who suffered when indeed the opposite was the case. If proof were needed one has only to look at the photographs of Mary taken at the time: an overweight girl with pimples. You don't get like that if you're starving. In fact she never ceased to eat. We kept the supplies Milton brought us in a special closet and when she returned from her practice the first thing Mary did was to raid this larder. My most telling memory of the occupation is of Mary bent double, reaching for handfuls of figs or nuts, her fat backside filling the doorframe.

Mother never tried to control her diet, though she attempted to lessen some of its worst side-effects such as Mary's boils and her generally spotty complexion by treating her with home-made face creams. It was a pointless exercise as it was only her weight that was the problem and had they both decided to deal with that then everything could have been resolved. I was to read later that Mary claimed to have kept us in food from her earnings at the Lyric Theatre which was laughable. She had no further productions at all during 1941 and her later fees were tiny and always spent on pastries and sweets for herself. Later in the war a sort of ersatz ice-cream made out of God knows what appeared and whenever she could, Mary scoffed tubs of the stuff. It was only thanks to Milton we survived that terrible year. Our worst period was the winter, the coldest in memory, with snow for the first time in twenty years. As fuel oil was one of those things that even gold could not buy we, along with the rest of the population, shivered our way through those desperate months. In Mother's favour it can be said that her skill at sewing helped keep some clothes on our backs. She was very inventive and even made some quite nice dresses out of some old curtain material she'd brought from America.

The one thing that sometimes united my mother and me was our anger at the way Mary never helped out in the apartment – she'd eat, then off she'd go to de Hidalgo without as much as putting her cup in the sink, let alone washing it. One day my patience snapped and I barred her way out.

'What's the matter?' she protested, trying to worm her way round me.

'The back stairs,' I said, pointing to the mop and bucket. 'They need cleaning and it's your turn.'

Amazingly she didn't even try to argue, not a single word was said. She simply picked up the mop and pail and went off and did the job.

Just occasionally we could behave like a normal family but only if it suited Mother's schemes. There was an evening when she thought she should impress de Hidalgo by inviting her to dinner. Mother was usually cautious about Mary's teacher, being a little put out by her daughter's devotion to the woman, yet not able to interfere because of her key rôle in the great plan. To give anything resembling a dinner party at that stage in the war was a miracle and poor Milton was obliged to go to extraordinary lengths in order to provide for it. He was invited as the only man present and Mother also invited Madame Filtsou, our piano teacher.

Mother and Mary went to great lengths to impress these leading lights of the Greek musical world and there was nothing to beat Mother when she decided to turn on the charm.

Overall, things were beginning to settle down after those first difficult months and when the bright Greek spring of 1942 followed that hard winter and the wild flowers were blossoming everywhere it was possible to be just a little more hopeful. The real occupying force were the Germans, though they kept in the background, trying to maintain a pretence that it was the Italians who were in charge. For the most part all we saw were the ordinary Italian soldiers, mostly poor conscripts, miserable and far from home and often nearly as hungry as the ordinary Greeks were. We found it hard to go on hating them, though we loathed the Germans. By and large both sides kept their distance. Those who had to work with the occupying power did what they had to do, the basic task no more, and no one blamed them. But overt friendliness was considered wrong.

Everyone knew this without anything needing to be said – everyone, that is, except Evangelia Callas.

One day she and I and two other women had gone out to Kiffissia to get away from the increasingly overpowering heat of the city. It was pleasant to spend an hour or so at an open-air café sipping a drink and enjoying the breeze. While we were chatting a group of Italian officers came and sat at the next table. They were accompanied by a Greek in civilian clothes who I recognised and who came over to speak to me. I was cold with him as was expected in those circumstances. He explained that he was working as an interpreter which was fair enough but didn't explain why he had to go out drinking with his employers. I nodded and didn't encourage any further conversation. Sadly, that was not the end of the matter for when I turned back to my companions I could not help noticing that Mother was staring at one of the Italians, a middle-aged man in a colonel's uniform, and that he was staring back at her. I gave her a kick under the table but she only flashed me a 'mind your own business' look and went on with her flirting. The other ladies began to look a little uncomfortable and I could see the soldiers joking and talking in a way that implied that we were included in their remarks. After a moment the interpreter came over and told Mother that the Colonel would like to have the honour of an introduction. That was too much for me and I began to protest. Mother sighed and told the man that she was sorry but she had to leave. She was in bad spirits all the way back to Athens and I hoped that that was the end of such foolishness.

By now the occupying authorities had ordered the reopening of the opera, largely to create an aura of normality and also to provide entertainment for their officers. Some performers preferred to withdraw but most went on, hoping that they would not be asked to do anything compromising. In fact the first full opera performance after the invasion was a singularly bizarre choice – *Tosca*, the story of an opera singer struggling against an occupying power, though it must surely have been approved by the Italian Command. They must have decided that as it was one of the most popular of all Italian operas there was no harm in it. Even allowing for those who had left the company it was doubtful whether Mary would have got the leading rôle at that stage, but when the woman originally chosen fell ill her chance came. The sets and the costumes were old and threadbare but none of that mattered to Mary who felt that her whole life had been moving towards this point. The tenor was Greece's most famous singer at that time, Antonis Dellendas, who was very large so the two of them were hardly likely to make a pretty sight. Although all the records say that it was performed at the old Royal Theatre with its plush boxes and gilded décor I somehow remember it taking place at an old open-air amphitheatre there used to be at Klauthmonos Square. As it opened on August 27th when the summer heat was fierce there is every reason for me to be right. Despite the size of the protagonists and Mary's inexperience, it was a wonderful evening. Of course Mary's voice was still far from perfect but she was already a wonderful actress and that made up for a great deal. Naturally, the greatest applause was reserved for Dellendas who was a great favourite with the Italian officers who made up a large part of the audience. Mother was of course in heaven. She loved the whole business of a first night even though the presence of so many enemy troops put a damper on the occasion. In any case she only saw part of the spectacle as she was for ever backstage helping Mary to adjust her costume or apply her make-up, or fanning her brow in the interval. Mother was everything to her: a nursemaid, a confidante, someone to build up her courage in those nerve-racking moments before she ran on stage with her 'Mario, Mario, Mario . . .'

There were only two performances of that *Tosca* but though she was only performing for the limited world of occupied Greece it was that production that propelled her out of the chorus and into leading rôles. It made her a star in our small community and although it was only a small step on the long road she was to follow it was nevertheless a tremendous advance for an eighteen-year-old girl.

Our mother had every reason to be proud of her handiwork and everything might have been fine if she had contented herself with her daughter's triumph. But not Mother. I came home from piano practice one day and as I opened the apartment door I overheard male voices in the living-room. I pushed open the salon door and found Mother offering drinks to the Italian Colonel and the two other officers we'd seen at Kiffissia.

She must have seen my astonished expression so she quickly picked up a bouquet of flowers that was lying on the table in front of her. 'This is Colonel Bonalti,' she said. 'He's come to congratulate Maria on her performance.'

The Colonel smiled and nodded.

*

Who was I and what did I want to be? With the occupation it was possible to stop asking such questions. Everything unconnected with basic survival had to be set aside. There would be a time to worry about such things in the future. The only worry that continued to nag away at me despite everything was my growing concern whether Milton would marry me or not. I now loved him very much and wanted above everything to be his wife. Mother still spoke of my having a career as a pianist though with less conviction than before. Her experience with Mary had shown her that you need more than talent to succeed. What Mother had seen of the infighting and backbiting at the Lyric Theatre had shown her that you needed the instincts of a killer to survive and, from what she had heard, Mary had them. Mary had quickly mastered the art of upstaging other performers, of using all the tricks that can win over an audience – and not merely on stage; she also knew how to get her own way within the company, an essential prerequisite for advancement when there were few productions and thus few good rôles to be had. None of these skills came from de Hidalgo; most came from Mother's 'lessons' in selfishness and ill-temper which had given Mary an unflinching desire to get her own way at all costs. She had inherited the soldier's genes from Mother's family, whereas I was my father's daughter. And Mother knew it. Had it been otherwise I would never have found myself in love with a man who showed less and less willingness to marry me. No. Mother knew by then that I just did not have Mary's fighting spirit.

So was I happy? Too strong a word – was I contented? I suppose the answer is that most of the time I just accepted the situation. But not all of the time – there were days when I longed to get away from them all, to leave them to their selfish schemes and make some sort of life for myself. I was twenty-five, there was still time if only the war would end and I could break free. My situation was brought home to me after Mary's *Tosca*. She was well known in occupied Athens and I was beginning to be introduced to strangers as her sister. Her sister, the sister of the singer Maria Callas. I didn't begrudge her the success she had had but why was I her *sister*, I asked myself. I was me. Often I would think over how we got to that point, how we came to be trapped in that city where everything was now bent towards furthering the career of just one sister, how I had been forced into a passive rôle in that plan. It was a pointless game of 'what-if'. 'What-if' we had got out of Athens on that boat? 'What-if' we had never left

America or if I had stayed behind? 'What-if' we had never gone to America in the first place? I often thought about Meligala, often wondered what it would have been like to have been brought up the daughter of a prosperous country pharmacist with a handsome well-to-do wife with no ambitions other than that her daughter Jacinthy should succeed at school and make a happy marriage. I would certainly have been far better off than I was then, for nothing that the great adventure had brought to us had benefited me. No, I often remembered Meligala, the ivory white house, the heavy polished furniture, the curving staircase.

And then Meligala came back into our lives. My father's sister had heard about Mary's success and, realising where we were, got in touch with an invitation to visit. She probably had no idea about relations between Mother and Father. There was no mail and in any case Mother never revealed that they had effectively separated. I doubt, under normal circumstances, whether Mother would have wished to go back to our old home; her feelings must have been impossibly confused about that whole experience. She had always argued that they should never have left, that that was the cause of all her problems. Yet, on the other hand, without the disruption of their lives she might never have found herself in the position of pushing Mary into the theatre and thus into the success which she was now sure lay before her.

I doubt she would have gone but for the occupation. It was rare then to have the opportunity to get out of the city and we all felt trapped and in need of a change of air. In any case the countryside held out the promise of fresh fruit and vegetables which even with Milton's money it was hard to find. So Mother, Mary and I set off on the train, retracing that journey we had made when I was six and she was pregnant nineteen years earlier. As the last houses of the city fell away and we chugged slowly into the countryside I wondered what she felt. Surely this was a journey back to the place where for a time she had been in love with her handsome husband, where they had believed they had a marvellous future before them. Having experienced love myself, I couldn't imagine how she could be other than very moved by the experience of revisiting so poignant a place. Ah well, I had reckoned without Mother's complete single-mindedness – the entire journey was taken up with talk of what Mary must do next, of how best to tackle the next stage in her career. It was important, she insisted, that the success of *Tosca* should be built on, there were enemies in the opera house who were jealous of that success; they must not be allowed to hold Mary back. Whatever the next production was to be, Mary must have a leading rôle. And so on and on and on almost in time to the rhythm of the wheels. It didn't matter, I had long ago perfected the art of sleeping with my eyes open. She didn't require any response. She was talking to herself.

When we arrived we were met by my aunt and taken to her house. Mother and Mary were quite happy to stay there and tell a new set of people all about 'their' music. They showed not the least interest in seeing their old home. I, however, could not wait and, making my excuses, set off on my own.

There had been little new building in the town since our departure and I found the main street instantly. But I remembered so little it was hard for me to be quite sure which our pharmacy once was. I walked up and down and saw that there was now no druggist at all; the business had presumably changed after Father left but which of the present stores had it been? Then I realised what had happened. One of the shops was boarded up, its window covered with slats of wood. The windows of the apartment above were just vacant holes. This was our home, it had been abandoned, no one had occupied it after we had left. The street itself was unswept and the gutters strewn with rubbish. The town had declined, much of the life had gone out of it. I tried to peep through the wooden barrier into the hallway but I could only see a broken box near the door. It was too dark to see as far as the staircase. I looked around and saw a young man walking down the street. He passed me with a polite nod and I realised with a shock that he must be Vassily's age. I felt suddenly crushed. There was no past, nothing to go back to, no world of childhood preserved so that you could enter into it and start again. There was only the world we have now, whatever that is. And all I had was my life with Milton; there was no way out of it and if that was so then I had to ensure that I made the most of it. I was sure Mother looked on it as a useful temporary measure and that as soon as I was needed for other 'duties' she could use me as she wanted. That was what I had to fight.

On the way back to Athens I decided to clear the air.

'That Italian Colonel? Bonalti?'

Mother looked up, sensing trouble. 'Yes?' she said cautiously.

'I don't think he should come to the house. It's not good. People notice these things, they talk.'

'He's a gentleman,' she said. 'He loves opera and he's an admirer of Mary's voice. He came round to congratulate her. I could hardly refuse to let him in when he was standing on the doorstep with a bouquet, could I?'

In one way I had to concede that she was right. Bonalti was a gentleman. We had long since realised that the Italians were not brutes and after the initial months any friction had been eased. If there had not been a war a man like the Colonel would have been more than welcome. But there was a war and as I quickly gathered when I found him at our home, he and Mother must have been meeting since that first encounter in Kiffissia. That did not bother me. By this time there was little criticism of social contact with the enemy provided it was discreet and did not involve financial or other advantage. The only people to arouse public anger were profiteers who used the enemy to get rich at the expense of their own people. No one could accuse Mother of that; she wasn't bothered by such things, she just liked Colonel Bonalti. In fact that was what worried me. There was a terrible reckless naïveté about her. I tried to point out again that there was no reason to bring him home, that she could as well see him outside and thus avoid any criticism. I had forgotten how perverse she could be. How even the most well-meant criticism could immediately provoke her into wilfully adopting an opposite position from which she would then resolutely refuse to budge. It would have been better to keep quiet but after that visit to Meligala my thoughts were centred on making something valuable out of my life with Milton and Mother's behaviour looked set to jeopardise it.

'What will Milton say?' I asked.

'What's it got to do with Milton? It's my business.'

'But everyone knows we're together and if they see enemy officers at the apartment he'll have trouble. They know he pays for the house, they'll think he's mixed up with the Italians.'

I shouldn't have said it.

'I told you Bonalti is a gentleman and a good friend. Are you to be the only one allowed to have a gentleman friend? Is Milton not supposed to see me invite who I want to my own home just because he *helps* . . .' She spat out the word. 'Just because he *helps* doesn't mean to say he can control whom I choose to invite.'

It was useless to protest that that was not what I had meant. She had now fixed upon her own interpretation and that was that.

'I think it might be good if Milton met the Colonel,' she said slyly.

I said nothing. I realised I had provoked her and that she was determined to organise a confrontation.

I now dreaded coming back to the apartment with Milton as I never knew whether that would be the night I'd find soldiers waiting for us. After a week or so it happened. I slipped in first and there was Bonalti with his two friends and Mary and Mother chatting with them. As Milton walked in I could see the look of dismay on his face. The officers stood up with correct politeness, bowed and shook hands. Again the story that they had come to congratulate Mary was trotted out and I could only hope that that would go some way towards pacifying Milton.

It didn't. When they had gone he was angrier than I had ever seen him.

'What does that woman think she's doing? And in front of Mary. She's only eighteen, that's a terrible example. Everyone will know they've been round here. God knows what might happen after this is all over. Doesn't she know they are the enemy? You must talk to her, you must tell her that after all I've done for you she can't do this to me, it's too dangerous. The Italians won't be here for ever and when they go there'll be a lot of trouble for anyone who helped them.'

Judging by the look of triumph on Mother's face when I next saw her I decided to say nothing. She was unstoppable and if she decided to ruin us all there was nothing I or anyone could do about it. The worst thing was that Milton's prediction about the effect on Mary proved all too exact. Her work with the Lyric Theatre had already involved her with the occupying force who saw the opera as some sort of symbol of Italian culture at the heart of Greek life and were determined to foster it. No one blamed the singers for this but it put them in a difficult position that needed careful handling – just the sort of subtlety Mother was incapable of. While other, more experienced, performers knew they had to work for the Italians, they did only the minimum necessary. But Mother was still fighting to get Mary into leading rôles even in those productions where it would have been cleverer to stay out of the limelight. Thus Mary came to be the main soprano at a command concert given for the Italians in Salonika that October where there was to be a programme of Rossini arias to celebrate the hundred and fiftieth anniversary of the composer's birth. It was evidently as much a political as a cultural occasion and one that common sense said was best avoided. But worse than Mary's participation was Mother's insistence on accompanying her, despite the initial refusal of the theatre to have any extra personnel go along. Inevitably Mother prevailed. Of course the singers were fêted by the Italians who were starved of music and of course Mother lapped it up. It was just what she wanted out of life, her daughter's success, with herself in the wake enjoying all the praise, the glory, the attentions of the admirers and, of course, all the salami and prosciutto the Italians paid the singers with. Naturally word of the concert and the luxuries heaped on the performers quickly leaked out.

'She's mad,' Milton groaned, putting his head in his hands. 'This war can't go on for ever. One day she'll regret all this stupidity.'

Fortunately, that concert was followed by a quiet period. There were no further performances by the Lyric Theatre until mid-February 1943 when they put on the only modern opera Mary ever took part in: Calomeri's *Ho Protomastoras*, though in that first performance she only had a choral rôle in the intermezzo between the first and second halves. Happily for her reputation she agreed to give her services in a fund-raising benefit concert at the Sporting Cinema in Nea Smerni to endow school meals for poor children. If she had only done more of that all might have been well but it was not to be . . .

While Mary might frequently have flouted Mother's wishes in small things, over the larger issues she still followed in her train. Finding it impossible to emulate my successes with men she had only Mother's example to copy and at the moment that was a particularly bad example. What none of us realised at first was that she had found an admirer, a man who religiously attended all her concerts and who had quickly made himself known to her. It was only when she announced that she was going to give a concert at the Casa d'Italia that we began to suspect that something was going on. The Casa d'Italia was a sort of cultural centre supported by their embassy which before the war had put on little musical evenings, lectures and exhibitions. It was housed in an elegant turn-of-the-century corner house across from the archaeological museum, not far from our apartment. Today it has returned to its original functions but during the war it acted as a sort of social club for the occupying forces and was thus no place for a Greek to be seen. What we now discovered was that a Major di Stasio had personally arranged for Mary to sing there and that this di Stasio was no ordinary major but something shadowy in the intelligence sector of the Italian Command. In other words a man to be avoided at all costs. I begged her not to do it but she was by then beyond control, and she and Arda Mandikian sang Pergolesi's *Stabat Mater* to a room crammed with Italian officers on the afternoon of Thursday, April 22nd. For once I decided not to attend and cannot say how it went though she seemed well pleased with herself afterwards.

Sadly, I knew too well what poor dumpy Mary wanted; she just longed for someone to be nice to her, to flatter her and tell her all the things she believed as a woman she had a right to hear. If di Stasio had realised that, then he would have everything he wished. Of course I tried to talk to her about it but by then it was useless.

'Jealous, are you?' she demanded.

What could I say? All her complexes were there in that one situation: her desire to be loved and her desire to compete with me, her sister. Why? What had I got? I was trapped in an affair that looked like never being resolved, my life was frozen, held in a vice I couldn't unlock and yet here was my sister doing herself so much damage out of a senseless envy of what she thought I was.

'Don't,' I said softly, but she wasn't listening any more. She had gone to the piano and was singing 'La Paloma' at the top of her voice.

The main consequence of all this was that we saw less and less of each other as both considered it wiser to avoid a confrontation. In the middle of July there was a revival of the previous year's *Tosca* and later in the month she gave her first major solo concert with another staggering variety of pieces: 'Care Selve' from Handel's *Atalante*, an aria from Rossini's *La Cenerentola*, and another from Cilea's *Adriana Lecouvrer*; these were followed by an aria from *Il Trovatore* and the evening ended with a Greek song by Lavda. But any good this might have done was almost immediately negated the next month by another concert in Salonika for the Italian troops, this time of works by Schubert and Brahms.

By this time I was too distracted to care. Most of my concerns were based on Milton and his increasingly difficult family. His younger brother Harry had recently married for the second time. His new wife was the elderly widow of a prominent banker and Milton's father was absolutely furious. He immediately nicknamed her Sarah after the biblical character who had no children and refused to go anywhere near her. In truth old Mr Emberikos was distraught about almost all his offspring. He considered me an unsuitable companion for his eldest son and refused to entertain the idea that we might marry. He had plans that Milton should get engaged to one of the girls in the Goulandris shipping clan who were astronomically wealthy. Fortunately for me, Milton was not attracted to the young woman and after one encounter he refused to even discuss the matter. One of the Emberikos daughters made a marriage that infuriated her father. Only the unmarried daughter Moska remained in favour. It all seems so strange today but then it was considered utterly appropriate that the head of the family should ordain who his children allied themselves with and that he should be outraged if they flouted his wishes. To Mr Emberikos I was a loose woman who had seduced his eldest son away from his filial duty and that was all there was to it.

All Milton could do was promise to try to sort it out after the war was over. I suppose that today we would say he was weak in not standing up to the old man. If he truly loved me he could have married me but then what? Everything he had came from the family. His father would certainly have cut him out of the family business and we all, he and my family, depended on that. In a very real way we were all trapped which was what made Mother and Mary's behaviour so grotesque. Without Milton there was no roof over their heads, no food and no more lessons with de Hidalgo, so why did they persist in doing things that could only cause trouble for their benefactor?

In the end the Italian situation resolved itself. In early September 1943 the Allies advanced into Italy and the Italian government surrendered. This did not apply to the troops in Greece but they had no stomach for a war they had already lost and longed to go home. The Germans, who had always despised their half-hearted approach to the conflict, now thoroughly mistrusted their so-called allies and started to shunt them aside. Finally they surrounded their barracks, shot any resisters and shipped the rest of them out, either to forced labour or concentration camps. The Germans were now our masters and di Stasio and Bonalti suddenly disappeared.

What this sudden, even violent, end to her first real romance must have meant to Mary I can only imagine, for she showed nothing to the outside world. Pride? A hurt too intense for normal reactions? Or just total self-control? I cannot say. She knew I was not sorry that di Stasio was gone and I could understand her not wanting to confide her feelings to me but it must have been a terrible time for her. That she was able to go on performing showed how much the theatrical life had already replaced the world of real emotions for her. A little more than a fortnight after the Italian withdrawal she gave a benefit concert at the Olympia Theatre to endow scholarships for needy students and another in December at the Cotopouli-Rex Theatre to raise money for tuberculosis sufferers. Then there was a void while the Athens musical world, as all other sectors of Greek life, tried to take stock of our new situation under German rule.

Although the changeover meant little in terms of the way we lived, it nevertheless had a profound psychological effect. We had all felt some affinity with the Italians; as a people we had always been very close and we admired their attitude to life, music, most things. Though they had invaded our country we tended to blame their leaders and heaven knows we'd had a few rotten ones ourselves. In the main we found little fault with the individual soldiers. But the Germans were another matter. We loathed them. They seemed to us arrogant and interfering. They clearly despised our easy-going Mediterranean ways and were determined to knock us into shape. They, too, saw the opera as a useful symbol of how they planned to deal with us. One of the first things they did was to announce that there would be a production of *Tiefland* by Eugen d'Albert, a choice that had even our experts running to their books to find out why. D'Albert, it transpired, was a renegade Scotsman of mixed parentage who during the First World War had gone over to the Germans. His rather nondescript opera, rarely performed, was thus an emblematic choice. Reading the signs, even more singers quietly withdrew, but Mary was there as the lead. In fact she confessed that she rather liked the new sense of discipline that had been brought into the workings of the opera house, which had been notoriously slack in the past. Mary was always a fanatical professional, always on time for rehearsals, having memorised her part before the first day's work. She was already notoriously sharp with anyone who fell below her own exacting standards so she was hardly popular with her fellow performers. So it was easy to see why she found a little Germanic discipline very much to her own working tastes and delighted in seeing her rivals in the company discomfited.

If she ever missed di Stasio she did not show it. Now she was very close with the tenor Magliveras who shared the lead in *Tiefland* and who did much to help her with advice at this stage. He was an experienced performer who had some success outside Greece and he had just the sort of knowledge she needed to draw on.

While Milton was glad she was no longer compromising his position he was nevertheless amazed at her choice.

'Magliveras is twenty-five years older than she is,' he protested. 'And look at the size of him.'

He would have stopped complaining if he had known what would happen next. *Tiefland* opened on Saturday, April 22nd, 1944, at the Olympia Theatre. A few nights later someone came to our apartment door and when Mother opened it she found a very handsome, very young, German officer who had called to pay his compliments to Mary. He introduced himself as Oscar Botman and despite our terror at his uniform, with its jackboots and Nazi insignia, we soon realised that he was an extremely gentle and cultivated person. Unsure what to do Mother invited him in and let him say his words of praise to Mary. We all knew that this was the most dangerous visitor of all but as neither Mother nor Mary were to blame for his sudden appearance it was hard to know what to do about it. Mother offered him coffee and while he was drinking it I heard Milton arrive and hurried to the door to explain the situation. All might have been well if the young officer had concentrated on the main reason for his visit, his wish to compliment my sister, but that was not to be. When Milton had sat opposite him, Botman began to explain that he had been badly wounded during the invasion and was not in good health. He then went on to say that he had had another tragedy in his life with the recent death of his fiancée in a motorcycle accident. We were all making the appropriately sympathetic noises when he suddenly turned to me and said: 'You remind me of her, she was very beautiful.'

The look that crossed Milton's face was classic and I hurried to the kitchen, hoping to stop that line of conversation. When I came back the young soldier was saying his goodbyes and after Mary had seen him out Milton began to lay down the law: he was never to be invited in again, if Mary was to see him it had to be outside, away from Patission. For once both Mother and Mary saw the sense of what he was saying even if it was motivated by jealousy. For once, his rules were strictly adhered to. Mary and Botman walked out a few times but that was all. He was much weakened by his wounds and his only real interest in her was a deep admiration for her voice. In the end he became part of that great mass of lost souls swept away by the maelstrom at the end of the war. Years later Milton told me that he had heard that Botman had made his way home only to die shortly afterwards, but as he had no way of knowing such a thing I merely assumed it was the last ripple of his crazy jealousy over an innocent remark.

As for Mary's career, after that symbolic *Tiefland* the authorities seemed disposed to leave the Lyric Theatre to its own devices and things got back to normal with a production that May of *Cavalleria Rusticana* in which Mary again sang with Dellendas. On Sunday, May 21st, she and other performers gave a morning concert for a fund for poor artists and in July they revived *Ho Protomastoras* with Mary now taking the rôle of Smaragda.

We all realised that the end of the war was approaching. Illicitly listening to the BBC, we were aware that the Germans were losing. Nothing, however, could stop their senseless cruelty and Mother received a terrible message to say that Colonel Bonalti had been badly tortured in a concentration camp and was seriously ill. To her credit, she stood by him, just when it would have been most to her advantage to ignore what had happened. She sent two parcels of precious food, praying that they would get through to him.

Perhaps it was this sense that liberation was at hand that prompted the opera house to propose putting on Beethoven's *Fidelio*. The authorities could hardly object to their doing one of the greatest works of German music yet must have realised that that great hymn to freedom was hardly what they wanted to hear. Having acquired the necessary authorisation, the company then rubbed salt in the wound by announcing that it would be performed in Greek. This was thankfully to go some way towards erasing the past and although the rôle of Leonore is one of the most demanding Mary had Magliveras to help her and her old friend Dellendas was to play Florestan.

I knew she had rehearsed to the point of madness over *Tiefland*, calling for extra rehearsals and begging the conductor to give her private briefings, but with *Fidelio* she was even more obsessed. It was as if she knew that this was far more than some minor piece put on to placate our invaders, but somehow a sign of our impending freedom. During rehearsals there was a major upset in the form of bad news from the family: one of Mother's sisters sent word that Grandmother was dying. It is appalling to realise that since her ridiculous quarrel seven years earlier Mother had kept completely apart from her relatives and had gone on forbidding Mary and me to see our grandmother. It was an abominable situation and one that Mother would live to regret bitterly. Did she ever stop to think what we, her daughters, would make of this lesson in how a child should behave towards its mother? If she did not, then she was to have years on which to reflect on just that subject. For the present, social convention ordained that she should at least pay a courtesy call on the old lady. Mary and I were ordered to accompany her and we set off on the embarrassing business of seeing the relations we had so thoroughly snubbed for so long. Did they know that Mary and I were not responsible? I hoped so.

Grandmother was propped up in bed, resting on the pillows. She had had a heart attack and looked sallow and exhausted. The sight of her lying there upset me dreadfully though Mother seemed hardly bothered and treated the situation as if we were visiting a distant acquaintance in a strange hospital. After the minimum decent interval she announced that she didn't want to tire her and would be going. When I bent to kiss her goodbye she hugged me as close as her waning strength would allow. I was shattered. That night I couldn't sleep, I was so haunted by the sight of her lying there and I went back to visit her often in the few weeks until she died. It took all Mother's skills as an actress manquée to shed a tear at the funeral.

Mary of course was full of her new rôle and I cannot blame her for being preoccupied. It was her duty to her art and what was now her public. She opened on a hot August night at the open-air Herodes Atticus Amphitheatre and I can say that for the first time she was unreservedly magnificent. Her weight problem was irrelevant in the rôle of the woman dressed as a man, and, as acting is as important in *Fidelio* as singing, she was able to reveal her unique dramatic gift, that ability to perform which was later to lift her above all other sopranos since Malibran in the last century. That summer in Athens, with the war drawing to a close, I suddenly knew that my sister would be great; I had long known she would succeed as a singer, but greatness I had not glimpsed until then. Now I had and it was an awesome feeling. We were so close, the same blood, the same inheritance, yet there she was on that stage alone, while I was only one of thousands staring down at her.

Mary ought at last to have found a measure of contentment in this triumph but something always seemed to come between her and any sort of true happiness. In this instance it was the sudden death of Magliveras from a heart attack. And yet again, as with di Stasio, she showed no sign of grief at this second loss. It was if she was able totally to erase the past. As if affection, love, or whatever, only existed in the here and now and could be completely wiped away once the object of her affections was no longer there. I found this deeply disturbing. I, who was supposed to be a creature made for love, was in fact profoundly attached to the single man in my life; whereas my sister, supposedly unloved and in search of deep affection, was turning out to be a butterfly. I tried to shut out these thoughts and to think only of her performance in *Fidelio*. With Mary, it seemed, it was better to dwell on the rôle rather than on the person behind it.

If her career during the occupation had ended with *Fidelio* then I would have been well content, but within a month she was back in Salonika for her third recital, surely unnecessary now that the final collapse of the enemy was imminent.

And then at last they were gone. Athens was emptied of troops and the city held its breath waiting to see what would befall it next. The British and the Free Greek forces were preparing to land and the celebrations began but somehow the Callas household was rather subdued. Each of us had looked no further than the end of the war. We had survived it each in her own way, making whatever compromises we thought necessary. In many ways it had not been a bad period for Mary, allowing her to go on studying with de Hidalgo and to make a respectable début in her career. None of us had really considered where we would go next and this sudden void that opened before us left us curiously untouched by the general air of relief everyone else was experiencing.

'What is Milton proposing to do about you?' Mother demanded almost as soon as the enemy had evacuated the city.

I shrank into my chair. Milton's father had been unwell recently and with his current feelings about his children's behaviour this was no time to bother him. In any case Milton had explained to me a plan whereby he would try to set up some business deals with America which would enable us to go there and once away from Athens he promised we would get married. Naturally I did not wish to share any of this with Mother but there was always the risk that she would blunder in and spoil everything.

'I think I should go and see that father of his,' she said, as if reading my thoughts. 'He ought to oblige his son to marry you. It isn't decent.'

I looked to see if she was joking but she wasn't. 'You mustn't,' I said.

'Mustn't!'

'I'll leave if you do.'

She shrugged. It was a pointless threat, the war was over, she had no further need of Milton now, no further need of me if the truth were told. She was free to do whatever she wished and she knew it. It suited her book to have me married off and if she believed that an encounter with Milton's father would achieve that, then that was what there would be.

'No!' I shouted, jumping to my feet. 'Just leave me alone. Please leave me alone.'

She too got up, muttering about never having heard such a thing and announcing that she was going round to the Emberikos' house in Kolonaki at once. Mary said she would go with her. I looked at my sister, begging her not to encourage our mother but it was no use, they had both scented a fight and that was just what they loved best. As soon as they'd gone I dashed out into the road, determined never to go back.

I don't know how long I walked around the side streets near the museum but eventually I was accosted by a friend of the family who must have been watching me and was worried that I was unwell. At first I couldn't tell him what was going on. How could I involve him in our private affairs? But he was sympathetic and could see that I was in considerable distress and tactfully enquired whether I had had lunch and if not would I care to join him. I was grateful for the chance to sit down and went with him to a nearby taverna. He ordered a meal but I was too upset to do more than toy with the food. He didn't question me too far but after a while I began to explain what had happened. He knew my mother and so it didn't take much to convince him that she was out and about causing trouble.

'You should go and see Milton,' he said. 'It's the only thing to do. If you're determined not to go back then he's the one who'll have to sort it out.'

He was right but what could I do? The rules forbad me to go to his office and I never broke them.

'You could go to his house,' he suggested. 'You could wait nearby till he comes home. Come on, I'll wait with you.'

It was the kindest offer I'd had in a long time. I nearly started to cry but I knew there was nothing to be served by cracking up so I sat quietly while he settled the bill.

We had a long wait in Kolonaki and all I could do was torture myself thinking of what must have transpired between Mother, Mary and Mr Emberikos that morning. Despite his opposition to my marrying his son I had considerable admiration for the old man. He was very dignified and had been a great help to the poor when he was in government by bringing in cheap corn from America to keep food prices down. It seemed wrong to think of him being lectured by my mother. He was no doubt fully aware of what had happened during the occupation years and as a great patriot he of all people would not have approved of Mother's behaviour. To find himself being scolded by such a woman would surely have been intolerable to him.

When Milton appeared he was stunned to find me waiting there. My friend had discreetly withdrawn and I went into the house and poured out the whole sorry tale.

'Quite mad,' he said. 'What does she think she's doing? All that could happen is that she'll make more of a split between me and my family.'

'Maybe that's what she wants,' I said. 'I can't go back. If I do she'll find a way to end everything. I can't say no to her if I'm there.'

Thankfully Milton saw the sense of that. He said the best thing would be for him to get me a hotel room where she couldn't find me, no easy task with the city full of celebrating soldiers. We set off on a trail round whatever hotels were still open for business and he eventually managed to bribe his way into a small room in the Hotel Park on Agiou Konstantinou. It was worryingly near to our apartment which meant I would have to be careful if I went out. He left me there and went to see what had happened at the meeting with his father.

He came back that night with an air of grim satisfaction. It seems that Mother had made a great fuss when she was told that his father could not see her without an appointment and that they had only admitted her to keep her quiet. She had then loudly insisted that the Emberikos family make an honest woman of her daughter. Old Mr Emberikos had watched her performance from behind hooded eyes and when she had played herself out he rose to his feet and addressed her like a naughty schoolgirl: 'Madam, you speak about my son at this moment. I forbid you to speak in this way. Let me remind you that I know the whole story – I heard that your daughter is a very nice girl and I am sorry that my son cannot marry her. I realise that the objections come from our side but you must understand that we have a different way of thinking and it is my wish that my son should marry someone from his own background. So, regrettably, I must forbid you to speak further on this subject.' He paused here and just as Mother was about to protest he continued: 'I think, however, that you ought to have some gratitude for what my son did for you during the occupation. He had no need to put his life at risk in order to get supplies to you; I understand he was manhandled by some Italian soldiers on one occasion – he had no reason to suffer that. So you see, madam, I know the whole story. And now I would like you to leave me in peace.'

And that was it. Apparently she went, as quiet as a lamb. But I was devastated by the tale. There I was and that was what his family thought of me. They had paid a price, they owed me nothing and Mother knew it was true. At last I wept.

I stayed at the hotel, I had nowhere else to go. I stayed *in* the hotel, I had nothing else to do. Milton came when he could, bringing food which at that time the hotel could not provide. I was dreadfully lonely and worried. I could hear the noise of drunken celebrations in the streets outside but I had nothing to celebrate. Then one day Milton did not come. The next afternoon he sent word to say his father was very ill and that he couldn't leave his bedside. My rations got lower and lower until a messenger brought some supplies and word to say that the old man was worse. I sent a message back, hoping all would be well but the next day the boy returned to say that old Mr Emberikos was dead. I crossed myself and said a prayer for him. He had not hated me; he simply had not wanted me in his son's life. I did not wish him dead but now that he was I could not help but think that here at last was the opportunity Milton had said he was waiting for. Surely now we could get married. Suddenly I no longer minded being alone in that dull room; there was a future for me, there was a way out of the trap that I had been delivered into.

Perhaps it is better not to hope, perhaps the dull neutrality of the first of my hotel prisons, with only the distant echoes of happiness in the streets beyond the shutters, would have been better than the disappointment I would shortly face. Why? Why me? It was so unjust.

Milton came two days later to say that there were terrible problems at home. The funeral had been a grandiose affair even for those days of wartime austerity. His father had been a leading political and business figure and in the wake of the occupation people felt the need for a little pomp and circumstance. It had not been easy for Milton. Harry, as usual, had not been much help. But there had been worse to come. Following the interment in the family plot, the will had been read, only to reveal the full extent of the father's opposition to his children's various liaisons – only the unmarried daughter Moska was to benefit. The bulk of the family fortune was left to her. Only the building opposite Zonars which had been given to their mother was to be divided between all the children, but even there half was to be Moska's. The family business was left in the hands of Milton and Harry but the assets were hers. There had been an uproar that had nearly come to blows with everyone accusing everyone else of treachery. In the end the entire family had split into several camps and each had charged off to see their respective lawyers. Massive litigation was under way over the Emberikos millions and even I, in my innocence of such financial matters, could see that it would take years to resolve. As he paced up and down, furiously recounting the events of the past few days, I realised that he had said not a word about me and my problems or about him and me or about how any of this would affect us. I had been relegated to the shadows again. Any dreams I might have had were over.

I sat alone in that room after he'd gone and let it all slip away. I was beginning to discover that I could empty my mind. That I could let everything drift off and leave a sort of nothingness. It was not a happy state but it was far better than the tortured unanswerable questions that hung around my consciousness if I tried to think. I began to acquire the skill of just sitting quite motionless, my mind a void. If Milton came, I spoke with him, ate with him, did whatever was required of me. If he was not there then neither in a sense was I. I absented myself from myself.

That was why it was some time before I realised that no one had been to see me for perhaps three days; neither Milton nor the messenger. I had little left to eat. I tried hard to concentrate on the world, I even drew back the curtains to try to hear what was happening beyond the closed shutters. Gunfire. Yes, gunfire, just as if the invasion had begun again. Perhaps I was hallucinating? Should I leave the room and try to ask someone what was going on? No, that was impossible, I couldn't face anyone, couldn't deal with what they might ask me. But I couldn't go on without food, without knowing what the gunfire meant. I opened the door and stepped out into the corridor. No one! I walked to the head of the stairs. Deserted!

I began to descend; perhaps I could skip down. Skip, jump, but, no, that wasn't allowed. There was a man at the reception desk furiously trying to telephone. As I approached I could see that the apparatus was not functioning. Nearer to the door the sound of shots was louder and louder.

The man put down the telephone and peered at me as if trying to work out who and what I was. I announced my name and room number as if these were essential evidence. He relaxed slightly and asked what I wanted.

'What is happening?' I said, aware that the question sounded hopelessly inadequate against a background of rifle fire.

'Communists,' he said. 'Fighting.'

My incredulity must have sparked off some sympathy in him. He came round from behind the desk and led me to a chair while he tried to explain what had happened. It took some time to sink in, a story of guerrillas from the mountains, the fighters of the resistance, many of whom had been members of the communist party and who had entered the city and tried to take over the government.

'But the British wouldn't let them,' he said. 'The British are here.' He gestured in a circle to take in the area where we were. 'They are holding the palace and the parliament and all this, from Syntagma to Ommonia.'

I tried to picture the heart of Athens encompassed by that description: a wide circle from the foot of the Acropolis to just where we were now. We were at the edge of that defended zone, on the front line as it were.

As if to ram home his point there was another burst of gunfire and then I suddenly thought of the implications of what he had said.

'What's happening over there?' I said, waving beyond Agiou Konstantinou towards the museum, towards Patission and the apartment.

He turned down the corners of his mouth and shook his head in exaggerated gloom. 'They're murdering and looting,' he said, clearly cheered at the prospect. 'It's terrible: snipers on the rooftops killing anyone who moves. No supplies getting in. They must be near starving over there.'

'Can anyone go in?'

He laughed. 'Only if they want to die.'

I thanked him for his help and went back to my room. As I lay on the bed I tried to tell myself I didn't care. Why should I? Think, I told myself, remember what they have done to you. Then I thought, how can I blame Mary? She was as much a victim as I was and yet there she was trapped in that place. She would be starving by now. She would suffer worse than anyone. As for Mother, despite everything how could I just do nothing? If anyone nearby was a member of the party she would be a prime target; they all knew what she had done in the war years, now would be a chance for revenge. Maybe in some ways she had asked for it but she was my mother. How could I do nothing and yet there was nothing I could do. Once again I felt the total inadequacy of my life, my complete inability to control events. All I could do was lie there and pray that Milton would come and sort it all out for me. It was at that moment that I began to hate being a woman.

When Milton came he told me more about the fighting; the death toll was worse than during the war. The biggest problem was snipers on the rooftops who fired at anything. It was a time for settling scores and many people had old weapons that they'd hidden away and which were now brought out for vengeance. Inside our 'island' those loyal to the democratic government and the few British troops who had been part of the liberation of the city were trying to hold out until help could come. They were outnumbered by the communists but were still hanging on to the line of streets that made up our border. The real terror was starvation. We were trapped and under siege. There was no longer the possibility of going out into the countryside to buy food. All the money in the world was useless now and we would have to survive on whatever was left at his home. He apologised for having brought only a bag of dusty raisins but I told him I knew how precious they were. I thought of Mother and Mary imprisoned in Patission and wondered if they had anything at all. I kept trying to tell myself not to care, to abandon them as they had abandoned me. They had thrown Milton's gifts back in our faces, now let them see what he had done for them. Mother had simply taken for granted her home, her servant, her food and clothes, all of which came from Milton and thus from me. As soon as she thought she didn't need him any more she had tried to throw everything aside. For a moment I almost welcomed that terrible civil war as a just punishment for her arrogance – but no, people were dying all around us and they must have been terrified beyond all reason. I asked Milton if there was anything we could do.

101

'It's death to cross beyond Ommonia,' he said. 'There's a sort of no-man's-land for a few streets. There are bodies lying in the gutters. Then the communists are in control and they shoot on sight. If they don't get you, then there are the snipers on the rooftops. If someone did get through they'd meet the same problem coming back the other way. It can't go on for ever and as soon as there's any sign that it's easing I'll see what I can do but for now it's absolutely impossible.'

For nearly a week that was the same story. I sat in the hotel room and listened to the rifle fire. Sometimes it was worse at night. Occasionally, unable to bear the four walls any more, I'd go down and stand at the hotel entrance and look into the street. Clusters of armed men moved to and fro, sometimes a cart with bodies draped over it would be hauled back from that invisible front line. It was a nightmare. Quite early on the electricity supply failed and half our lives were passed scrambling about in deep darkness. No one dared make a light for fear of snipers. There was a terrifying combination of utter blank dullness with sudden nerve-searing fear. One minute one was bored rigid, the next jangling with terror.

After that first week, Milton came to say that the fighting had eased on the 'border' and that people were able to pass to and fro. He knew someone who was going across and had given him some gold coins for Mother that might get her out of trouble if she was picked on – assuming she was still alive. I went through agonies of fear until Milton came again to say that the messenger had returned and had managed to see the two of them. They were terrified and had been threatened by the janitor of the building, a crazy drunk who had decided to join the communists and seemed to get a thrill out of scaring two defenceless women. Apart from that they were hanging on. Food was a problem, there was only a bag of dried beans in the flat but that was more than some had, so they could survive. As with everyone, the main fear was the indiscriminate gunfire. They begged us to do something to get them out.

Relieved as I was to hear that they were alive, I was nevertheless appalled at this news and I too begged Milton to try to do something. Who knew what might happen? If the communists found themselves losing they might decide to avenge themselves before pulling out. And what about the crazy caretaker? He might want to cover his tracks and how easy it would be just to knife the two of them. In all that carnage no one would ever know. As we found out later, a great deal of that kind did indeed happen.

But even Milton with all his connections was powerless at first to effect such an escape. A solitary messenger could flit across the line at night, but could two women? Over a fortnight went by before the situation improved. The British were determined to deny the communists our country and were pouring in aid as fast as they could. Our little island began to feel stronger and better supplied, there was the beginning of a feeling that the enemy within were edging back. This time Milton found a young boy who was going over and hired him to go to Patission with the idea of leading the two women out in daylight. If they walked slowly and openly through the streets, two ladies and a young boy, there was a chance they would be left alone now that the initial crazed bitterness was falling off. It was a terrible risk but what else could be done? Left there, anything might happen, not least starvation. But when the boy returned it was without Mother and Mary – they had refused to believe the story that he had been sent to help them.

Milton sent him back the next day and we gave him things to say, stories from our lives that Mother would realise only we could have told him. We stood in the street near the hotel for hours, hoping against hope that they would appear and when I saw a group turn into the road and I recognised Mother and Mary I was overjoyed. How could I ever have thought otherwise? Despite everything they were my closest family, there is no choice in these matters. And how bizarre they looked: their faces were predictably haggard from the deprivation of the past twenty days but their bodies were ludicrously fat as they had put on all the clothes they could wear and had stuffed the family icons underneath rather than leave them to the looters. But something was missing – the canaries. As soon as I asked they started crying and it was some time before they could blurt it out. One night they had gone to feed them a little dried fig that they kept just for the birds. Their shadows must have fallen against the blinds and that had been enough for the snipers. Fortunately, they had both left the room before the burst of gunfire smashed through the windows. The stream of bullets had mangled the cages and sliced the little songbirds to pieces. Those poor tiny creatures who had been part of our lives in America, who had been with us all through the years of war, who had been Mary's constant inspiration, had been murdered.

I took the two of them into the hotel and we made them something to eat. Supplies were starting to come through at last. As soon as she'd tasted food Mother perked up and launched into her chronicle of events: the janitor scribbling slogans on their door, his shouted threats that he was going to kill Maria, then Mother, then me! The poor drunken fool must have thought I was still there. According to Mother there was no end to the terrors they had suffered and for once I could tell she was not exaggerating. There had been gun battles on the roof, shattering explosions from the street below. Once, desperate for air, they had gone down below and edged open the door only to find a dead soldier in American uniform sprawled across the entrance. At one point Dorentis, the old Minister of Culture whom we'd met on Milton's boat, had turned up asking for sanctuary. He was a prime target for the communists and was trying to get across the line. Mother had taken him in but he was a difficult man, constantly complaining, and they were glad when he decided to slip away again one night. Fortunately, he was one of the few to make it to safety.

Using all his influence and at considerable expense, Milton managed to get Mother and Mary a room at the hotel and we settled in for a long wait. It would have been the most miserable Christmas imaginable if it hadn't been for a living message of hope in the form of Winston Churchill who, along with Anthony Eden, flew into Piraeus and at considerable personal risk was driven through Athens to Constitution Square where he met the surviving members of our government to promise them aid. Mary heard about the demonstration celebrating his arrival and hurried to see what was happening. She got to Syntagma just in time to watch the great man get back into his car for the return journey and along with everyone else was thrilled when he waved his famous 'V' sign to the delirious crowd. She returned to tell us all about it; it was Christmas Eve and the best present we could have had. We knew now that it was only a matter of time, though it was to be nearly another two months before the terrorists were finally driven back into the countryside and even then it took years ultimately to stamp out the menace of civil war.

While we waited in that hotel, word gradually filtered through of what had happened to people we knew. Miraculously no close family or friends seemed to have been killed, but many people we knew or knew of had died. There were a number from the opera whom Mary had worked with. There were awful stories of people being accosted by groups of thugs shouting that they would take their clothes – 'and you'll take mine.' They'd come up and tug at a dress or a coat, the victim not daring to speak in case that provoked them. And then the worst news of all came: my mother's younger brother Filon, who had fought in the resistance, had stood up to the communist take-over and been murdered. For so many it was the same story. Greece had been tearing itself apart. It seemed for a time that it would be impossible to repair the wounds we had inflicted on each other.

For Mary the wounds were to be most apparent when she attempted to pick up the threads of her career. By mid-February the fighting in Athens was over and the government once more in control. People started to return to their places of work to sort out the damage. But it wasn't the physical damage that mattered so much, though in many cases there was a great deal of clearing up and repair work to be done. No, the main restoration was in human relations. Everyone had been politicised by the fighting. Everyone had taken sides; even to have no declared side was taken to be a position in itself. And just as with the killing this was a wonderful opportunity for settling old scores. In some ways Mary was very naïve about things like this. Following Mother's lead she had adopted a rôle of permanent aggression towards everyone she worked with. Each was a rival to be bested. During the war she had been offered parts that would have gone to older members of the company had not Mary combined promise with furious determination and had she not been backed by de Hidalgo. Inevitably she had made enemies who now saw a chance for revenge. All the details of what she had done in the war, much exaggerated and out of context, were now repeated and enlarged. In truth Mary had done no more than thousands of others; perhaps she had not always acted wisely but she was young and inexperienced and was only following the example of someone who certainly should have known better. But for those intent on putting her down these were mere details. When Mary returned to the opera and applied to have her contract renewed she was faced with a wall of hostility. Eventually her application was met with an astonishing reply: 'Miss Calogeropoulou has not had her contract renewed. She has played too active a part in the last months of the occupation.'

I doubt if any of those responsible for that answer would have survived much scrutiny of their own activities during those bitter years. Everyone had compromised in order to survive and nothing Mary did was so very terrible. But that was the answer and there was no gainsaying it. She had believed that she had achieved something with *Tiefland* and *Fidelio*, something she could build on. She had

105

imagined the Athens opera would receive her with open arms and offer ever more challenging parts. If she had been asked to map out her career then, I imagine she would have said she expected to do two or three seasons in Athens building up a reputation, improving her technique until the inevitable offer of a part in Italy came. Then she would be launched on her international career. It was as simple as that. Now the whole thing had been torn away from her.

At first she was furious and inconsolable. Mother was no help, simply stoking the flames of her discontent. De Hidalgo tried to calm her down and give her sensible advice. She wanted Mary to go on training until she was ready to move to Italy to start auditioning. But Mary was by now impatient. Athens just after the civil war was a broken, dismal place. After the years of deprivation it seemed intolerable just to go on as before. We all longed to break free, to get away, but most of us had no opportunity to do so. Mary felt she had, so why wait?

While she was trying to work out what she would now do she had to finish her old contract with the theatre. Astonishingly, after the high moral line they had tried to take over Mary's personal life, they proved just as inept by deciding to revive the wretched production of *Tiefland* that had been wished on them by the German authorities. One can understand their not wishing to waste sets and costumes but this was surely one production that should have been willingly consigned to the dustbin of history. Sadly, Mary did not play their own game and refuse to take part in this foolishness; instead she accepted the rôle of Martha again when it opened on March 14th. But at least six days later she improved her position by giving a 'musical afternoon' for the entertainment of the British troops which contained such unusual items for a Callas recital as Vaughan Williams 'On Wenlock Edge' and the traditional 'Willow Song'.

But by then nothing mattered but her determination to leave Athens.

It was a letter from Father that clinched it. Since the war ended he had been trying to track us down and eventually a letter got through. As he was almost permanently on the road selling his products he could give us no address but he sent a welcome one hundred dollars and asked if we intended to come 'home' after all we'd been through. He reminded Mary that she was technically an American citizen and might find that useful, and indeed in April the American authorities advertised in the newspapers to say that there would be places on the first boat out of Piraeus later that year for any citizens wishing to be repatriated. Against de Hidalgo's advice but with Mother's strident encouragement, Mary went to put her name down for the voyage. She would have five months to wait but at least there was something now to look forward to.

Mother had been somewhat subdued since the humiliation of having again been rescued by Milton. Now, with Mary's impending departure, she sprang into action again. Her first concern was to organise a concert at the Cotopouli-Rex Theatre in order to raise money to help with the trip. After the war years we were all wearing patched-up clothes made out of bits and pieces. Some things were virtually threadbare and despite the shortages Mother was determined to use her skills as a dressmaker to ensure that Mary had something decent to wear in New York. As for me, she reopened her campaign to get me to confront Milton with the fact that he ought to marry me. At first I tried to shut out her endless nagging but that was difficult as she had cleverly touched on the one subject where we agreed. I could see no reason why we could not be married. We were supposed to be secretly engaged, he always referred to me as his fiancée and now that the principal opposition, in the form of his father, was no longer there to embargo the idea he could surely have volunteered himself. But no, he said nothing. When I broached the subject he became evasive and went on about wanting to marry me in America and how that was impossible just yet because he was not allowed to leave Greece until the family's legal squabbles over the will were resolved. It seemed then and still seems now a pretty feeble excuse and it was some time before I managed to squeeze out of him the real reason: his fear of marrying me sprang directly from the one person forcing him to do so – Mother. Her last gesture in this regard, her visit to his father, had horrified Milton. The woman was clearly out of control, or, put another way, her control over me was something too difficult for him to handle. The great fear in his mind was that in marrying me he would also be taking on the utterly unmanageable Evangelia. I had shown no ability to control her. When she had gone too far I had simply run away. No, he could see no reason to fall into that trap.

Not that Mother's intentions were entirely straightforward. It would have suited her at that time were I to marry Milton and thus ensure a source of funds to help her with the next stage in Mary's career. But were he to show no signs of wanting to marry then she would have been equally happy to see us part and thus have me available for other, as yet unworked-out, schemes. Content either way, she prodded away at that sore spot, telling me he couldn't possibly love me if he wouldn't marry me. Telling me that at twenty-eight I was getting on and that if I didn't find a husband soon it would be too late. Telling me he'd ditch me when it suited him if I didn't have it all legally tied up. On and on and on as only she knew how.

Of course in the end Milton's view that I was totally subservient to her proved a self-fulfilling prophecy. Goaded beyond endurance I tried to force him to make a decision and when he again prevaricated I told him I was leaving. Ever ready to throw petrol on the flames, Mother arranged for me to leave Athens so that I could not change my mind and in July I was bundled off to my relations in Salonika.

It was a grim experience on all counts. Salonika had been badly bombed and the harbour front was a mass of shelled and burned-out buildings with half-submerged vessels tragically poking up out of the water. There was rubble and filth everywhere and the process of clearing up had barely begun. As July turned to August the heat combined with the dust to make life intolerable. My uncle, Colonel Mondooris, and his family did all they could to cheer me up but I was inconsolable and mooched around the house or went for depressing walks among the ruins or just lay on the bed in my room feeling sorry for myself. No matter what Mother said, no matter whether or not Milton was behaving as he should, the basic fact was that I loved him and that was all I could think or feel. The tragedy was that we had allowed things to get to this point and there seemed no way out of it.

After a week it looked as if I was going to be seriously ill. My uncle was a kindly man and tried to talk me out of my black mood but he soon realised that he was having no success. His next move was to behave like a Greek uncle should and write formally to Milton asking him what his intentions were. A friend took the letter to Athens and delivered it personally and reported back that Milton opened it and said: 'Why can't she wait? Why doesn't she trust me?' The friend said that it was common knowledge that Milton had completely withdrawn from view. He went nowhere where he would be seen by those who knew him and had become a recluse.

'There's no doubt he loves you,' the friend said. 'Won't you go back?'

108

But how could I? I now doubted he ever meant to marry me. I could tell his reasons were getting more and more improbable. I heard later that Father had found out about our relationship and he too sent a letter politely demanding an explanation, only to receive Milton's by now standard response that everyone should trust him, that he had many problems just then but that as soon as these were resolved and he could get to America he intended to do the right thing. I no longer believed this and as miserable as I was I now determined to see it through. Whatever latent streak of toughness lay buried within me surfaced and I vowed to be strong.

There was no point in staying on in Salonika, the place only added to my depression. In any case the biggest test would be how I faced being in Athens without Milton. I returned to Patission, by then fully taken over with preparations for the great departure. Mary's concert, organised by Mother, had taken place that August – another tour de force of Mozart, Rossini, Verdi, Weber, with Greek and Spanish folk songs. This had raised enough money for the wardrobe Mother considered essential for Mary to make her way in the musical world of New York. It was amazing to me that neither ever seemed to doubt that what were essentially Mother's fantasies might not prove hollow. Now Mary was preparing for her last rôle with the Lyric Theatre, the lead in Millocker's *The Beggar Student*. She and Mother were frantically busy, both with the new opera which was to open on September 5th and the impending departure, and for once I was grateful that no one paid me any attention. I decided just to get on with my own life and even went back to the Conservatory to resume my piano lessons.

CHAPTER FIVE
1945–1951

The most noticeable change since I had been away was the presence of so many British soldiers in the capital. True to his word Churchill had sent a large contingent to help flush out the communist insurgents in the mountain villages and those released from the front line were able to spend their leave in Athens. Others were attached to the various branches of the Greek forces. Many were young conscripts called up at the very end of hostilities. They were unlikely now to face the rigours of their predecessors and for them it was a sort of fantastic interlude in their youth and education. Unlike we battered Greeks they were light-hearted and full of hope and we rather loved them for it. They were a breath of fresh air in our weary lives. I first came across one such visitor when an officer in the Greek navy, a friend of Mother's, came to visit and brought with him a young British marine officer whom he introduced as Anthony Barlow. He was a little younger than me and had barely been away from home before except for his boarding school. After all we had suffered it was hard not to think of him as a mere child but it was good to be with someone for whom life was full of exciting possibilities. When he asked if he could see me again I was more than a little pleased.

Poor Anthony, I don't know why he put up with our first encounters. I was so depressed because of Milton, I must have been terrible company. I was also a little confused about how to deal with the British. Americans I knew about but these strange reserved people with their sudden silly humour were quite different. One day we were out together and one of his friends ran up to join us. He kept referring to him as 'my Lord this and my Lord that' – I couldn't get the joke.

'Why does he make fun of you?' I asked when we were alone for a moment.

'Because *I am* a lord.'

I sort of knew what that meant but was not sure of the implications so when he had disappeared for a second I asked his friend to explain.

'Easy,' he said. 'When he marries you, you'll be a lady.' And then he burst out laughing.

I guessed I was the butt of a joke but there was no point in trying to find out what had made him laugh. It was the 'when he marries you' that bothered me for it had become clear from the start that Anthony, or Lord Anthony or Lord Barlow or whatever he was called, had fallen for me in a very serious way.

For once it was I who needed to talk things over with someone and who ought I to have been able to turn to but my own sister? To her irritation I interrupted her practice at the piano one day and tried to explain what was worrying me. I told her about this lord business but that seemed to cut right through her.

'Lady Barlow,' she sneered. 'You. Lady Barlow. An English lady.'

Clearly Milton had been bad enough, someone from a grand Greek family, but that I might suddenly transfer myself abroad with such ease, a rôle she evidently thought reserved only for her, was enough to awaken all that simmering envy that had so poisoned our friendship.

'*Lady* Barlow!' she snorted and began to crash out a tune on the piano as if to submerge the thought in a crescendo of clattering chords.

Shortly afterwards my worst fears were realised when Anthony suddenly proposed. I knew at once that it was no use being flippant and treating it like a first affair to be laughed away. He was far too serious and much too intense a person to be joked out of his first romance. There was also the fact that he had behaved impeccably. Many of those young men were after an easy thrill with a foreign girl in need of the gifts they could bestow. He'd tried nothing like that and I was deeply grateful. I owed him better than a quick brush-off. Thinking quickly, I told him I would marry him if his father approved but that he had to set out everything so that his parents could decide. He had to say precisely who I was, how old I was, and that it was I who desired their agreement. Unable to imagine that anyone would not be as drawn to the object of his affections as he

111

was, he wholeheartedly agreed to my suggestion. He seemed to think that that would resolve the matter. I knew enough about grand families and their ways to know that it would be the end.

While we waited for a reply Anthony and I continued to amuse ourselves according to post-war Athens' limited resources. We went to Mary's last production, *The Beggar Student*, held in the open air. It wasn't a very impressive piece and Anthony didn't feel that Mary shone in it, though I suppose her mind was then on the coming journey and not on the world of Athenian music which had rejected her. Indeed, when she was suddenly informed that the first boat for the States would be leaving in a matter of days and that there was a place for her on it, she happily abandoned the production and left the theatre with the difficult task of replacing her at short notice. It was her one act of revenge for their ridiculously high-handed and utterly unfair treatment of her.

When she left shortly afterwards she refused to let Mother and me accompany her to Piraeus. I could guess that she was now preparing herself for a new and completely different period in her life and thought it better to begin the change on the very shore she was leaving. But it was a cruel blow for Mother who sat at home and fretted while her precious daughter was given a farewell lunch by the mayor of Piraeus. It was just the sort of official function Mother adored and it was really rather mean of Mary to deny her it. For myself the supposed deprivation was a blessed relief. I wished Mary every success with all my heart but I at least knew that I would have no part of it and would have to get on with my own life. That was the hard lesson Evangelia Callas was going to have to learn for herself.

Although I will never know, it might be one of the ironies of fate that the SS *Stockholm* that carried Mary off to America had earlier brought in the reply from Anthony's father. Despite the wartime limitations his response came so fast it was clear evidence that here was a family with considerable influence. The reply was exactly as I would have predicted. In cool, unemotional terms the father congratulated his son on having found someone he loved and even more fervently on having chosen a lady of such good breeding that she had had the decency to ask him to refer to his parents in the case of his marriage. Given, the father went on, her own delicacy in this matter it was obvious that the only way to proceed was that Anthony should delay any hasty action until such time as the present restrictions on travel had ended so that Miss Callas could travel to England to stay

112

with his parents so that they could get to know each other and so that she could decide if the world that he, Anthony, moved in was one in which she would feel comfortable.

It was an unanswerable request, so finely put only a barbarian could have objected. But that wasn't all: before Anthony had time to rally his forces, he suddenly received orders transferring him to Malta on the first boat. This happened to be the next day, making it clear to me that his father was not without considerable influence in British military circles. There was nothing his bemused son could do except obey. I kissed him goodbye and prayed to God he'd get over it without too much distress. I knew all too well what a broken heart was like and had no desire to inflict it on someone as good and kind as he.

I returned home to Mother. Now we were two people for whom life seemed to have come to a full stop. She hung about near the door waiting for a letter from Mary long before the boat could have landed in America. I just waited for God knows what. The first three months of 1946 were the first of my empty days. I was to get used to them in the end but at first they grated. I had often had periods with little to do but there had always been something, however slight, to look forward to. Occasionally Mother would try to play Svengali with me, suddenly deciding that we should reactivate my career as a pianist but her heart wasn't in it. She was dreaming of New York and Mary. Eventually her first letter came. A curious surprise: Father had seen the passenger list of the *Stockholm* in one of the New York papers and had hurried to the harbour to greet Mary as she landed. I could tell from Mother's expression that she had mixed feelings about the reappearance of George Callas, though from Mary's point of view his arrival must have been a godsend. From then on the letters trickled through, the occasional one for me. They were tiresomely uninformative, a sure sign that things were not going well. Mary could never withhold a triumph but became sphinx-like if she felt she would lose face. If things were going badly then you would hear nothing. Mother wrote screeds begging for details, back came a page or so of chit-chat.

I seldom went out. Friends occasionally called and some would try to act as go-betweens with Milton, telling me how he never appeared anywhere, how he was broken-hearted, how he wanted me back. To which the only reply was that all he had to do was what he had always promised. I had never tried to trap him, I wasn't after his

113

money, which in any case he seemed to have lost in the will. I had been with him for nearly nine years by then and what I was asking was only just. That he never came forward with a response was answer enough. I felt terrible but that was only to be expected. I was sensible enough to know that the only thing to do was sit it out and let my misery subside in God's good time and that was what I proposed to do.

Then one day during the Easter festivities Mother rushed to grab a letter that had just appeared and snorted as she realised it was for me. It was a note from a young British officer just passing through on his way from Malta to say he had brought a letter from Anthony and could I come to the Grande Bretagne the next day at five to collect it.

I spent a lot of time the next afternoon preparing for the encounter. I wanted to look good but I also wanted to get his friend to carry back a message saying it was not possible for us to marry. It was not going to be an easy meeting but I was determined to carry it off. It was then that the peculiar national characteristics of the Greeks and the British collided in a way that was to have far-reaching effects for me. An appointment to a Greek is an approximate time meant to give you a rough idea of when you are expected – tell a Greek five o'clock he comes at six. To an Englishman the time is the exact time. I sort of knew that and it was only a quarter past five when I entered the lobby of Greece's grandest hotel. But even those fifteen minutes had been too long for Anthony's friend who, thinking I had not got his note, had hurried off to our house to sort the matter out. I hung about the lobby, wondering whether I was too early. I turned to ask the receptionist for the man's room and there in front of me was Milton. We both gasped with surprise.

'I had to meet a businessman,' he said without needing to.

'I came to see someone,' I said feebly, looking round in desperation.

'Come on,' he said, grasping my elbow firmly and leading me out. We crossed Syntagma without a word, hurried past the parliament with the Efzones at their sentry-boxes, and turned into the Zappion Gardens. Once under the shade of the pines, Milton lessened his pace and we could catch our breath. At first we just walked, then he slipped his arm round my waist, then we sat on a bench and stared straight in front of us. I don't remember that we said anything. We didn't really need to.

I don't know how long Milton and I were in the Zappion, not too long I think, but by the time I hurried back Anthony's friend had gone.

'So nice,' Mother said. 'Very polite, you should be ashamed of yourself treating him like that. Anyway he says he will come back tomorrow evening so you can see him then.'

I spent a lot of time the next day composing a letter to Anthony that I hoped would let him down gently. There really isn't much one can say in such circumstances except sorry, even though you aren't really responsible. His friend was very nice and we went out to a taverna where there was dancing and I asked him to take the message for me. I hadn't opened Anthony's letter to me; I would look at it later, for there seemed no point in making myself miserable thinking about how he would react. In the end he never wrote to me again. I suppose he felt deceived. I have never had news of him since and imagine he is happily married, probably a grandfather by now. I hope so.

And there I was at twenty-nine, still living with Mother in Patission, still seeing Milton. He had moved into an apartment in his office block on Ommonia Square a short walk from us. He was trying to re-establish his business from the little his father had left. His main income came from his share of the building opposite Zonars Café that had once belonged to his mother and he was using that as capital to launch new ventures. He was an active man, never happy unless he was doing something and he had very quickly set up a factory to refine fuel oil near Daphni, about an hour's drive from Athens. The site was near the local lunatic asylum and he used to make jokes about ending up there with all the work he had to do, which was true enough. He left early in the morning and did not return until late at night so I barely saw him except for his evening meal which he took with me as often as he could. His sister Moska who had inherited the family fortune had married but that was a subject that no longer came up between us. It just seemed to have faded away as if we had had enough toing and froing and had decided to accept life as it was.

It was an amazing time in Athens, a sort of explosion of happiness after all the people had been through. The city was still the beautiful place it had always been, pretty white houses, cool courtyards, countless outdoor cafés. The destruction would start fifteen years on when people began to pull down the old buildings and put up

115

concrete blocks. Today, almost nothing of the old Athens remains except in memory. Then, it must have been a good time to be young, with music in the tavernas and people out dancing until late. But for me, that was a closed world. I lived for Milton and he now lived for his work. I even gave up the Conservatory, there really was no point. I played a little at home but even that gradually diminished as time went by. In the end I concentrated on the home. We had a maid and she cooked for us but there was always plenty to keep me occupied. I found that I was increasingly concerned that everything should be tidy and in good order. I liked to see the apartment polished, with all our objects in their right places. That same attention I applied to myself. I couldn't let Milton see me unless I had washed and put on my make-up. If he came round before I was ready and if he tried to come and kiss me I'd run away and tell him to wait until everything was done.

At least Mother left us alone now. She seemed to have accepted that I was going to lead my own life and that it did not contain an amusing rôle for her to play. Not that she minded, she had Mary's great career to dream about. Although she had been shunted aside at the time of the departure she felt that that could only be temporary and that her daughter would soon find that she needed her mother with her.

For once she was quite right in her predictions. Gradually our letters from Mary were full of how wonderful America was – lots of details about all the food there was available – and how she was going to be such a success. But though she always tried to hide it, it became clear that the starring rôles she felt were hers by right after her success in Athens were simply not coming her way. Mother wrote and wrote demanding to know what was happening but Mary simply told her how Father had been so good to her and had bought a piano and had given her the money to furnish her own bedroom, news that only infuriated Mother who still hated any mention of her husband. Eventually the letters started to mention someone called Eddie Bagarozy who turned out to be a lawyer and businessman who was fanatical about opera. He was married to a singer called Louise Caselotti who had taken on Mary as a sort of non-paying student. Over that year the letters revealed that Bagarozy had a plan to create an opera company in Chicago and was hiring singers from Italy for the first production: *Turandot* with Mary in the lead. Even we in our ignorance, half a world away in Athens, thought this sounded a little strange. Why had she not been given a part at the Metropolitan Opera House, we wondered?

Then one day she wrote to say that she had auditioned there and been offered the starring rôle in *Madame Butterfly* but that she had turned it down because she felt she was too big and would look ridiculous. Turned down a rôle at the Met? Mother was almost speechless. What was going on? Her frustration at being so far away when all these peculiar, momentous things were happening was terrible to see. In my mother's book her husband was utterly incapable of coping with the situation and she had no idea who this Bagarozy was and whether or not his plans for Mary made sense. She paced up and down the apartment, smoking furiously and longing for the post to arrive.

It was a welcome relief to me when she announced that Mary's godfather Dr Lanzounis was coming to Athens on holiday and that he would be bringing all the news.

His first announcement made Mother cry with joy: Mary missed her and wanted her to go to the States to join her. The rest seemed an anti-climax. Father, it turned out, had a reasonable apartment in a not very nice district on West 157th Street. He took care of her as far as he could, though as a pharmacist in someone else's store he didn't have much money – much head-nodding from Mother here. The first problem had been Mary's eating. After the deprivations of wartime Athens, New York had seemed like heaven and Mary had spent much of her early days gorging on hamburgers, hot dogs, pancakes with maple syrup; she simply never stopped and was now huge. All her old problems had returned, pimples and boils and the swollen ankles that made her look so elephantine. None of this, as Dr Lanzounis explained, had helped her with the round of auditions she had embarked on. Mary, of course, never admitted that she had had a set-back; it was always her way to refuse to accept failure, there was always some other reason. But even someone with as little knowledge of the opera world as her godfather had managed to work out that the opera house managers who had heard her had doubts about the quality of her voice as well as her weight problem. That was why, as he explained, the Bagarozys had been heaven-sent. Mary spent every hour she could at their beautiful apartment working on her voice with Louise Caselotti. Dr Lanzounis had no idea whether Eddie Bagarozy's plans for *Turandot* would succeed, but as Mary had no other offers she might as well go along with them.

117

How Mother longed to jump up then and there and head off for New York, but it was weeks of impatient organisation before she could even start. Travel anywhere in those first post-war years was a nightmare and Mother was forced to take a boat to France and a train to England where she joined the *Queen Elizabeth*, arriving in New York on Christmas Eve 1946. For once Mary was overjoyed to see her mother. She had tried to go it alone, despite de Hidalgo's warnings that New York was too hard a nut to crack and that she would be better off in Italy. It must have seemed to Mary in those dark days that without Mother at her side nothing could go right. So there was the old team again, ready to challenge the world.

For Milton and me, Christmas that year was a strange affair. Now neither of us had families that we wished to or could spend it with. We ate alone, enjoying the calm while way across the Atlantic my mother and my sister prepared for battle.

Indeed, the first letters of the new year were full of strife, both domestic and professional. Mother had discovered that her husband had found a little comfort in her absence and the first upheaval was the dislodging of this unfortunate, with clothes and bags thrown into the street. But George Callas was not to be so easily thwarted and having lost his mistress he decided he might as well have his wife. His advances in this quarter were met with noisy hysteria as Mother barricaded herself in Mary's room and threatened to commit suicide if he so much as touched her. Father shrugged and decided his worst nightmare had enveloped him and that his crazy womenfolk were back in control again. A settlement was reached whereby Mother and Mary would occupy one room and he the other. The second great upheaval was that *Turandot* collapsed. The Bagarozys had brought over a number of Italian singers, including the young Nicola Rossi-Lemeni, only to run into trouble with the American Chorus Union who created so many delays poor Eddie went bankrupt. It really did look as if Mary was finished. Even Mother seemed to despair and wrote to say that Mary was considering taking a job at Macy's. Then suddenly everything changed. Louise and Eddie heard that Giovanni Zenatello, the ageing director of the Verona opera, was coming to New York looking for singers. He hoped to engage Zinca Milanov for *Gioconda* but the Bagarozys persuaded him, against his will, to audition Mary. From the first notes the old man was entranced, even leaping up and joining in. Mary was given a contract and Eddie Bagarozy was signed up as her agent at ten per cent of all her future earnings. Along with Louise, Mary set sail for Italy in June. Mother, who had given her a list of thirteen rules as a goodbye gift – concluding with the injunction to 'honour thy father and thy mother' – was once again left behind. God knows what our poor father made of all this.

Seen from the distant vantage point of Athens, with many of the finer details filtered out, Mary's early career looked very much like that of the dumpy ugly duckling trying to fly and at first only able to jump a little then fall to the earth with a bump. Then it was up and off again but, no, not quite. I heard nothing for some time but next came news that the *Gioconda* at the Verona Arena had not been anything exceptional and that she was again having problems finding work. Nevertheless the Verona conductor, the great maestro Tullio Serafin, had liked what he'd heard and had taken on the task of trying to develop her higher register which had always been her weakest point. For six months she trained with him, then he took her to Venice as Isolde at the end of the year. Again another awkward leap but no take-off. Then in January of the new year it happened. Still in Venice she sang the *Turandot* she had prepared so well in America but had never been able to sing till then. And up and away she went, no more ugly duckling but an operatic swan in full flight. Musically she owed everything to Serafin. He was not only one of the greatest conductors of his day but also a great teacher devoted to continuing the highest operatic traditions and Mary was blessed to have been singled out by him.

But what of Mother in all this time? Why was she languishing in New York instead of being there at her daughter's side? Well, as we both now knew there was someone other than maestro Serafin in Mary's life. Almost as soon as she had arrived in Verona she had met a rich local businessman, Battista Meneghini, who had immediately made himself indispensable to her. Although in his fifties, Meneghini was very much the local ladies' man and a passionate opera buff. Despite her size and her lack of success Meneghini, according to the dreamy letters we now received, was entranced by Mary. And I of all people knew just how my sister would react to such a situation. For all of her adolescence she had only ever been loved for her voice, now along comes this man and tells her he loves *her* – not *Maria* Callas the singer but *Mary* Callas the woman. He must have been irresistible and, indeed, as I was soon to discover she truly found him to be so. In that situation there was no longer any need for Mother. Back in New York she must have read the descriptions of Meneghini and his loyalty, his attentiveness, his constant presence, with deep foreboding. Those were precisely the functions Evangelia Callas had reserved for herself, yet here was this elderly Italian assuming her rôle and with an intimacy no mother could match. As Mary began her first triumphant tour of the major Italian cities, culminating with *Norma* in Florence in October, Mother's letters got more and more strident. Why wasn't she being sent for? What was going on? Why didn't Mary tell her anything any more? At home in my isolated apartment in Athens I watched all this as if it were a play, the strange antics of fictional creatures. It was too hard to imagine my sister up there on all those historic stages being cheered to the echo, too unreal for someone who remembered the awkward schoolgirl and the plump adolescent.

Yet in one respect I had to believe it: by now the Greek newspapers were giving extensive coverage to her appearances. Oh, of course they had picked up on what she had already achieved, she was after all a local girl making a name for herself abroad, but it had usually been short paragraphs; no more than a notice of a first night. Now they began to acknowledge that something strange was happening, something beyond the usual news of singers and performances. It is always hardest for someone to be accepted in the place where they began. Who in Athens could appreciate that our dumpy wartime soprano was really breaking new ground in the very home of opera? But by January 1949 that is exactly what we began to hear. It was the extraordinary combination of *Die Walküre* and *I Puritani* in Venice and the Italian reviews Mary received that finally alerted the Greek press to what she was becoming. And now I began to see almost monthly accounts of her progress.

The story of how Mary opened in *Die Walküre* on January 17th and then stood in for an indisposed soprano as Elvira in *I Puritani* two nights later, having had only a week to study the part with Serafin, is now enshrined in operatic history. It was an almost impossible feat. The rôles are, from a vocal standpoint, absolute opposites. She also had to learn the words and music, a task that takes most singers months, not days. But she did it and she triumphed. It was then that the world sat up and began to take notice. She was no longer just another promising singer with a difficult upper register and a weight problem; she was a phenomenon.

The only thing that soured that triumph was a letter from Mother angrily pointing out that Mary had shown her usual callousness to a figure from the past. The Italian Colonel Bonalti, Mother's wartime companion, had apparently read about Mary in the local press. He had indeed been badly treated by the Germans towards the end of the war and had been permanently hospitalised not far from Mary's new home in Verona. He had written to ask if she would do a dying man the favour of visiting him to remind him of happier days. She had not answered his letter but he had managed to track down our mother in New York to ask her to write to Mary. But the second letter that reached her was to inform her of his death. I was the one who had been against his visiting us in Athens while Mary had seemed to welcome it, so I felt the least she could have done was to cheer him up during his last painful illness. But then it was pointless to criticise Mary for such behaviour. Since her arrival in Athens aged thirteen, Mother had done everything possible to suppress any normal human reactions and to instil in her daughter those selfish, aggressive qualities that she believed would enable her to claw her way to the top. Perhaps Mother had been right; after all, the evidence was that the method was working. But it wasn't long now before Mother herself would learn to regret having been such a thorough teacher of these ways.

I suppose it must have been all those articles with their descriptions of first nights and admiring audiences that led me to suggest in one of my letters that I might come to Italy on holiday. I suppose I was beginning to realise just how boring my life had become compared to hers and was daydreaming that she might welcome her sister and let her share in some of the fun. I can only imagine that I had in my fantasy erased the last few difficult years with Mary and chosen to recall that earlier period when she had doted on me. In my dream we were sisters again, devoted, laughing at secret jokes, defending each other against Mother, telling stories after lights out. With that in mind it was impossible not to create a life in which I would have a place. Perhaps, I fantasised, I could take up the piano again and Mary and her new friends would help me get started. Anything was possible.

Did I really want such a thing? After all I was truly in love with Milton. But then we are all capable of yearning for opposites. I suppose what I really wanted was simply to get away for a while, to pretend, if only for a moment, that I was not a prisoner in Athens, that I could if I wished break free. Even if none of my fantasy came true at least I would return of my own free will. When Mary wrote to say that I should come in March it seemed that there was some hope after all.

When I arrived at Verona railway station I took a cab, as directed, to the hotel where she and Meneghini were living and where I was to have a small room in their suite. The receptionist told me to go straight up and a porter opened their door and left me inside with my single suitcase. There was a long corridor connecting all the rooms and I cautiously made my way down it, peering into the sitting-room and then on to another room until suddenly I was face to face with the two of them in bed. I was appalled and gave out a terrified gasp. Mary looked up from a score spread across her lap and burst out laughing. The bulky form of Meneghini in thick striped pyjamas turned on one side with a groan and fell back to sleep. I fled to the sitting-room where I sat on the edge of a sofa trembling with embarrassment.

A few moments later Mary followed me into the room and came up and embraced me.

'I'm sorry,' I stammered, but she only laughed it away.

'He didn't even notice,' she said. 'He's fast asleep, we were up late last night.'

I had guessed they were lovers but somehow I hadn't expected them to be sharing the same bed.

'You can sleep like that?' I asked.

'Oh, I love it, I love to feel him beside me to curl up round him. Don't you like holding on to Milton?'

'No. I like my own bed for sleeping in. I like to be independent. Anyway I'd hate to wake up in the morning and find him staring at me before I was ready for him. I hate a man to see me before I'm prepared.'

'I don't care,' she said.

And I have to admit it would have made little difference at that time. She was amazingly fat, and must really have eaten and eaten in America. Now that she was in the land of pasta and cakes she evidently wasn't stinting herself. When Meneghini came to join us he too was no oil painting, though for a man of his age he was strong-looking, fresh-faced with white hair. For someone so short and squat he walked like a young man, though side by side, with her height and bulk, they looked most peculiar. This clearly didn't bother her and she was soon holding on to him and kissing him and exchanging

122

Father and Mother, he smiling – she not!

Me, aged about three, with Christos, our servant, in military uniform.

Dressed for tap-dancing.

A day out in New Jersey, 1933: Maria with George Vasson, me with Claire Poretz.

New York, 1936, beside the George Washington Bridge.
Alexandra Papajohn, her sister, Katina Papajohn, Mother
and Father. Maria in the foreground.

Greece, 1938, at Vouliagmeni Beach. Nicos Evangeledes (a cousin), Mother, Maria,
Milton and me.

Milton Embericos during the war.

Me, 1944.

Athens, 1940, in Field of Mars Park. Maria at 17, Mother, and me at 23.

Mother in New York with Louise
Bagarozy's dog.

he top floor apartment in Patission
treet, Athens.

Mother's dolls of Maria's roles.

Publicity photo for my concert, 1957.

The Diva: Maria in Rome, 1958.

Father, Maria and Meneghini, 1950.

Maria with Aristotle Onassis, 1961.

Ready for a ball. Me in 1968.

Vasso Devetzi with Maria's ashes after the funeral.

Andreas and me in 1984.

lover's compliments. At first I thought this was an act for my benefit, an attempt to prove to me that now she too had her romance, but I soon concluded that it went beyond Mary's old fixations. She truly loved him, of that I am sure. In fact I would say she was infatuated with him. He had to go off on some business and was to join us at his sister's for lunch but he had no sooner left the hotel than Mary became nervous and irritable, constantly wondering what he was up to and asking me if it wasn't time for us to go and join him.

'He has work to do,' I said, trying to calm her, but she wouldn't be pacified and continued to pace the room. 'Are you going to marry him?' I asked, hoping to capture her interest.

'I'll do it if I can,' she said. 'In fact you've given me a very good idea.'

We set off for his sister Pia's house far too early, so impatient was she to see her man again. While we waited for him to arrive the two women talked together. I had noticed that on entering the house Mary had adopted a rather miserable expression, almost as if she were in pain, but when I'd started to ask her what the matter was she'd hissed at me to keep quiet. Now Pia enquired if she was feeling unwell and to my amazement Mary went into a long litany about how distressed she was because I, her sister, had come all this way and had found the two of them in bed although they were not married. Now she knew full well that I didn't give a damn who she made love to; she could have been sleeping with the chorus and orchestra of the Verona opera for all it would have bothered me. But I knew enough about Mary's antics to realise that I'd better keep quiet and go along with whatever scheme she was hatching.

Pia looked suitably disturbed. 'Two years my brother has been with you and you're still not wed. Yes, I can see that it's not right. I must speak with him.'

At that moment the poor Meneghini arrived, unaware of what was in store for him.

We went in to lunch and I was amazed at Mary's performance: soup, pasta, fish, meat, salad, ice-cream, fruit. It all went down with second helpings in places. Everyone else picked modestly at what was on offer, Mary gulped it down. Oddly enough Meneghini seemed to take a sort of strange pride in her capacity to digest large quantities of food. He smiled lovingly and helped her to more of what she fancied. I could see that if you were as big as Mary and had no intention of doing anything about it then here was the perfect mate.

While they lingered over coffee I went to the bathroom. Mary followed me and began to repair her make-up.

'You've put on weight,' I said. 'You don't think you should diet a little?'

I could see her suddenly scrutinising me in the mirror, assessing my slim figure.

'Why?' she said. 'Titta likes me like this.'

But whether or not her Titta liked her that way I knew there was the stage to consider. Of course there have always been really fat sopranos but it did appear to be the end of that era and if she wasn't careful Mary would find herself out of place, the last of the elephantine divas. But it was impossible to say such things to her. She went back, leaving me to finish arranging my hair and when I eventually returned I found an air of festivity at the table.

'Congratulate your sister,' said Pia. 'She's just been proposed to and has accepted.' The two were arm in arm beside each other. Mary was staring like a lovesick adolescent into the eyes of her betrothed and I realised that while we had been in the bathroom Pia must have given Meneghini the talking-to she'd promised so that when Mary returned he'd popped the question then and there. So my presence had already achieved something. I'd succeeded in getting my sister married. It was an astonishing change of rôle: I, who had always been held up as the one for marriage while Mary was the one destined for a career, was now scattering these prophecies to the winds. I, who had neither a career nor a marriage, was obliged to congratulate my sister who was to have both success and a rich husband. I wished her well.

And so began my fifteen days in Verona though not all were as eventful as those first hours. Because she could not bear to be apart from him for a moment we went nowhere except to eat meals. I saw nothing of Italy and precious little of Verona. Much of the time I listened as she practised, nothing as amusing as songs however, just the eternal vocalising to strengthen the voice and the diaphragm. Fortunately, her technique had improved since she had been working with Serafin. There was much less wobble in the higher register and a little less steeliness in her tone. But she was no less self-punishing than she had been and her practising went on and on and on. Which was just as well, otherwise she would have had nothing to do except fret over her fiancé.

Although I was disappointed that she didn't do more to show me around, I tried to tell myself that she had much on her mind. This was one of the rare periods of rest in her new life. She had had a punishing schedule and this was a chance for her to prepare for another season of new productions. Around Easter she would be setting off on her first overseas tour with a visit to the Buenos Aires opera and I was hoping that she might suggest I come with her. I had not told her of my dream that I too might have a chance to do something, but I hoped that when I got round to talking about it she would be sympathetic. For the moment, if it meant I had to sit and listen to her practising *Turandot*, then so be it.

The first sign of trouble came after about a week when we were invited to dinner by one of Meneghini's business acquaintances. The man's son and daughter had both got engaged recently so there was a party of young people which was very cheering after the rather elderly group that usually made up our suppers. It was strange that Mary seemed to prefer the old cronies of her fiancé and looked wary whenever there were people of her own age around. I think she felt out of it when there was any sort of youthful fun and preferred to be courted like a lady and be praised as a rising star of the opera. She was certainly not happy at the dinner party that night and when the host asked if her younger sister would like to go to a cinema with the other young people Mary was not best pleased.

'Younger!' she snarled. 'She's six years older.'

She had no sooner let fly than she realised how idiotic she'd been and there was an uncomfortable silence before some attempt at conversation could be restored. Much as I would have liked to go out I thought it diplomatic to refuse and to accompany her back to our hotel. It was a tiresome journey with lots of remarks about 'younger' and 'young people' being hurled about.

From then on she was markedly less friendly. She began to give orders rather than make suggestions and I began to see myself more as a sort of assistant than a sister. Things got worse after an evening with some of Meneghini's elderly friends when one of them started paying attention to me. I must say he was one of the most unattractive men I've ever seen, a gaunt creature almost like a skeleton, but he was obviously very well off and clearly smitten by me. As soon as she saw, Mary became agitated. Then out of the blue the man went over and clapped Meneghini on the back and announced that as he was getting married maybe his friend should too and who better than the beautiful sister of his fiancée. They all thought this a very amusing idea but Mary's eyes began to blaze ominously and I could tell the evening's entertainment had not long to run. Sure enough there was a whispered conversation with Meneghini and we were off in the car in a trice.

From then on I began to get bored with all the hanging about waiting on her pleasure. After those first days she had ceased to be warm and sisterly and had gradually adopted the sort of mannerisms I imagine she used in the theatre to give herself the authority she needed. Bit by bit she was becoming Maria the diva and was no longer Mary the sister. The crunch came over yet another lunch – that really was all we seemed to do; as usual the men disappeared back to their offices after the coffee but Mary stayed on to talk to our hostess. It was a hot day. I was a little tired and barely understood a word of Italian, so I tried to suggest to Mary that I might go back to the hotel for a siesta. She hissed at me to stay where I was and just went on talking and gossiping for over an hour. As we eventually went back she told me: 'You can't leave when I'm there. You have to stay until I choose to go.' It was truly Maria the diva giving orders to her companion. It was at that moment that I ceased even to think of her as Mary. Maria she wanted to be and Maria she had become.

'Listen, Maria,' I said, 'I think I should be going home soon. I've enjoyed being with you but I must be getting back to Milton.'

'As you wish,' she said and that was that.

She and Meneghini were married that Easter after my return. I heard that under Italian law it was difficult to marry near to the religious holiday but she had made an almighty fuss until Meneghini found some way round the rules. She just couldn't bear the thought of not being married to him. With Maria there had to be a single dominating figure at each stage in her life. She had worshipped me when we were children but as I grew up we drifted apart. Then there was Mother who took her and moulded her and gave her the force of personality to be what she became. Now there was Battista Meneghini who made her feel loved and who offered her total protection at a time when she was very vulnerable. Although it seemed impossible at the time, with all her protestations of love for him, I had an uncanny feeling that her marriage was not for ever. Each person in her life fitted a certain period, when the circumstances changed then the person had to change. When they went, like di Stasio and Magliveras, they were instantly erased. For the

126

moment Mary was a struggling artist and there was Meneghini to sustain her, but woe betide him if she no longer wanted to fit into that world they now occupied. The odd one out in all this was Mother who as yet could only have begun to guess that she was yesterday's support. In fact this was still in some ways a transitional period and had Mother realised what was happening and chosen to withdraw gracefully then she might have maintained some sort of relationship with her daughter. Indeed, I still had a relationship with Maria of sorts, though as I sank back into my life in Athens I could ask myself just what such a relationship mattered when it was evidently so one-sided. Maria was rising far beyond us and had no time for what we had once been. I wished her luck and was happy to keep well clear of the wash from that particular high-speed vessel. Poor Mother had no such instincts for self-preservation and continued to fire off letters in all directions demanding to know why she was not being brought to her daughter's side.

As if to warn her off, Maria married without telling our parents. She simply sent them a telegram in Italian: '*Siamo sposati e felici*'. As neither of them spoke Italian it was a clear notification that they now had to deal with another Maria. Father probably shrugged, Mother ranted. I foresaw trouble.

A year later, in April 1950, Maria made her début at La Scala but only as a substitute for Renata Tebaldi who was ill. It was an old production of *Aida* and gave little hint of the glories that were to come. Unbeknown to me at the time was the opposition she had found from the Scala Superintendente Ghiringhelli, a feud that was subsequently to make opera history. I had only the Greek reviews and Maria's increasingly sparse letters to go by. The only news that did come my way was that she was to sing in Mexico the following month and would be taking Mother with her. This would be the first encounter between Evangelia and Meneghini, both about the same age, but by then the old and the new protectors of La Callas. Mother had cunning and a will to survive but she lacked wisdom and patience; it would be an interesting encounter.

When Maria arrived in New York she was met by Father who told her that Mother was in hospital with iritis, a painful eye condition but one not likely to persist. Maria visited her, left money for the trip, and went on ahead. Surprisingly the two men, George and Battista, had got on famously though they had barely a word of any language in common. In fact this was the beginning of Maria's growing attachment to her father. I think we had both long realised that he had been shabbily abused by his wife when we were children and that there was no longer any reason for us to accept her version of events. But it was quite another thing to make the emotional leap needed to establish some sort of relationship with George the man. Maria had had more chance than I to get to know him and her references to him in her letters were now quite glowing when set against her irritable remarks about Mother.

Evangelia, on the other hand, was in seventh heaven. Mexico adored Maria. She gave a series of stunning performances: *Norma*, *Aida*, *Tosca*, *Il Trovatore*, which an older and wiser hand might have refused to undertake. She was reported to be singing at the very limits of her strength and every note sung is like capital spent. Great voices have only so much time and in Mexico Maria was a spend-thrift. But the opera public loved her for it and fêted her, and in her wake was Mother. It was the world Mother had seen in her dreams; first in those small apartments she so hated after the Depression in New York, then through the hard days of the war. She had always believed that the time would come when her daughter would be a star and she would be by her side. Every day there were fresh flowers in her room delivered by an adoring management. There were fans on hand to do all the little chores. There were official receptions, first nights, press conferences, the whole glittering round. So what if there was Meneghini, closer to her Maria than she could now be? It was still Mother in the dressing-room washing the dye from the Aida make-up out of Maria's underclothes, it was still Evangelia who received the congratulations of other mothers on the success of her famous daughter. Only gradually can it have begun to dawn on her that this was not a beginning of the great dream but its end. There were no longer the girlish intimacies of before, no longer the childish fears and worries that Mother would be asked to soothe. Those were now the province of the husband and if Mother became too close or too cloying there was now a sharp remark or an icy coldness.

Just before the Mexican season ended Mother wrote to tell me that Maria had bought her the most expensive fur coat imaginable. I, who knew only too well how stingy Maria was, had quite a shock when I read that. Only when I worked out that that coat was not a sign of continuing affection but a guilty farewell pay-off did I begin to realise what had happened. Mother wrote again to say that she was staying on in Mexico for a few days after Maria's departure. The hotel was paid for, the flowers continued to arrive, there were still those to fawn on her and for a little while she didn't even have to share the limelight with her daughter. I hope she really enjoyed her few days of glory for she had to live off the memory for the rest of her life.

For me in Athens, the last chance of a marriage to Milton had passed with my barely noticing it. As the year ended the dispute over his father's will was finally resolved with a more equitable distribution all round. I was hardly surprised when he told me this but did not follow it up by saying we could now get married. We both knew the time had passed. Waiting for the will to be settled had only been a fiction we had maintained, we both knew it. In any case we were used to living apart but with his regular visits and the thought of exchanging that for something resembling the scene I had glimpsed in Maria's bedroom seemed faintly comic. The idea of wrapping myself round a sleeping man dressed up in striped pyjamas made me laugh. That aside, the settlement hardly brought Milton much joy. He still had to work day and night getting the factories going and he had been feeling increasingly tired. Then one day he complained of a swelling on his neck and asked me to take a look. It was hard to tell what the matter was as he had been rubbing it and the redness could merely have been the irritation. Still, I told him to see the doctor but as he never did I supposed it had not been anything serious.

Nineteen fifty-one was the fiftieth anniversary of Verdi's death and it was also previewed as Maria's Verdi Year – she was to do her first *Traviata* in Florence in January followed by *Il Trovatore* and *I Vespri Siciliani* before returning to Mexico and then on to Brazil. As Mother's infuriated letters began to make clear she was not going to be invited along for the ride. Having tasted ambrosia she was having withdrawal symptoms. No need to exaggerate her reaction when she heard that not she but Father was the parent chosen to go to Mexico that year. Rather than witness his departure she left New York and came back to Athens. I could hardly bear it. I had forgotten her incessant nagging, her almost constant litany of complaint about how badly treated she was. My life had not been particularly exciting since her departure but I soon realised that I preferred my somewhat lonely existence to days passed against a background of Mother's perpetual whining. On top of everything else she had virtually no money. In the dark days of the war the little allowance Milton made us had saved our lives but he saw no reason to pay for my increasingly irritable mother and her presence ate into such funds as he gave me.

Mother then tried to get an allowance out of Father but he too saw no reason to support a wife who had long since made it clear that she considered their marriage a mere formality. Though I must say that if he had had any sense he would have paid her off on condition she stayed away from America. As it was, his refusal was my rescue, for she decided to return to New York in order to sue him for maintenance. She was also at the start of her long campaign to get Maria to send her money. Her requests, whenever she chose to show them to me, were intemperate and badly expressed. She kept insisting that as she had sacrificed everything for her, Maria was absolutely obliged to give support in return. If we hadn't long ago realised that Evangelia had been as much concerned about getting away from George as she had been about helping either of her daughters these pleas might have received a more sympathetic hearing. As it was, both Maria and I knew that Mother was utterly selfish. Gradually, Maria stopped even bothering to say no and long silences followed Mother's ever shriller protests. Her departure for New York was a blessed relief but it was to be short-lived. She succeeded in convincing a New York court that she was entitled to maintenance from Father set at twenty-five dollars a month and, honour satisfied, she returned to Athens. With her safely across the ocean George simply twirled his moustaches and refused to pay up. To get him to do so she would have had to return to America to sue him again; that was now impossible. Round one to Father.

Unfortunately for me she was now even less restrained than before and her letters to Maria bordered on the unhinged. She was further inflamed by a sudden change in the financial situation in Greece. The Finance Minister Spyros Markezinis devalued the drachma by over a hundred per cent against the dollar. To bring money in from America was now to get rich quick. Mother promptly wrote to Maria and proposed that she should receive a monthly allowance of one hundred dollars. Was it not her due after all she had sacrificed etc. etc. etc.? Sadly, with her unerring instinct for disaster Mother's letter reached Verona just before Maria returned from Mexico. That second tour had not been as happy as the first. Maria had agreed to far too punishing a schedule which had resulted in a very unsatisfactory *Rigoletto*. Despite the success of *Tosca* and *Lucia* that one failure rankled with my sister. Ever her own worst critic, she had torn herself apart to the point where she was in a deep depression on her return and what should she find waiting for her but Mother's most demanding and grasping missive to date. Her own reply matched Mother's in intemperance, word for word: not only was there to be no money and no further correspondence but she went on to tell Mother that as she, Maria, had to 'bark' for a living why didn't Mother also get a job. But it was the ending that shocked us both: 'It is now good weather. Now that it is summer, go to the shore and get some fresh air. If, as you say, you still have no money, you had better jump in the river and drown yourself.'

I was appalled. No one knew better than I how infuriating Mother was and I was not unsympathetic to Maria's anger. Nevertheless, she was now a successful singer and it was perfectly true Mother had nothing to live off. After the alteration in the exchange rate even quite a small allowance would have made Mother comfortable. Despite all the exaggerations Maria owed a great deal to Mother's obsessive promotion of her talents whatever her underlying motives may have been. And all that aside, Maria was a Greek, and our whole ethos is to stand by our families no matter what. So, reluctantly, I wrote to her and tried as gently as possible to make these facts clear to her. The reply was as swift and as brutal: I was told to mind my own business. She thought that I too was only after her money and made it clear that neither of us was going to get any of it.

I read it to Mother and then tore it up. For me it was the end. There was simply no point in trying to deal with someone who had got into that position. In some ways it was a relief. Maria had gone. She was now far beyond anything we could cope with and it was far, far better to let her get on with it. Any attempt to participate in her new life was, I realised, bound to bring unhappiness. The life I had was all I could expect and I was prepared for that now. It was Mother who took it hardest, Mother who knew that this was the end of everything she had dreamed of. I was quite calm, as if a cloud had been lifted. Mother, however, was unable to control her sobbing. I knew then that she would never have any contact with her daughter again but there was no way that I or anyone could help her cope with that fact.

PART TWO
The Sister

CHAPTER SIX
1951–1963

I had no sister. I knew it as soon as I read that letter. I was the only child, alone with Mother. Sometimes she would cry but I couldn't feel sorry for her. Nor in a way did I blame Maria. Mother had made her what she was, hard and ambitious, trained to exclude anything or anyone that did not advance her success. She had needed Mother in Athens and again during those first difficult months in New York but what did Mother know of Italy and the world of the great opera houses? Meneghini, on the other hand, might have been created for the rôle of her protector. Of course Mother refused to see this. In her heart she felt that this was just another of Maria's tantrums and that any day she would wake up and realise that she needed her mother as before. But the months of waiting were to lengthen into years, years made more unbearable by the increasing fame of the absent daughter who was now constantly in the headlines. Mother was forced to keep up a façade of lies within her circle, referring often to her daughter's letters, her solicitous telephone calls, the fact that any day soon she would be flying off to join her. Anything rather than admit that she had been cast aside.

When one remembers how close they had been – in some ways more like sisters than mother and daughter and certainly more sisterly than she and I had been at the end – when one remembers all that, it is hard to credit that throughout the fifteen years of her triumph Maria never once agreed to see her mother. Milan, Rome, London, New York, each year brought her to another great city, another great opera house, another huge success. We who had merely glimpsed the first suggestions of her greatness could only marvel at the speed and the extent of this victorious advance. For fifteen years, from the late forties through to the early sixties we watched from afar, by turns confused and delighted, saddened and elated.

When Maria's recordings started to appear in the Athens shops we would bring them home and listen to them much as we had listened to the operas borrowed from the New York City Library all those years ago. And each time she read the sleeve notes Mother was forced to imagine the missed first night, the reception, the adulation. Then, once more, she would be plunged into melancholia. She tried everything, even consulting one of Athens' many mediums. She wanted me to go with her but I refused.

'They only take your own thoughts and give them back to you,' I said. 'They're clever but you never learn anything.'

But every avenue had to be explored.

She came back elated; the woman had told her that her daughter would be separated from her man. To Mother this was great news; with Meneghini out of the way Maria was bound to send for her.

But I was less happy than she. What if the medium really did know something and what if the daughter she was referring to was not Maria? Mother never stopped to think of such an interpretation because as usual I was invisible. Only the absent Maria had any reality.

Milton did his best to keep out of Mother's way. His businesses were giving him a lot of trouble and he'd had to borrow money from Harry to keep them afloat. Working late at the factories exhausted him but I could see that it went beyond that. He was increasingly unwell. Sometimes in the evenings as we sat over supper he would stretch his neck and grimace in pain.

'It's my neck, just here.' He would massage the area immediately below his left ear.

If I went to look I could see the swelling but it grew so imperceptibly it was a long time before we realised that it was not something that was just going to fade away of its own accord. Only gradually did we accept that the pain and swelling were linked to the lethargy that often overcame him. One day he could barely get out of his armchair to move to the table and I told him he must see his doctor the next morning. But neither of us were prepared for the concern the man showed. I think we imagined Milton needed a tonic, maybe a rest. If anything we thought the swelling was just an irritating symptom of over-work and that it would recede if he could only get himself fit again. But it was his neck that the doctor concentrated on and he advised Milton to fly at once to Paris to see a specialist there.

I was surprised but only slightly worried. After all, Milton was one of those big, well-built men you don't associate with illness. He never seemed to be plagued by minor things like the colds that bother most people so why get distressed? But when he returned from France with a large dressing round his neck my confidence was shaken. I asked him what had happened but he only shook his head; it was one of those forbidden areas, I was not to ask. As usual I held my peace.

To take my mind off things, I took to playing the piano again and if Mother was out I would sometimes sing a little. I'd never sung before. I suppose it was quite enough to have Maria filling the apartment with the human voice. In a way I'd had almost a revulsion against the idea but now I amused myself by trying out some of the operatic arias Maria had practised during the war. It was very relaxing, though I was determined to keep it as private as possible. Then one day Mother overheard me. The lift had broken down and she had been forced to climb to the top floor, struggling with her purchases. I, of course, had not heard my usual warning, the lift mechanism clanking into action, so that as she stood on the top landing catching her breath she overheard me happily singing away. When she came in she looked very suspicious.

'Aren't you listening to records?' she demanded.

I shook my head.

'I thought you were listening to your sister?'

This caught me off-guard and I blurted out that it had been me.

'You,' she said. 'You've got a voice. For God's sake, why did you never use it before?'

There was no answer to that. She insisted I sing something and I had to oblige. Watching her out of the corner of my eye I was pleased at her amazement but when I finished I ought to have been worried by her reaction.

'We're going to do something about this,' she said, with that sharp look on her face that I knew so well.

It was years since I'd let her meddle in my life and I should have stopped her then and there but somehow, with all the worries over Milton and the fact that I felt sorry for the emptiness of her life, I hadn't the heart to dampen her sudden enthusiasm.

'We'll get you a teacher,' she said. 'The best.'

'Oh, come on, Mother, I'm not a child the way Maria was when you started with her. It's too late.'

'Never. You've got musical training, you know piano, you've got some idea about technique. You're way ahead. All you need is someone good to train the voice. But who?'

I left her to her musings. I was hardly in the mood to take her seriously. The night before Milton had come back from the clinic where they had removed the dressing. He could no longer keep from me the fact that he had had a major operation. The left side of his face seemed to have sunk and it was all I could do to disguise my horror at his appearance. That once handsome man now looked like some terrible victim of war or industrial accident. If anyone thinks that the ability to act was the province of only one of Evangelia Callas' children they should have seen me then. I did everything to show him I cared for him and that nothing mattered.

I suppose it was our joint determination not to accept the consequences of his operation that meant that we never really discussed it, that we never said that fateful, terrible word. It was taken as an event: he had gone to Paris, they had done this to his face; it went no further than that. His doctor in Athens told him to be patient for a year then he could go to London for cosmetic surgery that would make a considerable improvement in his looks. In the meantime he tried to mask the worst of his disfigurement with scarves, reserving the sight of it only for me. One always imagines that people who were as intimate as we were will discuss everything, that nothing need be hidden any more but of course the opposite is very often the case. As the years go by you stop talking and just accept what is there; so it was with his face.

I couldn't even talk it over with Mother. She was now completely obsessed with the idea that I should have my voice trained. But who could do it? she kept asking with increasing desperation. I'm sure she would have gone to de Hidalgo if the elderly soprano still lived in Athens but she had retired to Ankara. There were voice trainers in Athens but most were very second-rate. I gratefully imagined that that would be the end of the matter though I ought not to have underestimated Mother's extraordinary persistence.

A few days later, when I'd managed to put the incident out of my mind, she suddenly returned to the apartment full of plans. She had been browsing in one of the local stores when she'd been greeted by a man called Simiriotis, a relative of the famous poet. The young man had been a pupil of Trivella when Maria first started and had sometimes been round to the apartment in those far-away days before the war started. Naturally they fell to talking about Maria's success and he'd commented on the amazing news, recently in all the newspapers, that she was getting thinner. He asked if Mother had seen pictures of Maria in Visconti's *La Traviata*. 'Didn't she look wonderful?' he said. None of this was likely to best please Mother, as any suggestion that her former girth was less appealing than her new slimmed-down look could be taken as a criticism of the years when Mother was in control of events. Indeed the women's magazines were full of Maria's supposed miracle diets, the régimes that had achieved the impossible and reduced her to the shape of a beautiful model. I for one saw no miracle in the new image, she had always had the potential to be beautiful. When we were little she had been as good-looking as I and it had simply been gross over-indulgence that had ruined her. Stop that and all would be well, as had been proved. But Mother was for once less interested in the miraculous doings of her younger daughter and it was only when Simiriotis asked after me, 'the good girl', as people often referred to me, that she perked up.

'What's she doing with her piano these days?' he asked.

'Oh, she plays and now she sings.'

The man expressed surprise but Mother only wanted information and asked him straight out if he knew a good teacher.

'I need one for Jackie. The best.'

'No kidding, she has a voice. Well there's always Vithinos. He trained Zachariou and Engolfopoulos.'

The names of the two other Greek singers to achieve fame outside Greece aroused Mother's interest. We had heard that Maria had done a lot to help Zachariou when the young man turned up at La Scala and would only have done that if she believed in his abilities. So Mother returned to the apartment determined to track down this Mr Vithinos.

It all seemed a little unreal to me at first. There was Maria transforming herself into a beautiful svelte model while I was to be sent to music classes by Mother. It was as if life had jumped back twenty years and our rôles had been reversed. But there was no stopping Mother now. When she tracked him down Mr Vithinos listened to me audition and agreed to train me but he made it clear from the outset that this was to be no game. He trained only professionals and would only let me begin if I understood that this was a serious matter and if I really wanted to be a second Callas. The thought was unnerving: was that really what I wanted to be? But for Mother there was no hesitation. The answer she gave was yes, that was exactly what I wanted to be. She had seen a ray of hope after those dark days of isolation and now I was obliged to work for her dream with almost constant practice – *Tosca, Cavelleria Rusticana, La Forza del Destino.* It was the past returned, the apartment ringing to the sound of vocalising in the mornings, with the constant reiteration of phrases all day and silence only on the three occasions a week when I went round to the Vithinos' house for lessons. In one respect Mother had been right: my musical training was a great help. That I both knew the scores and could accompany myself was a major advantage and Vithinos was soon enthusing over my progress. After only six months he told me that if I was truly positive about making a career he would stop charging me. But he warned me that there was a great gap between being merely talented and having the guts to succeed.

'Your sister was a fighter,' he said. 'But are you, Jackie? Do you have enough spirit to claw your way up the way she did because it's that that makes the difference? I don't want to be disappointed, we have a lot to do and I don't want to spend all that time for nothing.'

Did I really mean it when I told him I would fight or was I just wanting to please Mother? It's hard to remember what I truly felt. I was confused about Milton and wasn't displeased to be the centre of attention for once. For years it had been Maria this and Maria that, now it was my turn and it wasn't unpleasant. Yes, I told him, yes I wanted to be famous, wanted to stand up there alone on stage listening to the applause. Yes, yes, yes.

Now Vithinos became for me what de Hidalgo had been for Maria. I was at his house whenever possible and often his family would insist I took lunch with them. If I had had any doubts about my getting anywhere these were allayed when Nicos Zachariou called to see him while on holiday in Athens and overheard me practising. He got very excited about my voice and told Vithinos that Maria would be furious if she knew what was going on.

When I repeated this story to Mother she grew very pensive and asked me to repeat exactly what Zachariou had said.

Shortly afterwards we saw a good example of what Maria's anger was like when the newspapers carried an astonishing photograph of her screaming with rage at an American process server who had just slapped a writ on her for not paying Bagarozy the money she agreed in that contract eight years earlier. She had signed him up as her agent and then forgotten about it. In fact her real agent was Meneghini who we heard was notorious for driving a hard bargain, but now in Chicago came this action by the man who had beggared himself trying to launch her career. The Bagarozys had lost all their money over that ill-fated *Turandot* and now he wanted some return. From Maria's standpoint that early contract had been signed when she was at the lowest point in her career, since when Bagarozy had had nothing to do with her life. Rossi-Lemeni had also signed one but he had wisely come up with a small settlement that had satisfied the Bagarozys. Provoked by the ever-greedy Meneghini, Maria had refused even to talk to her old supporters and now there was this much publicised court case. Dressed as a fragile Madame Butterfly, by now thin and angular, Maria's howl of rage cruelly distorted her features into a twisted mask of fury. It was among the worst publicity she ever received and it marked the beginning of that universal awareness of her stinginess in money matters that was to tarnish her reputation. Already the newspapers carried the gossip of how unusual it was for the Meneghinis so much as to buy someone a cup of coffee, but so far the blame for that had been laid at the husband's door. Poor Meneghini was pilloried for being both grasping and parsimonious; soon these were criticisms that would fall upon his wife.

For the moment Mother studied the image of her screaming daughter with increasing interest and savoured Zachariou's words.

At this point Milton went to London for the cosmetic surgery that the Paris specialist had recommended. I imagined this would put everything right, that things would miraculously be as they had been before and I felt quite elated at the prospect of seeing him whole again. Then one day during his absence I was walking home from my lesson when I met his lawyer, Mr Kaminopetros.

'What word of Milton?' he asked.

I told him it was too soon for any news but that I was sure everything would be fine.

Kaminopetros gave me a worried look. 'You shouldn't build up your hopes too much,' he said. 'Cancer is something you have to come to terms with.'

Cancer. The word hung in the air as deadly as the disease itself. Cancer. The word we had chosen never to use.

Kaminopetros was shaken. 'You didn't know? But his face?'

All I could do was shrug. I felt foolish. How could I explain that I had known that Milton did not want the matter aired. The lawyer went on to tell me that when Milton had gone to Paris the year before they had told him that he was in a bad way. If only he had gone six months earlier things might have been different. By then it was virtually too late. They had operated and removed a massive cancer, hence the collapse of the side of his face. But they were not hopeful that they had ended its spread and had warned him that he probably had only three months to live. That he had survived another year was in itself a miracle.

So there it was: the truth. Was I better off for knowing? Did it change anything except that now I had nothing to look forward to but a dying Milton? But no, I told myself, these doctors are often wrong; three months to live and he had survived a year. They were already shown to be fallible. Even when he returned from London and it was clear that the doctors had been unable to do much to improve his appearance I refused to accept that this was anything but temporary. I tried again to show him that I didn't care and indeed in a way I didn't. I no longer seemed to see the new damaged Milton; to my eyes he was still the handsome young man I had first seen in the notary's office. It was only when others came on the scene that the illusion slipped. I used to greet him at the door of my apartment when he came and one day the neighbour across the corridor drew me aside and told me how brave I was.

'I don't know how you can do it,' she stumbled on. 'Kissing his face like that. I love my husband but if he was like that I wouldn't go near him. You're so strong, child.'

It took me a moment to realise what she was referring to, so far had I managed to ignore the reality she saw. I tried to explain to her that it was a different Milton that I kissed but she could never understand.

Nor could Mother – which in a way was just as well. Had she been at all sympathetic I might have broken down. As it was I fought off ever showing anyone what I really felt. I never cried. I never railed against fate or blamed heaven for what had happened. I kept it all to myself rather than add Mother's pity to my other sorrows.

She for her part had another enthusiasm. Vithinos had told me about a competition for young singers held every year in Italy with musical scholarships as prizes and when I told Mother her eyes lit

142

up. The only problem was my age. At thirty-nine I was beyond the limit by four years. Nothing daunted, Mother simply altered the date in my passport, the reverse of what she had had to do to get Maria her scholarship with Trivella. Vithinos entered me and another of his pupils, Irene Sakellaredis, and we both prepared our pieces. Irene travelled with her husband Aristedes, a bank clerk and, along with Vithinos' sister, we set off in early March to spend fifteen days in Vercelli near Milan. Vithinos was a shrewd man and he had warned me that if word got out that I was the sister of Maria Callas there would be nothing but trouble. It would probably prejudice the judges against me and I would certainly be pestered by the press. At his suggestion I entered the competition as Elena Montesanto.

It was glorious early spring weather. Vercelli was a delightful small town with a concert hall in a pleasant park where we were able to practise. The accompanists and the judges came down from La Scala, a sign of the prestige of the competition which had drawn entries from all over the world. It was strange to think that these men and women from the opera house in Milan had probably worked with Maria and I couldn't help wondering how they would react if they knew my secret.

We were all to sing in a preliminary selection, then the winners would go through a process of elimination until the final at the end of the fortnight. One day I had just finished practising with my accompanist when I noticed an old man seated in a corner, leaning on a walking stick, watching me intently. He summoned me with a wave and began to tell a long story about how he had come with his granddaughter who had entered to please herself, though he admitted he didn't think much of her voice.

'But you are different,' he said. 'I have listened to them all, from Galli-Curci to Callas and you too have a great voice though you're not going to win.' He chuckled as he said it which made me angry. 'The judges will never give it to you,' he went on. 'They'll pick an Italian in the end, wait and see. But you mustn't be discouraged. Promise me you'll go on.'

I didn't much care for his predictions but he seemed a kindly old man and to keep him happy I promised him I'd go on.

For the competition, the singers appeared on stage with their accompanists while the judges looked down from the first row of the circle. It was nerve-racking to sing in the almost empty hall save for those experts from Italy's leading opera house all staring down

143

intently. On the Monday, Irene went first and to my surprise she sang only a tiny extract from *Carmen*, barely more than a page and then an aria from another opera, whereas I launched into an extract from *La Forza del Destino* and finished with the whole of 'Vissi d'Arte' from *Tosca*, not unaware that this was Maria's most famous aria. As soon as I'd finished I could sense the interest coming down from that distant row of judges.

'Well done,' my accompanist said. 'You should be all right.'

In the end he was incensed when the old man's predictions turned out to be all too exact and I was ruled out at that first round. They let Irene through to the second stage of the competition, then she too was eliminated and that was it for the Greek entries. We stayed on till the end, enjoying the good weather and drifting in and out of the competition to see what was happening. The final winners were an Italian, a Bulgarian and a Chinese, so the old man had not been totally correct. And then to my surprise the judges suddenly relented and awarded me a special prize for the quality of my voice and issued a statement saying they were sure I had a great career ahead of me.

Back home, Mother of course was furious – why hadn't I done this? Why hadn't I said that? It was the old fighting spirit that she had instilled in Maria. She was right, of course; in my position Maria would have challenged the judges and made a scandal until they declared her the winner. I had meekly accepted what they had done. But that wasn't the end of the story – we were no sooner back in Athens than the story appeared in all the newspapers that the 'younger sister' of the great diva was now embarked on a career as a singer and it was this more than anything that must have provoked Maria into giving an interview, largely to go on record that it was she and not me who was the younger of the two.

Nicos Zachariou told me later that Maria blamed our mother for putting me up to it and for leaking the whole thing to the press in order to embarrass her. At first I'd assumed that it was Irene or Aristedes who had blabbed to someone but how could I be sure? Back in Athens I found Mother giving an interview about me to the popular Italian magazine *Oggi*. It was obvious that Mother hoped that publicity of this sort would goad Maria into ending the frigid silence she had maintained since the famous rift four years earlier. Although I had continued with my decision to let Maria lead her own life I had discovered the previous Christmas that Mother had continued to send her a card and I had no doubt she would also have

144

been writing to her. Maria simply ignored her. Hence the publicity about my voice. It was a clever move and the ruse most likely to break down Maria's indifference.

Whatever the reason, Mother insisted that it justified the decision to train my voice and that I should work even harder at my lessons. We had left our old apartment in Patission and had tried staying out on the coast at Paleo Filiron but the building was too damp and we soon moved back to central Athens. We were no sooner in our new apartment than we were contacted by a reporter from *Time* magazine who said he was writing an article on Maria and would we talk to him. I flatly refused. I really had no wish to embroil myself in her life any more. I had taken up singing because I had thought it would mean a life for me, a thing that I myself would do on my own, with praise or criticism coming because of my own efforts. Now the whole thing seemed to be degenerating into just another skirmish in Mother's campaign. She, of course, was only too happy to see the reporter and had him round one day. I stayed out of the way at the Vithinos' house.

'I hope you were careful,' I told her when I returned, though she had that look of victory about her that said that she had really enjoyed herself. But even I could not have predicted the lengths to which she had gone. When the issue of *Time* appeared it was a bombshell. Maria had just arrived in New York for her first season at the Met and there was her portrait on the cover of the magazine, a rare honour. But the article inside was all too clearly Mother's: it portrayed Maria as an ungrateful harridan who had abandoned her poor devoted mother to a life of misery. Mother had made it abundantly clear that she was the one who had discovered Maria's talent and who had single-handedly nurtured it. It was Mother's sacrifices during the war that had kept us fed and in music lessons and it was only when she was no longer needed that she had been so cruelly cast aside. As a final, and to me appalling, coup de grâce, Mother had given the reporter Maria's last letter to her, the end of which, with its injunction that she could drown herself, was printed in full.

The issue appeared two days before Maria was due to open in *Norma* and the American horror of anyone mistreating the sacred institution of motherhood meant that she was given a distinctly cold reception. I asked Mother just what she thought she would achieve by this, but it was pointless to try and reason with her. She was

145

convinced that Maria was just a naughty girl who needed a smack and who would come running back obediently. The problem was that she had still to find the right place to land the blow. The *Time* article was a very nasty surprise for Maria but it didn't provoke the required response. Mother then had the ignominy of being informed by letter that Father was suing for divorce in America on the grounds of desertion so it was *her* turn to feel that everyone was against her. With all these things piling up it was inevitable that she would come to feel that the only weapon left in her armoury was my voice and we were no sooner into 1957 than she conceived the notion that I should give a big public concert, something that would establish my existence and would act as a launch for my career. No sooner did she have the idea than she threw herself into the business of bringing it to fruition.

I was far too preoccupied with Milton, who was going through one of his ever more frequent bad periods, to attempt to restrain her. It was now four years since the French doctors had written him off with only three months left to live, so it was easy to delude oneself into thinking that they had been totally mistaken. Indeed there were occasional good periods when he seemed to rally and when one could imagine that it was somehow all over and that he would soon be restored to full health. But then those moments would be swiftly followed by an even sharper decline. It was all he could do to rise early in the morning in order to be first at the factories near Daphni and by the time he returned after a day's struggle with a difficult business he was too exhausted to do anything but eat and sleep. We no longer attempted to go out. I would practise while he was working and then be ready for him in the evening. When he heard of mother's plan for the concert he got very worried.

'Are you sure you can do it?' he asked. 'It isn't just your mother pushing you too far?'

He got so worried that one day he stayed off work and came round to Vithinos' house while I was practising. After he had listened for a while he interrupted us.

'Why didn't you say before?' he said. 'You can sing. Why did you wait all these years?'

As with Mother, what could I say to him? I had never wanted to let a note out of my mouth till then, that had been Maria's life not mine. But now that the taboo had been broken there was much to do. Vithinos wanted me to start with a bang and had chosen an

146

incredibly arduous programme that would leave no one in any doubt as to my abilities. I was to start with three solo arias from *Aida*, *Tosca* and *Un Ballo in Maschera* and go on to a large part of *Cavalleria Rusticana* and finish with the end of *La Forza del Destino*. For this I would need to be accompanied by a tenor and a bass so Vithinos approached Kostas Trogadis and Nicos Papachristos at the Lyric Theatre and they offered to help, provided I auditioned for them first, as they wanted to be sure I was any good before they could agree to appear with me. It was a great boost to my morale when they pronounced themselves well satisfied with what they heard and both agreed to donate their services to help me. Mother was delighted when she heard this as part of her plan was to raise money from the concert so that we could get back to America. She had developed the notion that what I needed was some sort of patronage, something or someone in my life who would correspond to Meneghini in Maria's. She reckoned that she had two candidates in a couple called Zarras whom she'd befriended on her last visit to New York and who were said to be bowled over by the Callas legend. We had, so Mother reckoned, only to get to New York and they could be prevailed upon to sponsor my career. With Maria safely in Italy she would be free to start getting rôles for me at the Met. It sounded incredible, but there was never anyone as convincing as Mother when she was determined to get somewhere and she *had* succeeded with Maria, so why not me?

Not that being promoted by Mother was ever easy. She nagged away at me over wasting time on Milton when I could have been rehearsing, then if I stayed on at the Vithinos' house she moaned because I had betrayed her by leaving her to eat alone. There was never any way to satisfy her and the only thing was to accept passively whatever she chose to say.

Thankfully, much of her time was soon taken up with booking the Parnassos Concert Hall, arranging for tickets and posters to be printed and then selling seats. Given that I was now using the Callas name these proved very easy indeed to sell and within a few days Mother could proudly announce that we had a full house. The Zarras in New York sent over a beautiful full-length pink silk evening gown, a sign that Mother's expectations from that quarter might indeed be fulfilled.

My rehearsals with Trogadis and Papachristos were going so well we had added a further selection from *Un Ballo in Maschera* to the already full programme and later, 'Retourna Vincitor' from *Aida*. It was clear from the selection that we were challenging Maria on her own territory as these were the very arias that had made her famous and, sure enough, a few days before the big night, word came to Vithinos via Zachariou that Maria wanted to know just what we all thought we were playing at. She said she knew full well that it was her crazy mother behind it and that I was just a foolish girl who had a bit of a voice and who'd allowed myself to be talked into it. As the day approached and I watched Mother's increasingly manic excitement at the prospect of once more queening it over a first night I began to wonder whether I was doing the right thing. My blood-pressure, always low, dropped dramatically and the exhaustion from taking care of Milton and trying to cope with Mother began to take its toll. I suddenly realised what Maria had been going through for all those years. The dread of the night itself, the sudden feeling that one cannot go on.

But of course somehow one does. There was the hall with flowers along the front of the stage. There was a sea of curious faces come to see a Callas and there at the back was poor Milton, accompanied by his lawyer and another friend, obviously as worried as I was. He'd told me how beautiful I looked in the silk dress with my hair piled high.

'The most beautiful,' he said, 'always that, my Jackie.'

The accompanist had walked to his place and I told myself to forget everything, even my own name, everything except the words and the music. I acknowledged the applause as if in a dream and signalled to the pianist who led me into Scarlatti's 'Son Tutta Duolo'. I took it very gently to begin with, feeling my way into the music, letting my voice find itself. When I finished, the applause was generous, and Milton would tell me afterwards that it was only then that he was aware that he was breathing again, so terrified had he been that I would open my mouth and nothing would come out. For me that first piece was the decisive point. I told myself to take courage, that everything was fine. I shut out the world. I wasn't even sure where Mother was sitting and certainly didn't want to see her fixedly staring up at me. I was alone, quite alone out there and as soon as I accepted that, I really began to sing with all my voice and with all my heart.

Trogadis and Papachristos were marvellous and when we finished the trio from *La Forza del Destino* they stood back and forced me to take the applause on my own, joining in as heartily as the rest. Clutching my flowers I returned to my dressing-room elated and relieved in equal measure. The biggest compliment came the next day when a friend called to say that after the concert she had gone to a nearby taverna where she overheard some Americans talking about me. One of them had smuggled a tape-recorder into the hall and they spent their evening replaying my voice and making appreciative comments.

Milton was delighted and full of pride. He looked transformed as we went out afterwards, as if the evening had restored his flagging spirits.

'What a career you'll have,' he said. 'You'll be as famous as your sister.'

The prospect suddenly saddened me. 'Mother thinks I should go to America now. She knows some people who'll help me.'

He looked thoughtful. 'Then you must go,' he said.

I shook my head.

'Yes!' he insisted. 'What's the point of getting this far and then throwing it all away? For once your mother's right, you need to get started and if these people can help then go ahead.'

'I'll just go and see,' I told him. 'I'll see if what Mother says is true but I won't stay away, I promise.'

They were desperate words and he must have known it. I was being torn in two opposite directions. Mother was holding up the prospect of a glittering future and there before me was the man I had loved since I was a girl and who knew as I did that any success I might have would drive us apart. I looked at his cruelly disfigured face and only then did I curse a fate that had put me in this terrible position. Why me? I asked again. Why me?

Mother of course had no such doubts and was busily counting up our profits and planning the details of our journey.

'You'll love the Zarras,' she said. 'They'll do anything for you, wait and see.'

That was little comfort, torn as I was between thoughts of a career and the wrench of leaving Milton behind. And yet another part of me, a part long suppressed, whispered, 'Why hesitate? He could have married you but he didn't.' Maria had got where she was by never hesitating, by never doubting that she should do only what advanced her career. She had even cast Mother aside, but then Mother had never really done a selfless thing in her life. Her whole

149

reason for forcing Maria on, for depriving her of the normal upbringing any child should expect, had been to provide Evangelia Callas with a life more amusing than that offered by her rather unambitious husband. Now that Mother was punished for this, who could blame Maria? And if I had to leave Milton, was there not some justice in that?

And so New York again. How to describe the feeling of sailing back with that skyline looming into view? Yes, Mother had been right for once, this was where I belonged, where I had been happy, where I could find myself at last. If only we had returned before the outbreak of war: if only we had gone back as soon as the fighting was over. If only . . .

Mr and Mrs Zarras met us at the docks. They were a nice, homely Greek-American couple full of excitement at our arrival. While Bessie Zarras fussed around seeing that we were all right after our journey her husband struggled to get our bags into the boot of his small family car. They were just like the couples we used to meet at the Orthodox cathedral every Sunday all those years ago. As we drove out of Manhattan and into the suburbs it was clear that Bessie was in awe of Mother who kept up a flow of stories of Maria's doings, mostly fantasies, to impress the stage-struck woman. We pulled up at a neat little house with a tidy garden and Mr Zarras made his excuses and went off to work. Bessie did all she could to settle us in. They had set aside a room for us and it was obvious that they had gone to a lot of trouble from limited resources. I couldn't help thinking about the silk evening dress and what that must have meant to them. As soon as Bessie had left us alone in the tiny bedroom I rounded on Mother.

'What do you think you're doing?' I demanded. 'You told me these people were going to sponsor my career. Can't you see how poor they are? They can't afford a thing.'

Mother was uniquely silent. It was obvious from her expression that the reality of her surroundings was falling far short of the fantasy that she had built up during her absence from New York. Desperate and driven into a corner, she had taken the name of her nice ordinary friends and invested it with all the glamour, the wealth, the position, she knew we would need if we were to challenge the world or, more correctly, challenge Maria. She was like some desperate general who, though aware that the war is lost is yet unable to surrender and who tries desperately to bolster his men with tales of a dream weapon that will save the day. With such a tale she had got me, her ragged army, to this point but now the ruse was exposed, the great new weapon of war lay revealed as a damp squib.

'It's no use, Mother,' I said softly but firmly. 'It's no use.'

She did not reply. She did not try to persuade me otherwise, nor tell me that she had an alternative scheme or was sure to come up with something soon. No, she knew it was too late for all that. She said absolutely nothing.

I would have liked to have seen Father before I left but he was on a sales tour outside New York. I thought about trying to look up Clare but the idea of trying to explain what had become of my life was too much for me. Better just to go back to Athens and the life that seemed to be my destiny.

Milton, too, said nothing. But then what could he say? He, who had refused to marry me, had no moral right to accuse me of anything. For my part I felt no particular urge to explain what had happened, I was back and that was it.

I went round to see Mr Vithinos to apologise and to explain that despite all his hard work, despite all the promises I had made that I would persevere, I was quitting.

He nodded his head slowly. 'It is difficult,' he said. 'I don't think you've got Maria's fighting blood.'

Mrs Vithinos was very kind and took me into her kitchen to comfort me. 'You must still come round,' she said. 'Come and eat whenever you want.'

She was a very good cook and that gave me an idea.

'Would you teach me to cook?' I asked her. 'It's for Milton. We can't go out any more and all he gets is something warmed up that the maid has left. I'd like to be able to make him something special but Mother never taught me to cook. He's so very thin. I think if he had something appetising it would help him put on a little weight.'

And so I changed teachers in the Vithinos household. While my former fellow students were practising in the salon, Mrs Vithinos began the slow process of transforming someone who had never as much as boiled an egg into an acceptable cook.

It was not before time. The illness was gaining on him now. He was forced to go for chemotherapy which left him dazed and enfeebled. His hair fell out and he began to look more and more wizened. It was no longer possible for him to be seen in public without attracting unwelcome looks or hurtful whispered comments.

I didn't mind so much but it upset him dreadfully and eventually he refused to go where there might be a crowd. Since my return from America I'd rented an apartment in Hypocratos where he came every evening for the meal I'd cooked him. I was a willing pupil and soon found great pleasure in the tasks Mrs Vithinos set me. I tried to make familiar Greek dishes but to make them lighter, using, say, fresh tomatoes instead of the richer purée. All this was much more appetising to someone in Milton's state and I found an appreciative audience for my performances. We were, after a fashion, happy. It was a sort of marriage with me now performing all the tasks of a housewife. One night we listened to Maria on the radio. She had come to Athens to give a concert in the Herodes Atticus Theatre but had made no attempt to get in touch with me. I thought she sang beautifully but Milton was dismissive.

'You were much better,' he said. 'Your voice was lovelier, more natural.'

Just before she left Athens Maria announced that she was donating her fees from the visit to endow scholarships for young Greek singers. Thinking of her refusal even to consider helping me I could only smile ruefully and wonder if other families were the same or whether we were unique.

About that time I received a letter from a lawyer acting for the impresario Sol Hurok. Hurok had acted for Maria for a time but as the letter explained they had fallen out. It continued by saying that Hurok had read about my concert and would like the opportunity to represent me. To get me launched he was prepared to pay for the lessons I needed to perfect my voice.

'Take it,' Milton said. 'Don't think about me just do it. It's the last chance. He's what you need and offers like that are rare.'

'But does he really want me or does he just want to annoy Maria? How will I ever know whether people are really seeing me or only her shadow?'

'Don't even think about it. If it helps you get started go ahead.'

But I couldn't. I had to hang on to whatever it was that was me, alone and unique. In the shade of that towering figure I needed something, no matter how small, that let me live as myself. And if that meant turning down Hurok's offer then so be it. I didn't even reply. His people tried two or three times to persuade me but as I never responded they eventually gave up.

Convinced that I had surrendered everything for him, Milton at last realised that he ought to do something for me. Towards the end of 1957 he bought me an apartment of my own.

We spent our evenings like any other long-married couple except that he continued to decline. Surprisingly he suffered little, there was almost no pain, but the combined effects of the illness and the severity of the treatment left him increasingly shrunken within himself and looking little more than a skeleton. It was now that I tried more than ever to be always looking good, always impeccably made-up whenever he arrived, always to have everything just the way he wanted it – what else could I do for him?

From time to time a letter would arrive from New York with Mother's news. Of course she spent a lot of time complaining but there was enough to suggest that her life wasn't so bad. She seemed to have been absorbed back into the Greek community in New Jersey where, as the mother of the most famous Greek of our time, she enjoyed a certain celebrity. She had a lot of invitations to the sort of family celebrations, weddings, anniversaries, baptisms that were the lifeblood of the community and by and large she seemed to get some satisfaction out of being a sort of permanent guest of honour. She certainly went out more than I did. It was true that money was her perennial problem but she managed to get a job in a boutique run by Zsa Zsa Gabor's mother Jolie and when that proved too hard on her legs she used the dressmaking skills that had kept us in clothes during the war to make dolls dressed in the costumes of Maria's principal rôles. Thus there was the *Tosca* doll, the *Norma* doll, the *Lucia* doll and so on. While she was far from rich she apparently made a reasonable income from those wishing to get close to the divine Callas through the homely images produced by her mother. With one letter I received a photograph of Mother and in the background were some of the dolls. It was an extraordinary combination. There was the woman who had rejected all the normal expressions of motherhood as she struggled to turn her youngest daughter into a machine dedicated to success, yet she was now surrounded by those symbols of sweetness and caring. Mary and I had never played with our dolls when we were children and Mother had never encouraged us to do so, but here she was actually making them. It was hard to believe.

In a way, time was running out for Mother's dream of sharing Maria's success. It was becoming clear from articles in the newspapers that her life was taking a different turn. She was now as famous for her doings off stage as she was for her performances. It was strange that the moment that all the critics were won over to her interpretation of opera she should be losing interest in the art form to which she had so far sacrificed her life. When she started out there had been a hard core of writers who refused to be seduced by her performances. They were the ones who put a pure voice above all other qualities and in this they found Maria, with her slightly unsure upper register, somewhat deficient. She, on the other hand, had another view of opera, believing it to be more about music drama than fine singing. If she needed a harsh, perhaps even unpleasant, sound to convince an audience of a character she was playing, as in *Macbeth*, then she would use it. At first the purists had squirmed and Italy had been divided into the Tebaldi camp who adored that singer's superb voice and the Callas camp who believed that she was transforming opera from a concert in costume into true lyric theatre. By the end of the fifties, it was clear from the newspapers that Maria had won.

But it was equally clear that time was running out for her. There were ominous reports of her voice refusing to do her bidding, witness the sudden crack in her top note during an opening night in Dallas. Perhaps it was the realisation that her time as a great diva was limited that made her long for some other kind of life. As I studied the newspaper reports I wondered if Mother had also realised what was happening. If she had, then she would also be dreaming that Maria would now return to her. But I knew that it could never be like that. Maria always needed someone new to help her into a different stage in her life. First it had been Mother, then Meneghini. There would be no reason for her to return to Mother, it would have to be someone completely new, from an entirely different world. But who?

For a time there seemed to be nothing but upheavals. There was Maria attacked by the Italian press for walking out of a gala performance attended by the Italian President. Her cancellations were becoming as prominent as her first nights, her squabbles with theatre directors legendary. And there she was photographed in nightclubs and restaurants, elegant, soignée. I smiled as I thought of the Mary I'd known. She was now a combination of what she had been: a nervous, ill-tempered, self-willed fighter and what she had wished to be: desirable and loved.

And then it happened. Nobody could talk of anything else in Athens – Maria Callas and Aristotle Onassis, the two most famous

Greeks of our day, had come together. He was notoriously rich and could obviously offer her a completely new life but I stared at the photographs of them together in frank disbelief. There they were aboard his yacht the *Christina* and there was poor old Meneghini in the background looking the part of the cuckold. I could imagine Mother's satisfaction if she saw it; she would be pleased to see him getting the same treatment she had got when he had first appeared. So the new man for the new life was to be Onassis. A new figure to cling to. Soon the stories of their being together turned into reports of divorce, she from Meneghini, he from his wife Tina. I remembered how she told me she liked to cuddle up to Meneghini in bed. I had found that pretty unpalatable but now the thought of Onassis was little better. And yet here was I with the wraith-like form of Milton that I had to kiss and pretend no revulsion for, and there was Maria, about, so it appeared then, to embark on her second marriage when I had been denied even one.

Never able to keep quiet when there's trouble to be stirred up Mother now delivered another bombshell – in 1960 she published her autobiography, a long justification of her actions and an extended lament for the way she had not been rewarded. The book was high on special pleading and low on accuracy. Again she reinterpreted the war years so that it was largely she and not Milton who kept us in food. Milton, who had done everything for us, was here reduced to someone who had helped out a little. There were stories of Mother and Mary struggling out of Athens to buy food in the villages and much was made of Mother's dressmaking skills in keeping us in clothes, even though I distinctly remember that much of what we wore was bought with great difficulty by Milton.

Father was reduced to a feeble layabout and at every opportunity Mother portrayed herself as the one who held the family together. But worse than all that was the fact that she included details of Bonalti and Botman that could only have been intended to hurt Maria. Why did she do it? I suppose she must have thought she would make money out of it but here she was wrong. For once Maria did the sensible thing and kept quiet. She refused to give interviews and if cornered by reporters said only the mildest things about Mother. Any hopes that the publishers may have had that the famous Callas temper would spark off a public row and send sales sky high were dashed when the issue died for want of a quarrel.

To me, the worst part of the book was her suggestion that she had been reduced to penury and that her rich and successful daughter refused to help her get out of it. I knew full well that she was leading a reasonably comfortable life and was much fêted in the Greek-American community. She had kept away from Father who was no doubt very grateful. Since I had been in America we had written to each other and in his last letter he had told me that as he was going to retire he thought he might come home to Greece where he could live more comfortably on his pension.

I was pleased to see him. I felt closer to him than ever before and I spent some time with him each day either in his hotel or out for a peaceful stroll. And just as I had learned to set aside the antipathy Mother had fostered between us so it seemed had Maria who now corresponded with him. It appalled him that his two daughters had also fallen out because of their mother.

'No need for that,' he said. 'Let that woman fight her own battles, she's good at that. But you should see your sister; you're all that will be left one day, and you might need each other. Look how she used to love you when she was little.'

She had written to say that when she next visited the mainland with Onassis she wanted him to come and see her and he said he would try and patch up our differences.

I told him not to bother as Maria would never give way once she had decided to exclude me from her life. In any case what had I to do with the great diva she had become? What on earth had I to say to a woman like that? But Father was not to be deflected and he vowed that when she next sailed into Greek waters and contacted him he would make a point of mentioning me to her.

I wasn't really bothered either way. I had too much to worry about with Milton. By early 1961 it had got to the point where he could barely get to work and the task of running the factories had to be left to others. He had a maid at his flat who could help him when I wasn't there but things were getting more and more difficult. One day I took Father round to meet him at last. I suppose if he had been in good health Father might have told him off for not doing the decent thing by me but as soon as he had been introduced to what was in truth a living skeleton it was clear that he could do little more than make polite conversation. As I walked him back he was clearly overcome by the experience.

'What will you do, child?'

'See it through.'

156

'How long will it be?'

'Who can tell? Years ago they said it would be three months and he's still here. He was very strong, thank God, and he still has some fight left. It's just that it gets more and more difficult to cope with.'

Father looked deeply miserable and gave me a hug. 'You didn't deserve it,' he said. 'You were the beautiful one, my Jackie, you should have been happily married. Not this.'

I understood how he felt but I had got beyond self-pity. My main thoughts were all on practical matters, how to cope with Milton's increasing weakness. Would I be able to handle the physical strain of nursing him? Not long after Father's visit I went round when the maid was out and found him collapsed on the floor, having tried to get to the bathroom. He may have been a skeleton but he had once been a big man and even in his emaciated state I couldn't lift him. I ran up and down the corridors trying to get someone to come and help me but no one was in. Finally, in desperation, I rang Harry and told him to get over quickly. He came at once and we manhandled Milton into the lavatory and then into the bedroom.

I took Harry into the salon to talk about what we were going to do. It was impossible to go on like that. Without the maid to help me I couldn't cope and she had to have her time off. But then instead of listening to what I was saying Harry went off at a tangent.

'You know you're still a very beautiful woman,' he said.

'Thank you very much,' I said with a dry laugh. 'Tired as I am and looking this way you say I'm a beautiful woman.'

But he wasn't to be deflected by sarcasm. 'Look, Jackie, I'll make a proposition to you. You'll need someone soon and I could do a lot to help you.'

'I don't need your help. Milton will take care of me.'

This time it was Harry who laughed. 'I know all about that famous Foundation of his and your share in it but you might as well know that he's been borrowing money from me for his business and that I have to be repaid before anything goes to the Foundation.'

I didn't want to listen to him. I told him I didn't care what he said, I didn't care if there was no money left, I was still not interested in any offer he wanted to make to me.

He was furious and went off, banging the door.

Milton wanted to know what all the noise had been about but I just told him it was the wind that had slammed the door shut. We talked a little and I told him I was worried in case he fell again. His

157

legs were almost paralysed and it was only a matter of time before he would be completely bedridden. He did not argue, he could see I could never cope with him at home and agreed that he would have to go into a clinic.

He went into the Pamakaristo Hospital which was run by Catholic nuns and where he was wonderfully looked after. I went three times a day to be with him and if for any reason I missed a visit the nuns would tell me how it made him worse. If I was not there he would refuse to eat. There was nothing for it but to dedicate my days to being with him.

Being so preoccupied, I must have been the last person in Greece to realise that Maria was coming back to perform at the ancient theatre at Epidaurus. Posters announcing both *Norma* and *Medea* had been up for weeks before I realised and when I did I could only suppose that as before I would be ignored except by the odd journalist who would try and get me to say why it was the family were being shunted to one side. Father, of course, was going to meet her and he kept telling me he was going to bring us together. I shrugged that off as an old man's delusion. He went to see Maria in *Norma* though the first performance was rained off and it wasn't until the following evening that it was able to go ahead. The *Christina* was moored at Glyfada and Father went to visit her and Onassis there.

'I like him,' he said when he returned. 'We get on fine.'

No doubt they did, two Greek womanisers with a passion for sitting in cafés drinking ouzo. I'm sure they got on famously.

But then Father dropped his bombshell. 'She wants to see you,' he said.

For a moment I was confused. It was the last thing I had expected.

'She's got nothing against you,' he continued. 'It's your mother she loathes. You were just tied up with her but now she's not here Maria wants you to come and see her.'

'I'm not sure I can,' I said. 'There's Milton to think of. I can't leave him for long.'

'I know, but I'm sure something can be arranged, eh?'

After some hesitation I agreed to go with him the following night to join her at a restaurant near where the yacht was moored.

That next day seemed to go on for ever. I hadn't seen Maria since that visit to Verona just after the war and we had had no contact for nearly nine years, during which time she had become one of the most famous women in the world. I went to see Milton before I joined

Father for the bus ride to the coast but he dozed most of the time and I had no one to talk over my fears with. It was as if the only thing I had was melting away slowly before my eyes.

Father and I waited at the restaurant for a small boat to bring Maria from the yacht. While we waited we were joined by Dr Papatesta and Mrs Xakousti who were friends of hers and I tried to make conversation though all I could think of was the encounter to come. After a moment I could see the boat approaching; she was there sitting upright, the image from the photographs. A sailor helped her ashore and I noticed the assurance with which she moved. Her hands were long and she used them with a sense of drama, her clothes were very stylish and I suddenly realised that I didn't know this woman at all. Here I was standing and waiting to be introduced to a total stranger. The Maria I had last seen, the Maria I knew, was fat and awkward, ill-tempered and greedy; here was this vision of refined elegance. She walked purposefully into the room, embraced her friends then Father, then turned to me.

'Jackie.'

'Maria.'

We embraced.

'You look tired.'

'It's Milton. I visit him all the time. It's exhausting.'

'Strange,' she said. 'I've just realised we've both ended up with ship owners. Who'd have thought it? Come, everyone, let's eat.'

I watched her closely throughout the meal. I had read about how she ate little but picked from other people's plates which is precisely what happened. She was really good fun and kept the conversation going. When Mrs Xakousti started to drool over the *Christina* which was by then lit up and reflected in the calm waters of the Aegean, Maria proposed that we should all visit it after we'd finished eating. I looked across at Father who winked as if to say, 'See, I told you everything would be all right.' How easy it all was for him, easy-going old George Callas, quite happy to sit back and enjoy the good life his daughter was able to offer him. I suddenly felt a twinge of sympathy for Mother who had at least done something to ensure that we were able to sit in one of Greece's most expensive restaurants with the prospect of visiting one of the world's most luxurious yachts. But it was impossible to criticise Father. His delight in it all was too infectious. Once on board he strolled about as if the boat were his and not Onassis'. And when we moved to the bar and the man

159

himself was standing there with some business colleagues, Father and he greeted each other like lifelong buddies. Maria introduced me to Onassis and he seemed genuinely interested to meet the sister at last.

Inevitably it was his appearance that most intrigued me. He was short and stocky but clearly tough, a man who had fought his way up in a hard world. He made me nervous but I could sense some of the energy Maria evidently found irresistible and for the brief time he was there, he was the life and soul of the party. Laughing and telling jokes, he moved around to speak to each of us in turn. He asked after my health, the usual things and when he moved on I had a chance to take in the sumptuous surroundings. This was not so much a yacht as a cruise liner. The bar would not have been out of place in a grand hotel. Servants circulated, constantly replenishing our drinks. But Onassis was busy and as soon as politeness allowed we were deftly led away so that he could go on discussing money with his associates. Even as I walked through the door I could see him hunched down with them, deep in conversation.

Maria took me to her room to freshen up. She led me down a wide corridor, pointing out the suite for every guest, each named after a Greek island. There were gilded fittings everywhere; the effect was dazzling. Her own suite was inevitably a riot of gold and I don't know what made me do it but I couldn't resist asking her if she were happy with it all.

'Oh, I'm happy with Ari but I get tired of this boat. First I'm tired of the sea then I'm tired of being in port with so many people waiting to see me. I'd like to be alone with him more. I'd like to have a baby. And what about you? Are you happy?'

I shook my head.

'No, how could you be. Come to *Medea* next week. You've never seen me sing, have you? Or not since I was a kid anyway. Come and see me. Now we'd better get you back. Ari didn't want visitors tonight but I had to let the Papatestas see the boat.'

On the way back Father seemed delighted with what he'd achieved and I had to admit it made life a lot less miserable to have that old quarrel patched up.

In fact life just then seemed to be all sisters and brothers – the next day when I arrived at the hospital I found Harry there and I could tell by the unhappy look on Milton's face that their conversation had not been very pleasant. The only thing that would have brought

Harry to a sick-bed was something to his own advantage so I assumed he had come to talk about the loan. Whatever it was they stopped when I arrived and I tried to cheer Milton up with my account of the previous night's events.

'I'm glad,' he said. 'It's as well that you've seen her again.'

Harry left us but I did not stay long. Milton was increasingly tired and would drift away after a few moments. Even a little conversation wearied him.

It says everything about Maria's greatness that her performance a few nights later was able to completely lift me beyond all these bitter things. From the moment she appeared, the worries that were crowding in on me seemed to recede. Whether Norma or Medea were her greatest rôles others must decide but I needed only to see that one great performance to understand everything that she had achieved. She acted with her whole being, even the sandals on her feet seemed to project the rôle. And was there ever a more magnificent setting for *Medea* than that great ruined amphitheatre eerily lit under the stars. Afterwards my fumbling praise must have seemed genuine enough.

'I didn't realise,' I said, and then let it trail away . . .

We embraced. We understood each other, then I left her to be devoured by her admirers.

Could I really have hoped to do that? To be out there in that vast arena controlling the emotions of thousands with a phrase of music and the gesture of a hand. I had wanted it but now it would never be. What I didn't realise then, seeing her at the height of her powers, was that the thing which I so fervently desired, Maria no longer wanted. She had grown tired of the struggle, the nerve-racking effort wearied her, she dreamed no longer of curtain calls and applause: she had had them in abundance. What she wanted now was a child and that too I had been denied.

I told Milton about the performance when I sat with him the next day. He lay there listening; the cancer had spread through his jaw and speech was increasingly painful. Mostly we both sat silent, I suppose we had said everything there was to say and it was only my company he needed. When the nuns brought food I would help him cut it up and then I would feed it to him, not unlike a child really. It was strange to think that just a short bus ride away Maria would be greeting visitors to the yacht, leading them to a table set with gold cutlery and crystal glasses while Onassis moved among his guests, slapping them on the back, pouring out more champagne. Still, I had nothing to complain of with her now; I had a sister again. How stupid all our quarrels seemed, how much we had been through and how foolish it was not to be together. I wondered about Mother. Would a reconciliation between them ever be possible? If only the poor woman had kept quiet, had not talked to journalists, had not published her book, then perhaps Maria could have slowly forgiven her, seen her from time to time. But Mother would never stop fighting. I knew she was living a modest but perfectly reasonable life in America, enjoying her starring rôle in her little Greek-American community, but every so often a journalist would go to see her and come away with a juicy story of how La Callas' mother was eking out a miserable existence in a cheap rooming house, hardly able to make ends meet. Why did she do it? I think she had some sort of death wish in relation to her daughter. Where common sense must have told her to desist she just couldn't. But despite everything I still had some pity for her and I wondered if I might be able to suggest to Maria that she do something for her, even if it didn't go as far as their having to meet again.

Of course I had been fortunate in my two meetings with Maria – she was on top form on both occasions. Her appearances had been a huge success and no doubt Onassis, who longed to be accepted as a major figure in his native land, was very satisfied with her. As her life revolved round his whims that would explain her sunny disposition when we'd met. But I ought to have known that I could not expect so smooth a ride every time and when we next met I could read the storm warnings from the start. Father and I had been invited to lunch at the Glyfada home of Onassis' brother-in-law – his sister, Artemis, had married a Dr Garoufalidis, a professor of orthopaedic medicine at the University of Athens. Maria arrived for the lunch looking cross; clearly something had happened on the yacht that had spoiled her mood. Everyone was slightly on edge, having sensed the situation and no one wanted to be in the firing line. Everyone, that is, except Father who was blithely indifferent and would have smiled contentedly through the day of judgment. Dr Garoufalidis was also a good-natured person who was quite unable to imagine what a phenomenon like Maria was actually like. The lunch began cautiously with rather stilted conversation as everyone kept to safe topics. I tried to make myself as inconspicuous as possible, fearing the worst and was duly appalled when the doctor leant across to me.

162

'Jackie,' he said. 'Where I heard it I don't remember, but someone told me you had a lovely voice. What did you do with your voice?'

Fortunately Maria appeared to be talking to someone else at the other end of the table and there might just be time to close the matter.

'I left it,' I replied. 'I gave a concert but my fiancé was ill so I couldn't go on and I left it.'

But it was no good, Maria had heard the word 'voice'. 'Are you talking about me?' she asked, equally at first.

'No,' said the doctor smiling. 'It's your sister here. I heard she had a voice.'

'Doctor,' said Maria coldly, 'the donkeys bray and think they have a voice.' She turned towards me and let fly. 'It was your crazy mother who thought you had a voice. She was behind those lessons. Don't you know how old you are? Don't you know you're too old to train your voice? Singing is for young people, it needs years of study, not just braying like a donkey.'

It was no use trying to keep out of it. Silence would only provoke her further. I knew the signs, she wanted a row and must have one.

'Maria,' I said, 'anyone can have a voice, a maid, a painter, anyone. It's what you do with it. I had a voice but I threw away the chance to do something because of Milton. You know that.'

'You a voice,' she yelled. 'Do you want me to start breaking dishes?'

The doctor quickly got to his feet. 'I have to go and rest,' he said. 'I have surgery later so I must lie down for a while but do go on with your family talk.' He shook my hand and said how happy he was to have met me.

The interruption seemed to take the steam out of Maria, her discontent evaporated. As we moved from the table to the salon she came over and was friendly again.

'So how is Milton?' she asked.

'At an end. Like a skeleton. It's making me ill too. Yet if he dies what am I going to do? I'm going to be so lonely. He's been a father and a husband since I was eighteen. Who else can I trust now?'

The outburst must have been too intimate for her, the reality of my sorrow was not something she wanted to be confronted with.

'You have to hope,' she said, turning away. 'Hope is a wonderful thing. God gives us hope.'

I looked at her and realised there was no point in saying any more.

Father, too, was staring at her, a look of pity on his face as if to say here is someone who has forgotten how to feel for another and that is a terrible thing. I felt sorry for her: she was so wrapped up in her own daily worries no one else except she and Onassis existed.

We said goodbye and left her there.

In the taxi Father held my hand and shook his head. 'She cannot change now,' he said. 'It's too late.'

Two days after I got a message from her inviting me to come to the yacht for tea. When I got there she was preparing to go out, a maid handing her jewellery from a box which she tried on and discarded. Her hairdresser must have been and she looked very soignée. She told me to sit and continued putting on earrings and taking them off.

'Oh, what people are,' she said with a sigh. She dangled a heavy gold bracelet, making it clink as it swung. 'I hear you're jealous of me, Jackie?'

'Maria, I was never jealous of you. Why should I be? I'm proud of what you've done. History will remember you.'

She let the bracelet drop and picked up a string of pearls with a diamond clip. 'Really. But someone said you were jealous of all this.'

She was longing for me to say I was but I refused to play along with so silly a game. 'I'm lucky,' I said. 'I'm not a jealous person. I'm sorry for anyone who is, it must be a terrible feeling.'

She clearly decided to give up. 'Yes, people are so silly. But enough, tell me what to wear. Which dress, which of these diamonds.'

I helped her pick something, second-guessing what she really wanted herself. Tea was brought and we sipped, talking inconsequentially of people we'd known. When she rose to leave she put on dark glasses, completing the image of the famous femme fatale, elaborately made-up, elegant and forbidding. I walked a step behind her in my cotton frock.

When we disembarked at Glyfada she gave me a peck on each cheek. 'You should be able to get a bus over there,' she said, then she walked over to the house of Dr Garoufalidis which was close beside the marina.

As I waited at the bus stop, to go back to the hospital and Milton, I could see her Mercedes parked by the jetty with its bored chauffeur reading a newspaper and I realised that Father was right, it was too late for Maria truly to change.

Shortly afterwards the *Christina* sailed away and life returned to normal: the thrice-daily journey to the hospital, the silent vigil, the meals. Milton clung to life for another two years, two weary empty years. As time passed only his deeper preoccupations could provoke him into saying anything, old worries that were nagging away at him would slowly struggle to be released.

'We should have had a baby,' he said one day. 'You should have just done it, then I would have married you.'

I said nothing but on another occasion his argument had come full circle.

'I couldn't marry you. Because of your mother. You listened to her too much.'

By May 1963 he was slipping in and out of consciousness and his remarks were less and less lucid but one day in early June he suddenly seemed to rally and although speech was by now an agony he made himself sit up and talk.

'Get a priest,' he said. 'I want you to bring a priest here. I want us to be married.'

I tried to calm him, afraid that the excitement would make him worse but he was adamant and, afraid of upsetting him, I said I would do as he wished.

The next day I brought a priest with me and Milton repeated his wish to marry me. The old man agreed and told us to call him when we had spoken to the doctor. When he left I went to see Dr Katakuzinos, the specialist who took care of Milton, and he came and spoke with him.

Outside the room the doctor weighed up this unusual request. 'If he really wants to I have no objection, but I'll have to inform his next of kin. That's usual but in the end it's his choice and your decision.'

When I went back inside I could see Milton's eyes begging me to agree. Was his conscience bothering him? Had he decided that this was the only way to placate it?

'I agree,' I said.

Dr Katakuzinos informed Milton's family. I phoned the priest and went off to tell Father.

'It's only right,' he said. 'You've given your life to him and it's the only way he can protect you after he's gone.'

The following morning I tried to make myself look a little special; after all it was my wedding day. Nothing else was different. I still waited as usual at the bus stop and still made that long lonely journey to the hospital gate.

When I opened the door to Milton's room I saw Harry and Nina, his sister, standing by his bed. How strange, I thought, that they should have come.

'I've sent that priest away,' Harry said without warning.

I looked towards Milton but he was beyond speech, his eyes pleading with me to come to him.

'What are you doing here anyway?' Harry demanded. 'What do you want? You don't belong here?'

'I don't belong here? I've been coming here three times a day every day. You've barely come once a fortnight. How can you say I don't belong here?'

Harry waved this away. 'The family are not having you make a quick wedding behind our backs, oh no.'

Milton's eyes followed the argument but there was no way he could intervene.

I turned on Harry. 'God will punish you. I have done everything I should.'

I ran out and left them. There was nothing to be done now. How could I fight a man like Harry, so rich, so powerful, so unjust?

I shut myself up at home and wept, wondering what would happen to me, desperately worried about Milton alone at the hospital. After two days the nuns sent word that he was refusing to eat and was fading fast. My arrival changed that, he took a little nourishment, but the shock had hastened his decline.

The periods of unconsciousness were longer now. Having had his say, Harry kept away and Milton was left to me for the few remaining days. He no longer spoke at all, only his eyes could say anything. It was a terrible death, a pitiful wasting away so that there was little but skin and bone at the end. I left him in a deep coma one night and somehow I knew I was saying goodbye. I was woken at four in the morning by Harry who said that Dr Katakuzinos had insisted he ring me to tell me it was all over. I dressed and went to the hospital. The family were all there. No one spoke. I simply went into the room and stood by the bed looking down on him, the first dead body I had ever seen, the man I had loved. I waited a moment then I turned and left.

Father took care of me for a few days. I did not have the courage to go to the funeral and Harry and the family had certainly not made an effort to invite me.

On the day Father and I sat together so that I shouldn't feel too lonely. It was strange that the man who all my childhood I had been taught to reject was now the only person in the world I could turn to for comfort.

I thought of Maria with her rich lover, his priceless yacht and all the glittering company that surrounded her, but deep down I knew she had no more than I had. That autumn she too was shunted aside when Onassis took Jacqueline Kennedy for a cruise on the *Christina*, declaring that it would not be correct for his mistress to accompany the wife of the President of the United States. How strange, two Greek ship owners – I had sacrificed my life for one, now she was doing the same. They buried Milton in the family plot at the First Cemetery beside his grandparents and his parents. The next day Father took me to lay some flowers. I was forty-six years old. I had given him twenty-eight years of my life.

CHAPTER SEVEN
1963–1977

Almost immediately, the small allowance I'd received from Milton was cut off without explanation. I had no other source of income. Had he only done the decent thing and married me or at the very least made a settlement on me, even something as simple as some property from which I could have had an income, then I would have been secure. As it was, all he ever gave me was the small apartment I lived in. He had been ill for so long he had been unaware of the changes going on around him and had had no idea how expensive life had become. Unwilling to sour our last years together, I had almost never mentioned money and had made do with an ever-decreasing income. Now I had nothing and what he had planned to leave me was hardly very much. His will was not the reward for all that I had given him that I might have expected. He had left everything to a medical foundation which was to finance two research scholarships into cancer every year and I was to receive ten per cent of the income of the Foundation, which was to be administered by a council. By the time of his death the sums were already greatly reduced and my ten per cent was very small but at least it would have been something. Unhappily for me, there was one disastrous clause in the testament: the money that Milton had borrowed from Harry was to be repaid first, before any other claims could be honoured. Although the documents specified that he was owed nearly twenty million drachmas borrowed in sterling, Harry maintained that the loan had been given in gold sovereigns which radically altered the value. The newly formed Foundation found itself having to challenge the brother of its benefactor in order to save the research grants. The will was immediately put into litigation. All hopes I might have had of a small income were lost for years. I was reduced to poverty and if it had not been for Father I might well have ended up on the streets.

That much wronged old man now took it on himself to protect his eldest daughter. He had only his small pension from America but every day he would come round with a dish of food from a restaurant and sit with me for a while. For months I was in a state of nervous collapse, both emotional from the loss of Milton, and physical from the sheer exhaustion of the long years of keeping vigil at the hospital. My doctor told me the only cure was total rest and whenever possible sleep. He prescribed tranquillisers and vitamin injections and I sank back into a state of total withdrawal with only Father to comfort me. Occasionally dear friends like Mrs Vithinos would come to see me but in the main I preferred my solitude. After so many years I needed to hide away until I could accept that there was life without Milton, that somehow there had to be a way to live now that he was gone.

Father was wonderful. He never cajoled or offered advice, or tried to cheer me up. He would bring the food and sit and let things take their course. He was far too wise to try to lie to me. He understood what a loss like mine meant and how only time could heal it.

Milton had died in June 1963 and it was only after three months that my strength began to return. Seeing this, Father suggested we take a little holiday on one of the islands. It was September, the worst of the summer heat would be over and the crowds would be gone. I was indifferent but unwilling to contradict him and went along with the suggestion that we go to Rhodes for ten days.

He was right of course; the sea air, the white boat on the blue water, were wonderful after the long days of seclusion. It was as if I was sailing away from all the grief of Athens and by the time the boat docked at Rhodes harbour I was feeling more and more alive. We stayed at the Hotel Alexandra and spent a gentle first day strolling about the old town or sitting looking out to sea, listening to the sea birds and watching the boats bobbing about as the setting sun sent washes of colour over the waters.

On the second day we went to an open-air café for lunch and Father asked two men at a table near to ours if the fish was fresh. One of them said yes and recommended what they were eating and soon we were in conversation with them. The man who'd advised us was from Rhodes itself, his friend from Athens; they offered to show us the town. They came for us the next morning and as the day passed they gradually worked out that we were related to the famous diva. They admitted that they were journalists and were naturally excited at the prospect of a story but as soon as they saw that this upset me they were gentlemen enough to leave the matter alone. I liked them for that and was grateful not to have my holiday ruined by the usual nosey intrusion of Maria into our lives. We saw more of them during our stay and as they were both going to Athens Father suggested they visit us.

'It'll be good for you to see someone,' he said when we were alone.

But I only smiled at his kindness in wanting to take me out of myself. I knew that what he was hinting at was impossible. All my thoughts were still on Milton.

Still, they were nice people and I went out with them and Father when they came to Athens. The one from Rhodes called at my apartment bearing twenty-five hyacinths, the flower I'm named after. They were enormous blooms and when I'd put them in vases they seemed to dominate the bedroom.

That night in the restaurant I explained to him about Milton and what I still felt and he had the kindness to say he fully understood. Still, it had been cheering to be taken out and flattered and made to feel alive again, though there was to be one curious after-effect – I woke up in the middle of the night nearly suffocating: those great blossoms had used up nearly all the air in my room. There was a sickly overwhelming scent of hyacinths everywhere and it was all I could do to stagger to the salon and open a window.

Despite that mishap, the Rhodes trip and the kindness of that man had been very healing. As the death of Milton began to recede I was more and more able to see the events of my life with some sort of clarity. I began to regret that I had been forced into accepting his charity and was thus no longer free to marry him or leave him as I chose. I should have had work and been independent. After high school I had my modelling and in Greece there had been the possibility of an office job. But it was the joint agreement between Mother and Milton that I should not work but should only have my musical training that set my life on a course of dependency. Of course I had been happy with Milton, I'd loved him, but I was not happy with the consequences of our affair. I should not have been obliged to him, no matter that he was a good man, unless he had been my husband – for now I knew that the marriage contract does indeed make a difference: a wife has rights, an unmarried woman exists on favours.

This was strikingly brought home to me when I was forced to sell the apartment Milton had bought me. It was the only tangible inheritance I had had from him and now I needed such money as I could raise. How could he have left me like that? Other people leave their pet animals better provided for. I bought a small flat in Fokionos Negri which meant I had further to travel to see Father at the hotel where he was living but otherwise it was not too bad. Now that I had a little cash I thought I would travel a little more; the trip to Rhodes had done so much good I thought I'd repeat the process. My old music teacher Mr Vithinos came up with an idea. He told me about a letter he'd received from a Mr Vimercarti in northern Italy who'd read about my concert and had got in touch with him. He'd written to say that he was married to a Greek woman and that they had both been fascinated by the idea of Callas' sister having a voice as well. They would, he went on, be delighted if I wanted to take a holiday in Italy with them. The idea was fascinating. I didn't much care for the idea of imposing on complete strangers but I could always stay in a nearby hotel and they would be able to keep me company. So, in the spring of 1964 I set off for Crema near Milan and one of the strangest encounters of my life. The Vimercartis were very pleasant and welcoming, they had a daughter and a son so there was young company and the hotel, near where they lived, was perfectly pleasant. All that was unexceptional. It was an event a few days after my arrival that seems even now to be most bizarre. Mrs Vimercarti suddenly revealed that we were very near to Sirmione where Maria and Meneghini had lived together. He indeed still lived there, something of a recluse since she had gone off with Onassis. Would it, Mrs Vimercarti wondered, be interesting to ring him up and tell him I was there. I don't know where I got the courage from, but I said yes and she was on the telephone to the villa straight away. I could tell from the enthusiastic noises on the line that Meneghini was very keen that we should go over and the next day the two of us were driving through the beautiful park on the shores of Lake Garda, heading towards the home my sister had occupied during her decade of marriage.

As soon as the maid opened the door I began to sense the unreality of it all. There was a woman's coat hanging on a hook just inside the entrance and something told me that it was Maria's. Meneghini came out to greet us and he was clearly delighted to see me. He embraced me like a sister and looked me up and down, as if trying to soak up the presence of a Callas. He was soon reminiscing about my visit to Verona and in fact his conversation never strayed from the subject of Maria, though always Maria in the past. The maid brought drinks and I could see how solicitous she was of his welfare. Helping him to get a glass and fussing to see that he was all right. He was no longer the strong, confident man I had met. He had shrunken noticeably and his mind was a little distant. As soon as we had had some refreshment he insisted on showing us the house though what we were given was really a sort of guided tour to the museum of his love for my sister. Nothing had been changed. Her room was as it had been when she last occupied it. Such clothes as she had abandoned still hung in the closet. He opened it to reveal the contents with a certain sad pride. It was as if the place were ready for her to step back into at any moment should she ever choose to do so. Which of course was the whole point of the display. He was close to tears at several moments on our tour. Everything was so vivid for him and I in my loss felt a wave of sympathy pass over me for this lonely old man abandoned to his memories.

Having shown us the house we returned to the salon and he went off to find some press cuttings he thought might interest us. As the maid cleared away the glasses she told us how wonderful life had been in the old days before Onassis had come along.

'She really loved him,' the maid explained. 'If she woke up late and he wasn't in bed beside her she'd go crazy, running round the house demanding to know where her Titta was. He'd come back and explain that he'd only gone to buy his paper but it would take ages to calm her down again. And then to think this could happen.'

He returned with his scrapbook and we leafed through the years of his glory: Maria fat and ungainly at that first season in Verona, Maria svelte and glorious at La Scala, Covent Garden, the Met.

'I negotiated all these,' he said. 'She was paid more than any other soprano.' He rattled off a series of figures to prove his managerial skills but the effort seemed to exhaust him. 'I hear that ship owner won't marry her?' he said, rallying at the thought. 'He only wanted her because she was famous. The money he wasted. And now he won't marry her. Maybe he'll find someone else . . .'

He left the next part of his question unformed. Would she come back to this museum by the lake? Would she walk in the door, go up to her room, change her clothes, ask the maid where her Titta was? He clearly lived for the day when she would do so. What had I to add to his dream? I thanked him for his hospitality and despite his protests I insisted that we had to get back. As he waved us goodbye I knew that the visit had achieved one valuable thing; it had taught me to let Milton rest in peace and to try to look forward not back.

Though I returned to Athens in better spirits I was not yet out of the wood. My relations with Father were now reversed when he became unwell. He had had a bad attack of pneumonia in America and this had left him with some sort of weakness in the lungs. I can only suppose that the rather difficult climate of Athens had worsened the situation and he began to suffer badly from phlegm which made it hard for him to breathe. Eventually, an unpleasant reminder of my last years with Milton, I found myself taking Father to the hospital three times a week for treatment to keep his breathing passages cleared. After some months of this he felt he couldn't go on and decided to return to America for an operation. It seemed the wisest course as his pension rights included some medical insurance. It turned out to be more serious than we had imagined and he was to be four months in hospital before the problem was cleared up. During that time he wrote to me often and I soon gathered that among his more frequent visitors was Alexandra Papajohn, one of the four daughters of the family we had gone on picnics with as children. She was about his age and had never married and gradually the thought occurred to me that here was a perfect solution to several problems. I wrote, tentatively suggesting that Alexandra might make a good wife for him, someone friendly and familiar, someone peaceful with whom to spend his old age.

He wrote back rather astonished at the idea: 'At my age, how could I think of it?'

But I kept up the campaign, emphasising the fact that I couldn't go on looking after him for ever and that he couldn't go on living in hotel rooms for the rest of his life. Gradually his answers became less dismissive and eventually positively enthusiastic. As news of his recovery spread so did the certainty that as soon as he was up and about he and Alexandra would get wed. I was delighted.

When the day came he sent a telegram to let me know. He also cabled Maria but that caused problems. We all knew she was totally preoccupied because the newspapers at that time were full of news of her comeback in *Norma* and *Tosca* at Covent Garden and the Paris opera and we felt that it was pointless to try and bring her into our lives. Imagining she would be too busy to care, Father had not bothered her with news of his gradual decision to marry again so that

173

when the telegram came it was a complete surprise to her. Far from being unconcerned, Maria was outraged and as Father had just asked her for help with his medical bills, never an easy thing given Maria's stinginess, there were now two reasons for her wrath. Given her hatred of Mother, one might have imagined that she would have been totally understanding of Father's decision to find a little contentment at the end of his life, indeed she had in recent years shown considerable sympathy towards the man we had been taught to despise. But no, some bruise had been touched. Perhaps her increasing frustration at Onassis' unwillingness to marry her had been increased by the news that the old roué her father had done it again. Now he was to be ruled out of her life just as Mother had been.

When Father and Alexandra moved to Athens shortly afterwards I did all I could to help them settle in. She seemed a good soul, round but handsome, the exact opposite of Mother, essentially placid. I helped them find a little apartment not far from our old home in Patission and whenever I went round there I would find them sitting quietly, quite content to be together with nothing much to say to disturb the passing of time. They liked to go out to restaurants but their greatest pleasure was afternoon tea dances where they could waltz around the dance floor and Father could imagine he was that young rake who had won so many hearts all those years ago in Meligala.

'Are you happy, Father?' I asked him once.

He laughed. 'Wait a minute, what is that?'

'You're right, but quiet at least, are you?'

'That, yes. This woman doesn't say a word, she sits there and doesn't say a word unless I speak to her and usually I don't. She doesn't bother me. It's just nice not to be alone.'

From that first summer back in Greece in 1965 they took to spending the hot months in a little hotel in Kiffissia. It was in many ways the ideal marriage and it was sad that Maria had not the heart to see that.

For me, I was content enough. I had wanted Father to be independent and now he was, though in many ways it increased my sense of loneliness. With them away at their summer retreat and me forced to suffer the Athens heat without the money to get away, I felt more and more that my life was just drifting by. To cheer myself up I returned to the first love of our childhood and went out and bought three canaries. I wanted to call one Milton, another Maria and the

174

third Liz, after Elizabeth Taylor. Unfortunately my ornithological knowledge was limited and Maria had to become Mario, but no matter. Milton and Mario were yellow, Liz was dark. Having first been destined as Maria, Mario naturally turned out to be the best singer and it was love at first sight between him and Liz, much to the chagrin of Milton who would get very agitated if I let them out together. They were some company at least and, as before, I loved their singing. It gave me something to do, seeing they were fed, cleaning their cages every morning. Apart from that there was only the occasional tea party with some of the others from my days at Mr Vithinos' classes. We would sometimes get together at each other's houses. Most were married and for them it was a little break from the chores of domestic life – for me they were my only contact with the outside world.

Perhaps it was this that led me to accept with equanimity Mother's sudden decision to leave America and return to Greece once more. In a way this was made possible by Maria, though this time it was not altogether Mother's fault. Having reached the age of retirement, she had been receiving a welfare payment of about two hundred and fifty dollars a month from the New York authorities. They in turn invoked a law that obliged the children of destitute parents to come to their assistance, willing or not. In consequence a process was taken out against Maria's American earnings, which were considerable, and she was obliged to make Mother a regular income of two hundred dollars a month. Both sides in this unlooked-for dispute were somewhat disgruntled: Maria, who loathed giving anything to Mother, and the recipient, who was obliged to take a fifty dollar drop in income. Mother's solution was to return to the cheaper shores of Greece and to have the money advantageously transferred to her.

Just before her arrival Milton's Foundation settled its court case to Harry's advantage. There was now little of Milton's money left but such as there was added up to a three-year back-payment for me. It was a pitiful recompense for all my years of devotion but there was nothing I could do. I used it to buy a small apartment out on the coast at Glyfada near where Onassis had moored his yacht. It was at the time when Maria renounced her American citizenship and became Greek so that under our laws her marriage to Meneghini would be quite simply non-existent, having never been consecrated by an Orthodox priest. It was her last desperate gamble to oblige

Onassis to marry her and it was to prove as fruitless as my own encounter with that institution had been. As I read the articles in the press I felt for her. Clearly she worshipped Onassis and just as clearly he was toying with her. He had wanted the lustre of possessing the world's most famous singer; now that her performing days were clearly over, he had lost interest. For Maria it must have been a terrible confirmation of her worst fears. She had always convinced herself that she would only be loved for her voice not herself, then when her voice was deserting her she thought she had at last found real love. Now she was to be abandoned for the reason she had suspected all along; such a realisation could only destroy her.

Mother was utterly unsympathetic when she arrived in Athens. 'How could she leave her husband like that,' she demanded, ignoring her own example in this field. 'He did everything for her, she would have had no career without his backing. Then what? She treats him as she treated me. When you're no more use to her – pouff, out you go! So she's getting a taste of her own medicine now. Maybe it will teach her to appreciate what others have been through. Maybe she'll soon need a mother's shoulder to cry on.'

No, it was clear Mother would never give in, and equally clearly neither would Maria and here was I, once again stuck with one of the adversaries in this life-long war. I helped find Mother an apartment, again not far from where we used to live and spent all my time travelling up from Glyfada to take care of her. We were soon back in the old routine of my having meals with her and it wasn't long before all the frustrated complaints began bubbling up to the surface: Where had I been? Why was I late? etc.

As they were so close, I often wondered if Mother and Father would ever bump into each other. I could imagine Father handling it quite well; he had a certain way with awkward situations and I imagined he would not be put out about having to introduce the new wife to the old. Mother I did not expect to handle things with such finesse. Yet oddly enough, as near as they were, they never as much as caught a glimpse of each other. They could as well have been in different cities.

For me the problem was travelling up to Athens from Glyfada every day. As soon as she had her apartment Mother expected me to help her clean and cook and insisted I take my meals with her. It was an exhausting schedule for me and the only solution was to try to get another apartment in the centre of town. The problem, as ever, was

176

money. Flats near the archaeological museum where Mother and Father lived were becoming more and more expensive and I would need more than the proceeds of the sale of my little place on the coast.

It was at this point that I wondered if Mary would help out. She had seemed happy enough to see me when we met last and after all I was doing all the work of looking after our aged parents. I wasn't asking for a gift, only a small loan to help me move nearer them both. I wrote asking for two thousand dollars but predictably she never answered. Later we heard from Alexandra's brother, John Papajohn, that Mary had told him about my request as if it was just another example of her family's endless pestering her for money. She told him that if I'd put the apartment in her name then she'd think about helping me out.

In the end I took a bank loan and bought a place in Kallinikou not far from Mother, though it meant my living even more frugally than before in order to pay off the debt.

It was about this time that the Colonels took over in Greece, though what to the outside world must have seemed like momentous news meant little to our strange family. All the troubles seemed to die down after a week. We were like rare species in a cage, our lives limited to a few quiet streets of the capital away from the main administrative and shopping centres. We heard of great events taking place elsewhere but somehow they seemed utterly remote. Father sat with his new wife, happily at peace at last. I did my little shopping and went to visit Mother. If soldiers wanted to run the country there was nothing we isolated folk could do about it. Mother would sometimes talk about what was going on; she read her paper and listened to the radio but I doubt she ever got it clear in her mind. Life outside was a series of shocking events to be retailed as examples of the world's perfidy. Something to get incensed over but only in an abstract way. It was a break from her other hobby, nagging. She was still perfecting it. The years in America had not mellowed her and again there was only me to be the butt of all her discontent. Occasionally she would have some of her old friends over for gossip over an ouzo or she might go round to them. She loved any sort of social life but there was never enough of it to keep her happy and her discontent had to be directed somewhere. I always wondered as I stepped out of the lift and went to open her door just what sort of mood she would be in. Even a good mood was only a question of milder nagging – why had I not taken more care over my appearance, was I sure about the dress I was wearing? Little things like that. A bad mood meant more cruel, searching questions, a persistent wearing down of the object before her, now always me. No one else would have borne it.

She could nearly always get me to tell her everything. She had an uncanny sixth sense about my doings and would scratch away until I gave in and told all. But there was one thing I was determined to keep from her, my friendship with a man I'd met shortly after I'd moved into my new apartment. The matter was extremely delicate as he was my doctor. We had met way back in 1945 but only professionally. He was handsome and very gentle and what I didn't know then was that he had fallen in love with me. In all that time with Milton he had had the decency to say nothing but when we met again in 1967 he asked if he could see me and I said yes. I knew I shouldn't have and when he told me about his feelings I should have ended the matter then and there. But something inside asked me why I always had to be such a saint, wasn't I entitled to a little fun in life? Here was a good-looking man telling me he loved me. I who had so little in life being courted and flattered and told I was loved. Was I supposed to say no, don't say that, think of your wife, think of your child? Why should I?

He had only been married a year and a half. He told me he had done so because he had despaired of our ever getting together but now he knew it was useless and it was me he wanted. At first I was cautious, unwilling to believe him. What if he merely wanted another woman? But after a while it became clear he was telling the truth and I cannot deny I enjoyed the situation.

'What's going on?' Mother demanded. 'What are you smiling so much for? There's something you're keeping from me.' And there was.

The doctor was also finding it difficult to keep the story from his young wife and he told me of her distress. The worry was making him ill, the situation was getting out of hand. For a year I refused to let my ever-ready conscience interfere. Why not? I told myself. Everyone has used you and look where being decent and helpful and faithful has got you. But there was something more than conscience nagging away at me, something even more insistent than Mother's endless demands to know what was going on. It was the slow realisation that the pleasure I derived from the affair was the satisfaction of making him suffer. I was twisting him round my little finger. Leading him on, spoiling his marriage, dragging him down. It was my revenge against all the men who had hurt me and it was deeply cruel and unfair.

I told myself that it was not something I could allow to continue. It was like the aftermath of that party all those years ago when I'd made the boy Mary admired dance with me all night just to hurt her. I had only to think of what the results of that foolish game had been, to accept that treating people badly had the habit of backfiring. That autumn I told him it was all over, that I couldn't see him any more. I told him to go back to his wife, that I would see him from time to time if he wished, but only as friends. It was a messy business and he still came round occasionally but he knew I meant it and that it was all over.

I don't think his marriage was happy after that, how could it have been? But it was better that way than what I had been doing. I couldn't have married him even if his wife had agreed to a divorce. I didn't really love him and was only stringing him along. It was better to end it no matter how miserable he felt.

That October, 1968, Onassis married Jacqueline Kennedy and the papers carried huge photographs of Maria in Maxim's trying to look brave despite the agony she must have been going through.

'I knew that would happen,' Mother said. 'And you're not looking so good either. What *is* going on?'

Since her return I had discovered that Mother viewed with deep suspicion any move on my part to lead an independent life. Before, with Mary's career in its opening stages, she had left me to Milton. Now that I was all she had left, she was more and more concerned that I should go on being available. Even in the late sixties, marriages in Greece were still largely arranged, with people acting as intermediaries. One day Mother was approached by a downstairs neighbour on behalf of a gentleman friend who was interested in meeting me. In context it was a perfectly proper approach and one that should have been followed by discreet enquiries on Mother's part as to the man's background and status. If these had proved satisfactory then a chaperoned meeting could have taken place. In my state of mind then, I doubt whether anything would have come of such an encounter but one might have expected my mother to at least welcome such an approach for an unmarried daughter now aged fifty-two. But no, the first enquiry sent her into a state of nerves. She told the neighbour that I would never marry.

'As long as I live,' she said, 'I want my daughter near me.'

The one thing you could say for Mother was that she was never devious in her selfishness, she came straight out with it. She even justified her behaviour with a complete ethic about the duty of children to take care of their parents. This, she made clear, was my function in life. Useless to bring up the treatment of her own mother, or the fact that these rules did not seem to apply to Father whom I was obliged to see without telling her in order to avoid being nagged for treachery. In fact I much preferred Father, I now shared his sense of peace. I was getting used to the idea that life could be virtually static. Mother always fought against that: her ladies' parties, her outings to friends' houses, were all attempts to convince herself that her social life would never end. That's why she always spoke to any journalist who sought her out. She loved being interviewed and would say anything they wanted to hear. Father and I only wanted peace. His day began with a visit to the nearby barber to be shaved, and he was as dapper as ever. There were little shopping trips to be made but by and large just a lot of comfortable hours in the company of Alexandra. After his years with Mother they must have seemed like bliss. I, too, relished being alone with my canaries; my day was broken by the inevitable meals with Mother, but between times there was solitude safe behind my own door.

We heard less and less of Maria now. Her career appeared to have come to a halt and although the popular press still published photographs of her whenever she appeared in public, shopping or dining, the only news of her singing were occasional stories about the possibility of a comeback that never seemed to happen. It was as if we were a fleet of little ships that had been dispersed and becalmed in windless waters.

Given his age, Father was in remarkably good health except for a manageable case of diabetes, nothing unusual in an old man. He was very particular in this as in his appearance and tried to take care of himself. Ironically it was his concern that eventually caused him most harm: in 1971 he went to a health resort at Kamenavourla just outside Athens to take hot baths that he was assured would help with a mild attack of arthritis. Despite it being summer he caught a slight chill and this brought on otitis of the ear which in turn provoked a bad diabetic attack. At first Alexandra treated him at home but she, too, was in far from perfect health – she'd had a fall just before she'd left America and had somehow cut her thigh on an exposed nail which meant that she sometimes walked with difficulty. In the end there was nothing to do but get the old man to hospital. Every day for six months I took Alexandra to see him. It was becoming the theme of my life: the waiting at the bus stop, the slow ride, the long mornings and interminable evenings at the bedside. We could see he was not improving though he never failed to be sitting up and ready for us, his hair and moustache clipped and combed.

I suggested to Mother that she might care to see him but I might as well have saved my breath; George Calogeropoulou no longer existed for her, he was already dead.

When I could no longer go on pretending that he might rally, I realised that I would have to tell Maria. It would be our first communication since I had asked her to help me with a loan but there was no sense in being proud about it. I knew it would please Father enormously if she could come and see him so I had to do it.

It was not easy to make contact. The maid at her Paris apartment was clearly practised in keeping people at bay. She insisted that madam was out whenever I tried and it was pointless to ask her to get Maria to call me as she would only assume I was after her money and ignore the request. In the end I simply told the maid to tell her that her father was dying and that finally provoked a response.

'Have you had any reporters round?' she asked when she phoned me that night. 'I suppose the damned press will be on to it.'

I told her that no one knew so far and she seemed relieved.

'I can't come just now, I'm working again – recordings, can't interrupt them. You understand. Can you explain for me?'

I said I would try but in the end it seemed better to say nothing. He did not ask about her and I didn't bring the matter up. That December, 1972, when he died, there was just Alexandra and me and he looked quite contented with that. The women in his family had brought him little satisfaction and no doubt he felt relieved not to have too many of them crowding in at the last.

I telephoned Maria to say he had died and to tell her about the funeral arrangements. I had expected that she would at least come back for that, but no. Once again she was worried that the press would get hold of the story that she had ignored her dying father and was not coming to his funeral.

'You know it's not true,' she said. 'It's just these recordings. What can I do?'

Again she asked me to help her and I said I would.

She was right, of course, a group of reporters did turn up at the graveyard and started asking why Maria wasn't there. I told them firmly that Miss Callas was saddened but that she could not break her contracts and leave her recording commitments and that the family fully understood and supported her in this. I said she was heartbroken over the death of her father but as a professional she knew she had to carry on.

When one remembered all the contracts she had broken in the past, when one thought of all the opera houses she had walked out of, I wondered why they didn't just laugh in my face.

After the funeral it only remained to help poor Alexandra, who could hardly go on alone. Father's death had upset her dreadfully and worsened her health. I went every day at first and tried to see that she had food and assistance with the housework but it was soon clear that the apartment was too much for her, so I wrote to her brother John in New York to say that we would have to sort something out. He was a good man and he and his wife flew to Athens to see what they could do. By then she was walking on crutches and it was evident she needed nursing care, so John found her a room in an old people's home where he settled her in before his return. She was happy there in the three years left to her. I went every week to see if she needed anything and we would sit in silence much as she had done with Father. For me it was a welcome interlude from my daily diet of Mother.

How many people in the world are there living blank lives? Countless millions, for whom the whole business of living has no justification. I got up in the morning, did my exercises, meticulously washed myself and saw to my hair and make-up, I fed the canaries and cleaned their cages, I did my household chores then set off for lunch with Mother. I returned for my siesta, I woke, washed and made up and went back for the evening meal, then home again to sleep. Day in day out, week after week, year following year. Happy? Unhappy? After a time it gets beyond such questions. Happiness hangs on a fine thread – the sudden singing of Mario could bring contentment, Mother in a complaining mood could destroy an entire day. Prisoners must know these days of hovering between misery and elation with no especial reason for either. Should one question what a life like this is for? No. No one asked for it nor made it. Like a tiny silver fish in a vast shoal, turning with its numberless fellows in senseless, tide-washed patterns, such lives go on.

One day a puzzle: a cheque from Maria for two hundred dollars. I went round to Mother and she said that her allowance had not come. So, a mistake.

I telephoned Paris and to my surprise I was put straight through.

'I wanted you to have a present,' she said.

No point in asking why. I told her about Mother's allowance and she said she would see it was paid.

'But I want you to have something too. You're my only family now.'

I thanked her but didn't mention that Mother was still part of her family; she clearly thought of her as dead.

'How are you? How's Athens? I suppose things are quiet since Milton and Father died?'

I told her that quiet was hardly the word, that I had virtually nothing in my life.

'No love?' she asked.

I told her no, my life was quite empty.

'And mine,' she said. 'I don't go out much now – not since . . .'

Her voice trailed away but I knew to what she was referring; it was the explanation for the call, for the gift.

'It was terrible when Milton died,' I said. 'But I had years to prepare for it. He was dying for nearly thirteen years.'

'It was quick with Ari, very quick in the end.'

'You don't have to send me money,' I said.

'No, I want to, really. You can do something for me too – I can't sleep and all that helps is Mandrax but they've stopped them here. Send me some if you can.'

I told her I would and we said our goodbyes. I decided not to tell Mother. It would only upset her unnecessarily.

For two years Maria phoned from time to time. There was no routine, I never knew when the calls might come. Sometimes they were very brief, as if she only wanted to check that I was still there, available at the end of the line. Sometimes she only wanted to ask for more Mandrax or to say that she was planning this or that. I often had the impression that she was saying things as if to try them out on herself. Her 'I'm going to do this', was much more, 'Shall I do this?' On other occasions there were long late-night calls full of rambling talk about her loneliness, the betrayal of everything she'd lived for, the loss of Onassis. She came to Greece, to his tomb on Skorpios, without telling me but then rang me to talk for hours about how she had felt kneeling there, praying for them both. It was if she wanted me, her sister, as a disembodied listener, not a real person of flesh and blood who would have problems of her own. I soon realised that it was better if I said nothing beyond the conventional phrases that would keep her talking and simply let her work through whatever she needed to get it off her chest. How strange to think of it: two women, two sisters, utterly alone a continent apart, the one listening to the other as if they were adolescents again, sorting out the heartaches and fears at the début of life instead of rambling over the miseries of the past.

In early summer 1976 her godfather Dr Lanzounis came to Athens and visited me. After his return Maria called late at night and started on her longest call yet.

'Godfather says you have a nice place, a beautiful garden on the terrace. So tell me . . .'

I described the view of Mount Parnis and the big tubs of white and red roses and the real pine tree.

'And canaries?'

'Yes, just like the old days.'

That started her asking about people we'd known – how was so and so, what became of this one and that one. I told her, though it didn't make very happy listening.

'So many dead?' she said.

It was a theme she kept returning to whenever she called. For a while there was a long silence then in the summer of 1977 she began again. That September she spoke for over an hour, asking what happened to so and so.

'I want to die too,' she said. 'Since I lost my voice I want to die.'

I told her not to think like that, she'd done so much for her art she could retire happily now – her name would remain to history. But she only laughed.

'What for? Why retire? To do what? Without my voice what am I? Nothing. I don't go anywhere much; people ask but I can't be bothered.'

She rambled on and I tried to give her some comfort but I knew I was having little success and the thought disturbed me. She said she would call again soon but the days drifted by and I heard no more.

It had been very hot in Athens, and even in September I looked forward to my siesta when I returned from lunch with Mother. It was the seventeenth, though I doubt at the time that I singled it out from all the other blank days. I lay back on the bed and drifted away and suddenly there was a violent tremor and the whole building began to sway. With another sickening upheaval the walls began to crack and fall apart, the floor split and the earthquake sent me crashing through the debris to the earth below. I lay quite calm, observing the destruction, aware that this was a dream. Across the smoking debris and twisted metal I saw my father coming towards me.

'I'm sorry this had to happen,' he said. 'But it had to be.'

As I listened to him my first thought was that Mother was dead. He had returned to warn me and that was the meaning of my dream. Some way off I heard a bell ringing and I thought it must be an ambulance come to take her away. It rang and rang, getting nearer and nearer until suddenly I woke and reached for the telephone.

'Miss Callas,' said a voice with a heavy French accent. 'This is Jean Roire . . .'

CHAPTER EIGHT
1977–1982

Mother would sit at the window of her apartment writing poems. She would leave them lying about, unconcerned as to what became of them. I kept one:

> Little bird you have flown away
> and left me lonesome in the dark nights.
> You have gone from the nest's gentle warmth
> and have plunged me into sorrows.
>
> Little bird, I have heard tell
> that you will never come again to your home.
> All the nightingales have said it.
> Before the spring bursts into flower
> you wish to fly further,
> to flap your wings elsewhere.
>
> But I asked the flowers and green leaves
> and spoke to the waves,
> I begged them on my knees every night.
> But they only screamed at me
> that my beautiful bird has gone from me
> and will never return.
>
> With tears of grief I ask my Christ
> whether these things I have heard are true
> or have I merely dreamed them?
> Smiling, he tells me that the time will come
> when I will have her in my arms again,
> when I will kiss her dark eyes with joy,
> when her red lips will call me 'Mother'

as I comb her hair with a tiny golden comb
and plait with silk her long, long tresses.

When I returned to Athens after Maria's funeral her hysterical grief had given way to pitiful melancholia.

'Why didn't I die first?' she kept repeating. 'Why my daughter who was so young?'

I would go to her apartment twice a day to sit and eat with her. Much of the time was passed in silence but occasionally she would start to feel her misery more keenly and the cycle of grief and reproach would begin. Sometimes it was clear that she resented my being there instead of Maria. Though she never said it outright, I knew she would rather I had died than the adored one.

In between times we discussed the events and personalities in Paris but neither of us had much idea what it all meant. What might happen to all Maria's things seemed rather remote. We assumed that she would have left everything to those closest to her, and imagined that Bruna and Ferruccio would be the ones to benefit most. We never imagined that we would receive a cent, given Maria's attitude towards us in the past. If anything we were now much worse off than before, the tiny allowance she had reluctantly made us having terminated with her death. Still, we were by then quite used to living simply. It was only after a few weeks had passed that we received a letter from Vasso Devetzi, the woman who had organised the funeral and who had taken charge of me during my time in Paris. She wrote to say that she had been through Maria's papers and had found no evidence of a signed will. Maria had had a document drawn up which was indeed in favour of the two servants but she had never signed it. I understood why of course – someone as superstitious as Maria would never have dared tempt fate by foreshadowing her own demise in that way. To have signed the will would to her have been a recognition that she was about to die.

At first Mother and I were unclear what this absence of a signature could mean but Devetzi quickly informed us that without a will we were the legal inheritors of everything Maria left and of all her estate. We would, she hastened to add, be rich and she would be delighted to act on our behalf. Sitting in Mother's room watching her scribbling verses and sniffing into her handkerchief such a prospect seemed utterly remote. What did it all mean? Rich? Us? I think we knew from the first that such a prospect was not our destiny, so that when Devetzi wrote to say that there was a crisis in Paris we merely accepted it as inevitable. It seemed that Devetzi had been completely surprised by the unexpected arrival at the apartment of Maria's ex-husband, Battista Meneghini, accompanied by an Italian and a French lawyer. Having waited the statutory forty days, he had come to France bearing a will signed by Maria in 1954 at the height of their marriage which clearly left everything to him. He had the will presented to a French court which had sent a legal officer to seal the apartment until the validity of the document could be fully authenticated. Devetzi had arrived that night to find Bruna and Ferruccio confined to the servants' quarters while all the principal salons were locked with little wire knots and grey legal seals across the doors. She was absolutely furious but there was little she could do at first. She telephoned to Athens, repeatedly begging me to come before Meneghini got his hands on everything.

Mother and I were utterly confused. It seemed very nice of this strange lady to help us but why was she doing so? It was such an awful prospect, going to Paris again, getting involved in something that didn't appear to be our business at all. But Vasso, as she insisted I call her, was adamant, it was what Maria would have wished, she claimed, and I had to do it. That was an appeal Mother could not see refused and so I once again took the flight to Paris and returned to my hotel room and my curious, suspended existence. On the first day, Vasso took me to the apartment to see the sealed doorways. We sat in the kitchen sipping coffee while she begged me to fight – 'For Maria's sake.'

'But we haven't got the money for lawyers,' I protested.

'You'll have money if you win; there's always a lawyer who'll gamble on that.'

She began to tell me about all the things involved in Maria's estate; there were a lot of details about shares in a holding company that owned Maria's apartment, there were complicated matters of copyright and property – my head began to spin.

'It's too much for you, isn't it?' she said. 'Why don't you let me look after it all for you and your mother? You should get the power of attorney from your mother so that you can sign documents that are too upsetting for her and you could give me the "Moral Right", then I can look after it all.'

I had little idea what she was talking about but she explained that under the laws of most European countries, Maria's family inherited the right to protect her reputation – her standing as an artist. It was a very important right because it gave the family great control over the work Maria had left behind. As these things were very tedious to deal with, if Mother would assign the Moral Right to Vasso, then she would be happy to look after it for us. I was grateful. After all, what did Mother or I know of such things? I told her I would speak to Mother and try to persuade her to agree.

The next day Vasso took me to see a Maître Henri Bensusan, a lawyer she knew. He was charming and I found him sympathetic – rightly so because he was always to keep my best interests at heart. He listened to what Vasso had to say then he said that there must be some doubt about Meneghini's claim given that he had divorced his wife. However, he also pointed out that Meneghini was a rich man well able to afford expensive legal help. This might be said to tip the balance in his favour. As Maria had never made another will, his was the only one she had ever signed. I left more confused than ever but Vasso insisted that we should go on. As she said that this would cost us nothing it was hard to refuse her. Almost as a reward she persuaded Maria's bank to release a little more money for me and I returned to Athens in better spirits.

At least all this helped divert Mother's attention from her misery. She scented battle and something of her old spirit began to return.

'Why shouldn't we have the money?' she said. 'Who gave Maria life, who made all those sacrifices to get her started, who never received a cent in thanks? It's only fair that I should get something.'

I explained to her everything that Vasso had told me – the power of attorney, the Moral Right – and she agreed to it all. As with me, the details confused her; all she saw was the broad picture of Meneghini trying to claim her inheritance. As Vasso appeared to be our main ally in this struggle then of course she must be given all the weapons she needed. We went to a notary and drew up the documents.

We were now subjected to a barrage of letters and phone calls from Paris as Vasso took up the fight in earnest. Within a fortnight she was able to announce that Meneghini had agreed to come to Paris for a meeting and that I should prepare to return.

As I again flew to the French capital, I was nervous at the prospect of this confrontation. After all, Meneghini was a successful industrialist, a man of means, not used to being crossed by a pair of women. What would his reaction be to me? In the end I needn't have worried, Meneghini was as charming to me as he had always been in the past. He kissed my hand, made appropriately soothing remarks about Maria's death and asked after Mother, deploring the circumstances that had led to this unfortunate meeting, as he put it. I could see the disbelief on Vasso's face but I found it charming nevertheless. That first encounter was merely a preliminary to more serious discussions. He and Vasso hedged their way around the issues like boxers trying each other out. When he had left I told Vasso that Mother would feel happier if we discussed the affair with a Greek lawyer. She was worried that we might misunderstand something with our limited knowledge of French. I could see Vasso thought this was unnecessary but she realised it would be best to humour us. She went off to make the arrangements and I stayed to have coffee with Bruna in the kitchen. As I sat sipping the strong black liquid I noticed she had on the same old-style frock as she wore the last time I had been there.

The next day Vasso took me to see a Greek lawyer. He pointed out that although he had been divorced, Meneghini as a Catholic was in a sense still married to Maria and the will he possessed the only one she had signed. It might, he concluded, be best to come to terms with him. Both sides were strangers on French soil; were the French legal authorities to get involved who knows what might result and how many years of wrangling might ensue. His advice was that the two sides should come to an agreement and thus present a united front to a French court and obtain an early settlement. Although I didn't fully accept his advice it was hard to fault his logic and Vasso and I agreed that that should be the line to take. I telephoned Mother from Maria's apartment and she too saw the sense of that approach.

Sitting in that kitchen sipping coffee, I again found myself looking hard at Bruna. When she slipped out I asked Vasso why the poor woman always wore the same dress but Vasso only said that Bruna probably didn't have many things and I shouldn't worry about it.

But I couldn't let it be. 'She does still get her salary, doesn't she? They haven't cut that off?'

At first Vasso tried to wave the matter away but when I persisted she revealed the astonishing fact that Bruna and Ferruccio had never been given a regular income. Maria had fed and housed them, sent small sums to their families in Italy, given them gifts from time to time and that was it. I was appalled. There, so near, were those cupboards filled to bursting point with silks and furs and here was

Bruna with only the clothes she stood up in. Amazingly, she didn't seem to mind.

It suddenly occurred to me that it was very nearly Christmas. 'I want to get them some presents,' I announced.

Vasso shrugged but did not object. We went out of the apartment and crossed the elegant avenues, making our way to the nearest shopping centre where I bought Bruna a warm skirt, a silk blouse and a cashmere jacket and Ferruccio a cashmere jacket too.

That experience convinced me of what I ought to do. I was suddenly certain what Maria would have wanted and I was determined not to be dissuaded.

When we met with Meneghini the next day, Vasso told me that they had arranged a fifty-fifty split of all the estate. She looked at me expecting my gratitude but I had something else on my mind.

'And Bruna and Ferruccio?' I said, 'what is for them?'

'What about them?' Meneghini asked softly.

'Maria wanted them to have something,' I replied, nervous but determined. 'And I think they should too.'

I could tell that he was ready to flatly refuse but suddenly Vasso was with me.

'She's quite right. Of course we have to do something.'

She looked hard at Meneghini as if willing him to play along. He hesitated for a moment then appeared to see the sense of what she was doing.

'You have a very kind heart, dear lady,' he said, all smiles. 'A little gift for the loyal servants, such a thoughtful idea – a thousand dollars perhaps.'

Vasso too was smiling at me, humouring me.

'More,' I said. 'Much, much more.'

The smile left Meneghini's face, he began to object, but Vasso stepped in.

'Best to agree rather than fall out over this little matter,' she said sternly and that seemed to halt Meneghini in his tracks. He muttered something in Italian which I didn't catch.

Vasso took my hand. 'You are such a good person,' she said. 'I'm sure Bruna and Ferruccio will be very grateful to you.'

They agreed a substantial sum, enough to make the two secure for life and I felt easier in my mind. On behalf of Mother I signed the initial agreement with Meneghini and this was sent round to Maître Bensusan to get the French court to recognise the settlement. I said

191

goodbye to Meneghini knowing that we would meet shortly for the division of Maria's belongings. Alone with Vasso, I told her that Mother had agreed to her having the Moral Right.

'There's something else,' she said slowly. 'Just before she died Maria told me she wished that her money could help young singers. You remember the scholarships she set up in Athens after her concert, she wanted the money for that.'

This was the first I'd heard of it but it did not seem unreasonable.

'Of course,' Vasso went on, 'you and your mother must have an income but with so much money you should respect your sister's last wishes.'

She saw that I was not going to challenge her and went on, 'And you should think ahead. You won't live for ever and then what will happen?'

I shook my head. I'd never considered such a thing before. She said I should think about the future, I should make sure that after my death Maria's wishes would be carried out even after I'd gone. It would be best if I made a will leaving . . . She paused there as if thinking through a deep problem. Of course, she went on, there was a problem as there was as yet no foundation, or other institution for me to leave the money to. But never mind, she had a solution; if I made a will leaving everything to her, then she would see it went to the right source.

I was grateful she was thinking all these things through. They seemed so complex, so much beyond anything I had ever had to cope with. She said I shouldn't think about it, she would arrange the papers for me to sign. I said I would tell Mother about it all but that as it was Maria's last wish I was sure she would agree.

Back in Athens Mother never questioned it. Maria had wanted things that way then so be it. Vasso telephoned constantly to remind us of what we had agreed and I reassured her that she would have money whenever it became available. As she was one of the trustees of the original fund set up by Maria after her Greek concerts Vasso said I only had to make any cheques out to her and she would do the rest. As I sat listening to my canaries happily making their innocent music I thought to myself that I had at least done what Maria would have wished and that if any of her wealth came my way at least it would not be tainted by having been at the expense of those who had loved and cared for her.

When I went round to see Mother on the evening of my return I found her, as so often now, seated at the window staring out at the sky. I assumed that she was thinking of the little bird of her poems and I sat patiently waiting for her to turn and join me. I waited and waited but she just sat there. The light began to fade and I wondered how she could just go on sitting there motionless.

'Mother?' I said. 'Is anything wrong? You can't sit there for ever, it's getting cool now and you shouldn't sit so close to the glass.'

Still she didn't respond so I went over and touched her gently on the shoulder. To my surprise her head fell forward and I had to quickly reach out to catch her before she tumbled to the ground. She was no longer the slim woman she had once been and it was an effort to force her upright again. I shook her and called out to her but still she didn't wake. I propped her up in the chair as best I could and hurried to get help. A neighbour called for an ambulance and we were soon dashing to the nearest hospital, deafened by the plaintive wailing of an ambulance siren. As soon as we arrived she was rushed on a trolley and lost behind a curtained cubicle into which a troupe of nurses and doctors disappeared. I sat on a hard bench staring at a notice-board covered in yellowing memos, no doubt with the same vacuous expression as Mother had had.

After an eternity of waiting a young doctor came and sat beside me. 'Has your mother had any bad shocks lately, any strain at all?'

I told him who we were and he quickly made the connection with Maria's death. The name of Greece's most famous cultural figure made him doubly solicitous.

'Your mother was in a diabetic coma,' he explained. 'She's all right now that we've given her insulin but it was a dangerous moment. We'll have to keep her here while we stabilise her condition but I don't think you need worry too much. You can see her now if you wish.'

I passed through the tent-like break in the curtains and stood by the side of the bed. Mother lay quite still, her head propped on pillows, a tube snaking from her arm and up to a suspended bag three-quarters full of transparent liquid.

'The doctor says you're going to be fine,' I said but she only shook her head.

I tried again. 'The doctor says you had a diabetic attack but it's over now. They gave you insulin. They're sure they can control it.'

But again she shook her head and this time I could see that she was crying. 'It's my eyes,' she said. 'I can't see properly.'

I tried to reassure her, then said goodbye and went again to talk to the doctor. This time he explained that cataracts were sometimes a feature of her condition and that there was little they could do about it. 'We can put her on a strict diet,' he explained, 'and that should control the diabetes but her eyes may worsen.'

I went back to her apartment to put everything in order and then went home. I was too tired to cook and just nibbled a biscuit. It was dreadful that just as Mother was at last to get some money from her daughter her body should decide to deny her the pleasure of it.

Perhaps this thought crossed her mind too, for as soon as they had stabilised her condition and she had been allowed home she began to make plans to challenge her new disabilities. She announced that this next time she and not I would take charge of things in Paris. I was only too delighted to have the whole troublesome business taken out of my hands but it was not to be – alternate periods of lethargy and melancholia combined to deny her the will to go and in the end it was I who found myself once again in Bensusan's office listening to him explaining to Meneghini and me the final details of the agreement he and Vasso had drawn up. I doubted, as did Mother, whether the Will Meneghini so often brandished had any real validity – he and Maria had divorced and that was the end of the matter, but what could two women do about it? In any case the lawyer at the Greek Embassy in Paris had not confirmed these doubts. Who is to say that the fifty-fifty split was not the best we could have expected under the circumstances? At least that is what everyone, principally Vasso, kept on telling us, so why not agree? On Mother's behalf I signed and we agreed to meet in four months' time in order to divide the more portable items in the many cupboards in the apartment. For the larger stuff, the furniture, the pictures, the gifts and the kitchen equipment, there would be an auction later in the new year and again we would divide the proceeds in half. We shook hands and went our own ways. I was soon to be back in Paris for the division of Maria's smaller belongings but in between times Mother and I had celebrated an even quieter Christmas than usual.

In Mother's condition that was probably just as well. Her troubles had not made her any easier. Whereas before her nagging had been a by-product of her boundless energy, a constant attempt to push others into doing things her way, now the illness distorted this aspect of her character into an incessant grumbling. She went on crying over the loss of Maria and complaining about everything. Thinking that this would pass as she gradually got over the shock of her daughter's death I at first simply kept my head down and attempted to suffer her complaints in silence. Had I known that this was to be the pattern of our lives from then on I doubt I would have had the courage to continue.

Her worst moaning was reserved for the sparse diet she was obliged to follow in order to control the diabetes and avoid having to rely on insulin. She had always enjoyed rich wholesome food and had taken great pleasure in providing the young Maria with great quantities of heavily flavoured dishes. Now that the pleasures of the table were among the few things left to her she found herself limited to sensible though rather tedious recipes. Nevertheless, the régime worked to the extent that she needed no regular injections and felt less and less lethargic. Sadly for me, this gave her the energy to renew her assault on all the things that irritated her. Despite my discomfort in meeting the various people who had taken it on themselves to get involved in Maria's affairs since her death, it was nevertheless something of a relief to be flying out of Athens and away from Mother's whining. I returned to Paris on January 6th, 1978, for the first division of the property before the larger items went to auction. We all met at the apartment: Vasso and myself on one side, Meneghini on the other, though by then it was all perfectly amicable.

Meneghini had brought Signora Roverselli, the maid I had met on that visit to his home near Lake Garda, and his notary. For the family there was Vasso and myself. An officer of the court came to remove the seals and we were once more admitted to my sister's private world. We wandered round, not unlike naughty children in a parents' bedroom while the elders are out. We opened cupboards and pulled out drawers, fascinated by the sheer quantity of things, often still in the wrappers they were bought in. Everything was neatly stacked and folded. I who had so little could only marvel at so many pairs of shoes; they were to me far more fascinating than the jewellery and furs that so occupied Meneghini and Vasso. The two of them went into conference while I happily gawped at all that over-consumption. Eventually Vasso came to tell me that they had come to an arrangement over the more expensive items: the jewellery that had been bought during the Meneghini era would revert to him, that of the Onassis period would be Mother's and mine. Everything else would be simply divided into two halves and parcelled up. The mammoth task of stacking and wrapping all that stuff got under way. Everything seemed, inexplicably, to be in two hundreds – two hundred blouses, two hundred pairs of shoes, two hundred silk nightgowns. I wondered what significance the number had had for my sister.

To me, who had never wanted to see her things sold, the saddest moment came when Vasso and Meneghini set about splitting up the objects in Maria's museum, the blue room where she had kept the personal souvenirs of her career – awards and citations, the collection of mementoes of the great singer Maria Malibran with whom she had so personally identified – all divided in half. Vasso said she was going to put our half to one side as she intended to do something with them, an exhibition perhaps, but Meneghini's share was just parcelled up with the rest of his things.

The day stretched on into nightfall. I went into the small salon and found Meneghini sitting alone. He looked terribly sad and exhausted.

'Oh, you are tired, Signor Meneghini,' I said, 'and I am too.'

I went to sit near him.

'You know one thing,' he said. 'I am old but you are still young. You will enjoy all this but what is left for me to enjoy? I wish I was young.'

We sat silent for a while. I felt very sympathetic towards him. Of course he had his bad side – he really had no right to do what he was doing but I couldn't deny that he had loved Maria, so I found it hard to be angry with him.

Heaven knows how long we sat there, two unhappy people, but eventually Vasso's head came round the door.

'What are you two plotting?' she said, not altogether joking. 'You'd better come and see the results, it's quite amazing.'

We reluctantly left our chairs and followed her into Maria's bedroom. Piled high were one hundred and ninety-four large parcels – ninety-seven for Meneghini and ninety-seven for the family. Vasso said she would take our share to her apartment for safe keeping, and the jewels would all be sent to the Union de Banques Suisses in Geneva where the shares of the limited company that theoretically owned the apartment were kept, the idea being that we would all meet there at some agreed time for the final division of the spoils. For someone who had lived at a level of frugality just above the poverty line these antics seemed both alarming and not a little distasteful. I had wanted Maria's home kept intact as a museum; now I was part of the haggling, albeit amicable, over her things that would result in their being scattered far and wide. It was just as well that a downturn in Mother's health prevented me from being at the auction the following June. Judging from accounts in the press it was an unpleasant affair with Meneghini bidding to get back some of the things he considered his and with the apartment packed with souvenir hunters trying to get their hands on something that had once belonged to the woman they worshipped. One account said that as the bidding was taking place a huge mirror in the main salon suddenly and inexplicably cracked from top to bottom with a frightening report, as if Maria were expressing her ghostly displeasure at the unseemly proceedings. Very likely, I thought, when I read it.

As soon as Mother was well enough to be left I flew to Geneva and met with Meneghini and Vasso at Maria's bank. The settlement for the servants was arranged and the rest of the estate, with the exception of the jewellery, divided in two. The most valuable thing, Maria's Paris apartment, was technically the property of a holding company and again the shares were split between us. It seemed like an awful lot of money to someone like me, used to having next to nothing. The tiny sum I received from Milton's Foundation had dwindled into a pittance yet here I was dealing with a small fortune.

'So much money,' I said to Vasso after Meneghini had left us. 'It will be nice not to have to worry about paying the bills now and good for Mother to have a comfortable old age.'

Vasso looked up sharply. 'You haven't forgotten the Foundation, have you?'

I quickly reassured her that I hadn't for a moment forgotten the promise I'd made in Paris. As soon as the money was there she could have it.

'And the Will,' she said.

I reassured her that I'd sign that too.

Back in Athens she again kept telephoning to remind me of my promise and sure enough when the first major payment was made to my bank in February 1978 I transferred three hundred thousand dollars to her, the first of a long series of donations to establish the Maria Callas Foundation.

At this point Mother and I should have been able to relax at last.

We were comfortably off and had, so we thought, done all that could be expected of us to honour Maria. Why not sit back and enjoy a moment's peace?

I had, however, failed to take account of Mother's perversity in my calculations. Since the death, and with all the fuss about the inheritance, the press had begun to take notice of us. I would never have anything to do with them but, despite all my pleas that she leave well alone, Mother had a passion for being interviewed and photographed. It reawoke all her latent desire somehow to participate in Maria's glory. If she had been denied the rôle of Queen-Mother during her daughter's lifetime surely, she began to dream, it might now come to her posthumously. With no Maria to prevent it, why shouldn't Evangelia Callas now step forward and be lionised as the mother of the century's greatest diva? As the press were so keen to know all about her, she now reckoned that the adoring fans would be more than enthusiastic to encounter their idol's progenitor. She remembered the glorious time in Mexico: the receptions, the flowers in the hotel suite, the official lunches. If she could get to where Maria was still worshipped, then a new life could be hers. Thus she suddenly announced to me her decision that we should leave Athens and move to Paris. Maria had been queen of Paris society, she said; now that same society would eagerly welcome the Queen Mother. I was ordered to contact Vasso, to get her to arrange matters. We must move quickly, Vasso would find us an apartment and make sure we were introduced to the 'Le tout Paris'. I was horrified but at the same time paralysed like a small animal confronted with a predator. Long experience told me that this would be a disaster and yet it was unavoidable. Clearly she had been working the whole thing out in her mind for weeks. To argue now would be pointless. Not to contact Vasso would only mean that she would do so herself and create incredible confusion. Nor could I delay matters. 'Call Vasso now,' she ordered. And as usual I did so.

For once there was an immediate connection to Paris. As usual Vasso began in French then instantly transferred to Greek when she realised who it was. She always told me how happy she was that I had called and how keen she was to answer any questions I had. This time she listened to what I said in silence and did not immediately follow it up with her usual remarks about how pleased she was with what I'd just said.

'Are you sure?' was all she could say. 'I thought your mother wasn't well. It might not be good for her to uproot herself and come all this way.'

I was inclined to say how much I agreed with her but Mother was following everything I was saying.

'It's Mother's wish; she's decided it's what she wants to do.'

'But what do you want to do?' Vasso asked. I had no answer to that.

There was a pause while I heard her talking to someone, presumably M. Roire, in French. It was too rapid for me to follow but I could guess that she was passing on the news to her friend. I heard him speak and then Vasso came back to me: 'When do you want to come?'

'As soon as possible. Mother has set her heart on it and she hates any delay when she has decided to do something.'

'I'll see if I can rent an apartment near me in Neuilly, you'll be comfortable there.'

I thanked her and we talked a little more about the arrangements, though I rather wished that she had refused to go along with the idea as that was the only thing that might have made Mother change her mind. As it was we were now locked into this, to me, crazy scheme.

When I'd put down the phone Mother immediately began to take charge. 'We'll need a moving company.'

'What for?' I asked nervously and when she said that we were going to take all our furniture my worst fears were realised. We were to give up the Athens apartments, the move was to be irrevocable. There was no possibility that this would be a short trip just to see how things were or whether we could fit in to this new life. Mother entertained no such doubts. In her dreams we were already there, lionised by Maria's French admirers, the centre of attention. So why hesitate? she reckoned. Sell up and go.

When I got back to my own place that night I was exhausted and depressed. I looked at the canaries, at my room with its familiar things and wished that it could just remain the way it was. Paris was that bare hotel room with its view of the narrow courtyard. My place was no palace but it was mine. Sensing my distress the birds began to sing, with Milton struggling to outdo the others.

We travelled to Paris in November and went straight to the apartment Vasso had found for us in Neuilly. It had a living room, kitchen, three bedrooms and two bathrooms and was in a perfectly nice part of that leafy neighbourhood, but there was one sign that things would not go well – despite Vasso's having turned on the central heating before our arrival the apartment was bitterly cold.

'It's not the building,' Vasso explained. 'It's the whole of Paris. We're having the worst winter ever.'

She was right. M. Roire took us to a restaurant for lunch and we watched all the customers shivering in their topcoats. After Athens it was near unbearable. Of course Mother at first refused to admit that everything was not perfect and told me sharply not to fuss whenever I complained about the bitter cold. I tried to sleep with every coat and blanket I could get heaped on the bed but I always seemed to wake up in the middle of the night and just lie there shivering till dawn. Initially, Mother ignored all this as she awaited the flood of invitations she confidently expected would follow our arrival. Only gradually did I begin to suspect that she had misread the signs.

At first Vasso came often and there was much to keep us occupied, setting out the furniture when it arrived from Athens and generally making a home. I told Vasso that now might be a good time for us to have our half of Maria's things that we had parcelled up that day with Meneghini.

But she only laughed at the idea. 'In here,' she said. 'Where on earth would you put it all? No, leave that stuff where it is for the moment. You don't want to fill the apartment with a lot of packing cases do you?'

As usual what she said made sense. I could never argue with her even if, as I did then, I had a strange feeling that things wouldn't have been quite as she described them. The apartment wasn't enormous but nor was it so small we couldn't have fitted in a lot more things. But somehow I always seemed to think up these arguments when she'd gone and it was too late to do anything. Oh well, I thought, there's no hurry, I can always have them when I want.

It was a strange existence, knowing nobody except Vasso, and only speaking limited French there was not much scope for meeting people. My life revolved round endless trips to the supermarket where I could safely pick out the myriad things I needed while the setting-up process was under way at the apartment. As before, Mother sat disconsolately at the window, dreaming of her little bird. It barely made any difference having moved to Paris. Perhaps she imagined being nearer the Père Lachaise Cemetery where Maria's ashes were interred would somehow bring them closer. I can't be sure as we would never have spoken of something like that.

If we needed something more complex than could be found in Prixunis then I had to wait for Vasso to take me. Those outings and the occasional meal in a restaurant with M. Roire were our only entertainment. Otherwise we stayed in, Mother and me together, utterly cut off in that strange city. Thank God for Vasso, I thought, where would I have been without her? What puzzled me was that she was always available whenever I called. I couldn't help but wonder what had happened to her career. Why was Vasso Devetzi, the international concert pianist, never away touring but always in Neuilly helping Mother and I set up house? On the days she came round she would often sit with me while Mother took her rest. She was the only friend I had in the world and without her I would have been completely isolated in that strange city with only Mother's nagging for company. I felt very grateful towards her and told her all about myself and Milton, about my own short-lived career as a singer and the way Maria had treated us. She was very sympathetic, the first person who had ever really paid any attention to me. She told me I should never have abandoned my music and one day she insisted I go to the piano and practise. I was terribly nervous but with her encouragement I sat at the keyboard and ran my fingers over the keys.

'I'll leave you,' she said. 'You just vocalise a little to see how it goes.'

When she had gone I tried out my voice; it was out of training but still strong. I sang for a little and felt better than I had felt for months. Perhaps there was a chance for me to try again? Perhaps I could make another stab at it?

But what of Vasso herself? I was still puzzled by her lack of performances and the next time we had one of our long talks I asked her why she was never away. She looked down at her lap and I thought she was going to cry.

'What is it?' I asked, suddenly worried.

'These,' she said, slowly lifting her hands and opening the fingers out.

I could see at once that they did not lie straight. She was trying to force them out but evidently they wouldn't go.

'Arthritis,' she said. 'Worse and worse. I don't think I shall play again.'

What could I say? It was the most dreadful thing to happen. Here was this woman with her own tragedy to contend with doing everything to help Mother and me. We had never really questioned her rôle in all this, as if to ask might cause the little bubble of kindness to burst. She had always said that she was helping us because Maria had been her friend, so why was there any need to probe further? Milton and Mother having kept me at one remove from reality all my adult life, I had very little experience by which to judge people. If someone appeared to be nice and helpful I could see no reason not to accept them at face value and to wish to reward them for it. I decided that it was wrong of me to be enjoying some of Maria's money if Vasso was in need, so I planned to make some provision for her as soon as I could. Because I knew Mother would never agree, I decided not to tell her.

'Why doesn't she take us anywhere?' was Mother's constant refrain. 'Opera, theatres, concerts, receptions. Music is her field, she's in that world, she knows all the people who knew Maria. Hasn't she told them we're here?'

But no invitations came and Mother never ceased to raise the subject whenever Vasso appeared, only to be countered by more requests for money for the scholarships.

One day when I'd agreed to a further hundred thousand dollars and Vasso seemed to be in a good mood, I asked again if it wasn't time we had the parcels with our share of Maria's things. To my surprise she agreed to bring them round the next day.

But when she turned up the next morning she and M. Roire brought only seven parcels. I thought at first that this was all they could carry and that the rest would come later but as we spoke it became clear that this was all there was.

'What happened to the other ninety parcels?' I enquired, but Vasso only looked puzzled as if I had been imagining things. When I forcefully pointed out that I wasn't confused and was very well aware that there had been no less than ninety-seven parcels intended for me, Vasso was very shocked.

'It must have been Meneghini,' she said. 'He must have driven off with them. It's the only explanation. These seven are all I've ever had in store at my place.'

Mother was nodding furiously. It was clear to her that her ex-son-in-law had absconded with our share. I was confused. Meneghini may have had many faults but he had always seemed a gentleman to me and not the sort of person who would stoop to stealing parcels from women. But who was I to argue when they both seemed so certain?

Vasso said she would write to Meneghini via Bensusan the lawyer, asking if he'd accidentally carried off our share. 'We'll see what he says to that.'

But a few days later she called to say that Meneghini's reply had been: 'I did what I wanted.' So it seemed that he had taken them and was completely unrepentant. I was left with the unpleasant thought that my ex-brother-in-law had stolen my sister's things from me.

It was now that Vasso set about organising a public exhibition of our half of Maria's mementoes from the blue room, her 'museum'. The mayor of Paris, Jacques Chirac, had agreed that this should take place in the Musée Carnavalet, which meant that Vasso was now very busy and could no longer spend as much time with us as she had.

She found us a Portuguese maid, Odette, and she was a little company though not as much as Vasso had been. Odette would do her housework then sit entranced as I practised at the piano strengthening my voice, getting back to where I had been. Odette loved to listen to me and it gave me confidence to have an audience, albeit of one. But when Odette went home I was completely alone again, with only the canaries for company until Mother woke from her siesta and began to complain. By then even she, who had suffered many New York winters, was beginning to feel the intense cold of that unique year. Everybody moaned about it. The television was full of it. I can remember going shopping with Odette one day, well wrapped up in a heavy coat and boots and yet still standing on the edge of the pavement almost unable to move because of the freezing wind. I thought I would die right there and prayed to be allowed to return to Athens. But Mother would still not give in. Even a most miserable Christmas only dented her resolve. Odette was away with her family and our only outing was to yet another restaurant for Christmas lunch with Vasso and M. Roire.

'Shouldn't we go home where we have friends and family?' I asked Mother when we returned to the chilly apartment, though in truth I had few friends in Athens either. My real longing was for a more friendly climate. But I knew that Mother had always led a very sociable existence and might be persuaded to go back to it.

But if our Christmas had begun quietly it was suddenly and dramatically thrown into confusion. The morning following

Christmas Day I switched on the radio and heard the announcer say that the ashes of Maria Callas had been stolen from their resting place in Père Lachaise Cemetery. Mother was half-horrified and half-excited at the prospect of all the fuss that was bound to be made. We hung about the apartment waiting for the stream of reporters that Mother was sure would descend on the only relatives of the desecrated diva. Her fury when the evening news revealed Vasso making a plea for the return of the ashes may be imagined. She had offered herself as the official spokesman and had been accepted as such. Just as the bulletin ended there was a ring on our doorbell and I hurried to the entryphone where a solitary journalist announced himself. Mother was barely pacified, but one was better than none and she prepared to give him a good story.

'It was obviously her ex-husband Meneghini who has stolen my daughter's remains,' she announced unequivocally. 'The man is obsessed with Maria and seems to believe that everything that was hers must now be his – including her ashes it seems.'

The young man happily scribbled it all down and hurried away.

He was no sooner out of the door than the television announced that the ashes had been found in another part of the cemetery. It had evidently been the work of a madman.

'It couldn't have been Meneghini,' I said. 'He's in Italy. You'd better call that newspaper and tell them not to print what you said.' But it was no use, we hadn't asked what paper the journalist represented and Mother's wild statements were published the next day.

Vasso called the next day and said that she would see that nothing further happened to Maria's ashes – she had a plan, she said, but did not reveal what.

That month we again went to Geneva where we met Meneghini in a vault in the Union de Banques Suisses. He seemed much older than before, not nearly as sharp as when we last met, though his old-style courtesy never lapsed. He greeted me with his usual courtliness and I decided I could not bear to bring up the matter of the missing parcels. Indeed I tried to apologise for Mother's remarks to the press about the missing ashes but he rather grandly waved that aside. As we spoke a clerk brought in the metal coffer in which Maria's jewels were kept. As soon as I saw it I was gripped by a sensation of dread – the box was the same shape as that in which her ashes had been put, even the metal had the same colour and sheen. It brought back all the horror of that cold day and that hideous grim place. I watched appalled and fascinated as the lid was prised open expecting to see, what . . .?

In the end all that was there were the diamonds, the brooches and clips and earrings. But to me it was as if my sister had been transformed into hard stone – her heart a ruby, her eyes two dark sapphires. I couldn't speak and when I looked over at Meneghini I was equally transfixed by his reactions – there were two people struggling for dominance: a look of almost insatiable desire crossed his face as he set eyes again on this precious hoard. I thought he was going to reach across and plunge his hands into the glittering heap. On the other hand he suddenly looked unbearably downcast as he saw again the gifts he had given Maria during the happy years of their marriage. It was odd, they both had a reputation for remarkable stinginess; at La Scala people were said to rejoice if either of them bought so much as a cup of coffee, yet her love of diamonds had managed to overcome it. Now he sat looking at the final evidence of the one great passion of his life glinting there like so many shards of broken glass. I pitied him.

I barely glanced at the Onassis collection that was the family's share. Vasso had them returned to the strong-box for safe keeping and that was that. Meneghini gathered himself up and, still crestfallen, bent to kiss my hand.

'Goodbye, dear lady, until the next time we meet.'

I never saw him again.

On the flight back to Paris Vasso told me again about her difficulties now that her career was over and, much distressed, I told her not to worry, and that I intended to help her out.

But once back at the apartment in Neuilly I had other more immediate problems to deal with – Mother was again ill. The intense cold, the loneliness, the incessant worrying over her failure to succeed in Parisian society had provoked another attack of diabetes. As soon as Vasso and I entered the salon and saw her slumped in a chair we knew we would have to get her seen to. The ever-helpful M. Roire was summoned and he arranged a hospital bed at once. It was evident that things could no longer go on as they were but it took a further three months of this misery before Mother would finally admit defeat and it was Easter before we could pack up our things and return to Greece.

Not that our problems were instantly resolved – we now had no home in Athens and were obliged to move into a new hotel near the Champs de Mars not far from our old home in Patission. Strangely enough it was called the Park Hotel, the same as the place that we had taken refuge in during the civil war all those years ago when I still had Milton to take care of me. Our furniture went into store and there we lived with the canaries who seemed as happy as I was to absorb the warmth of a Greek spring. After that bitterly cold sojourn in Paris everything seemed to be blue skies and wild flowers. Even Mother forgot her complaints for a while as she took up with her old cronies who could now be invited round for coffee in the restaurant overlooking the park.

I must admit I rather enjoyed this interlude. I could escape to my room and only had to join Mother for our meals which were of course cooked by someone else. The allowance we drew from the money Vasso arranged for us seemed to be adequate for all this and we two women who had been used to living on next to nothing felt very spoiled and reasonably content. It seemed that at last I could make a life for myself – I even met an old friend from my singing days, Irene Sakellaredis who had gone with me to that competition in Italy. Sometimes, if her husband Aristedes was busy, she would come round and join me and from time to time we met up with other ex-pupils of Mr Vithinos. Irene was a good friend, though as she explained, she and Aristedes, who was a retired bank clerk, didn't have much money. Nevertheless, they worked hard to make ends meet and I tried to help by treating her whenever she came round to see me. It was good to have a little money to be able to do things like that and Mother felt that too. She arranged dowries for one of her sister's daughters and did her best to cope with the requests of the family. All in all it was quite a busy time. I could indulge myself with regular visits to the beauty parlour at the hotel and got to enjoy my chats with the manicurist who would tell me all the silly gossip of the place. After my years of solitude it was fun to be paid attention to and, along with the warm weather, I felt happy at last.

So much so that my mind turned more and more to the problems that Vasso had now that she had lost her career. As I explained to Mother, without her we might have had nothing. We could never have challenged Meneghini on our own and who is to say that, unopposed, the French courts might not have declared him to be the sole inheritor of Maria's estate? Such contentment as we now had was surely largely due to Vasso and yet she had asked for nothing.

She had told us she was working away setting up the Foundation and we were living happily in the Park Hotel. We had, I insisted, to do something. But Mother would not agree so I decided on my own that as we now had sufficient to live off we should find a way to give Vasso the same independence. I decided to sell off the Onassis jewels and give the money to her; that way she and we would never have to worry about her situation again. I wrote to Vasso and told her to arrange for the sale and that May I flew to Geneva to join her at the bank. We met a representative of a Swiss diamond broker who had come to examine the stones and a figure of four hundred thousand dollars was agreed. He handed over the money in cash, there in the vault, and when he had gone I pushed it towards Vasso.

'I think you should have this,' I said. 'To give you financial independence – for all that you've done.'

She looked at me with the same long, penetrating stare she had used when we first met and her thank you was almost a whisper.

'What are you going to do with the rest of the money?' she asked. 'You both need a place to live.'

I supposed that was true and indeed we had been half-heartedly looking for two apartments somewhere but the truth was that we were so content in the hotel there seemed little reason to rush things.

'You should invest your money carefully,' Vasso said. 'Property is always good. Get yourselves somewhere in Athens by all means but I have another proposal – why not buy out Meneghini's share of the Paris apartment? All the shares in the company that nominally owns it are here in the bank. Instead of selling the place and dividing the money, why not buy him out and sell the place yourself? With me to help you I'm certain you could sell it for more. In fact I know a very rich Arab who's looking for a place.'

I really had nothing to say. What did I know about such things?

'You have your mother's power of attorney,' Vasso insisted. 'You can decide. It's really the most sensible thing to do.'

I must have looked truly confused and miserable at this point because Vasso stretched over to take my hand. 'I know, I know,' she said. 'These things confuse you. There are so many things to decide about Maria's work, her copyrights, her recordings. There are many things already waiting for a decision.'

'I don't know about those things,' I protested. 'I really don't.'

She squeezed my hand. 'Don't worry,' she said. 'I'll deal with them all.'

As we left the bank and emerged into the bright midday sunshine Vasso revealed that she had resolved the problem of Maria's ashes. The Greek government had agreed that they should be scattered on the Aegean and that the ceremony was to be arranged for the following month. I wasn't at all sure about this; it seemed too far from what Maria would have wanted, just like the cremation itself. But what could I do? If the government was involved who could stop it?

Back in Athens Mother was as disturbed as I was but agreed that there was nothing we could do. She had heard about a new apartment block two streets from the hotel and a short walk from our old home in Patission. The block was just being completed and there were two floors, the fifth and the sixth, available if we wanted them. Although I was reluctant to leave the hotel I had to agree that such a move was inevitable and that this was an ideal arrangement. We decided to go ahead.

While the legal process was under way the day of the ceremony drew near. We received formal invitations from the Greek Ministry of Culture but to Mother this was a certain sign that far from being at the centre of the affair we were to be treated as ordinary guests. Once again, so it appeared, the starring rôle would go to Vasso, the prime mover in the whole affair. Mother promptly declared herself unfit to attend, so again the burden of representing the family fell upon me. I dreaded the occasion. Since the events of the occupation we had not been held in especially high esteem by the Greek authorities and there were those in the press who occasionally sniped at Maria, hinting that her behaviour during the war had been less than correct. On balance the Greek people were, by the time of her death, exceptionally proud of her international reputation and delighted that she had left her Italian husband for a romance with another famous Greek. This pride probably overrode any lingering qualms about her youthful reputation but my instinct was always to let things rest. This notion of taking part in a major national ceremony disturbed me. However, when Vasso arrived she was full of confidence and told me not to be so silly.

Much of that June day passed in a daze as I was introduced to dignitaries I had never heard of and whisked about from place to place. Vasso took me to the harbour at Piraeus where a destroyer of the Greek navy was waiting to sail us out into the Aegean to the spot chosen for the scattering. It was a sunny summer day but as soon as we left the safety of the harbour I realised that it was blustery with a high sea wind. I have little experience of sailing apart from the American voyages and that one cruise with Milton, but I do seem to be quite a good sailor. Others on board were not so fortunate. The warship bucked and heaved in a brisk Aegean swell and the wind howled in the turret. It was evident to me that Maria definitely did not approve of this business and I tried to shrink into myself and keep as small as possible. Unaware of any adverse signs Vasso was happily buzzing around the minister, playing hostess to the occasion. Far from feeling put out by this I was only too glad she was drawing attention away from me.

Why they had chosen one spot in the sea as opposed to another I could not say – for that matter I am still unclear why they imagined that my sister would wish to be put into the water at all. She had certainly enjoyed some of the period with Onassis on his yacht but that hardly seemed a reason to throw her ashes into that element. If asked, I am certain she would have wanted to be buried beside Ari but it is unlikely the family would have agreed to such a thing. So why not Paris where she had chosen to live out her last years? Anyway, it was too late. The minister made a speech. The usual things about Maria's greatness were said, much of them lost in the air, carried off by the wind.

Vasso held the casket, that same grim box that had so upset me in that cold vault a year earlier. She handed it to the minister and for a moment they both wrestled with the lid. The priest intoned a prayer and then the minister approached the rail and tipped the contents over the side. Precisely at that moment, the worst gust of wind of the whole day blew in from the sea and just as Maria's fluffy grey ashes left the receptacle they were instantly blown back over us all. Vasso received most of the fine powder full in her face and as she had her mouth wide open in order to catch her breath in the driving spray, a great deal went straight down her throat. She began to splutter and retch. Indeed we all got some in the face and mouth and were forced to spit and cough it up. The wind howled in the turret. The ship's horn was sounded in mournful tribute, though it appeared more like the moan of an anguished spirit. Rubbing my lips with my handkerchief I looked around at the illustrious party and realised that we were all swallowing Maria's remains. We were helplessly eating my sister; the greatest diva of the century was being consumed by those who had thought to placate her spirit.

209

It was a somewhat subdued crowd that said farewell at Piraeus.

When I got home Mother told me off for having a smudge on my nose. 'You should always check your make-up,' she said. 'What must the minister have thought.'

I said nothing.

Following the ceremony, Vasso turned her attention more and more on the outstanding problem of the Paris apartment. She said she had now contacted the wealthy Arab and if we bought the half share from Meneghini we could sell at a great profit. As we were about to move into our new apartments and had many outgoings, the thought of this money seemed very appealing. I was worried, having no experience of financial matters but Mother was very taken with the idea and agreed with Vasso that we should go ahead. As it turned out Vasso had already approached Meneghini and he was agreeable. All we needed to do was go again to Geneva and sign the papers. His lawyer would handle his side of things.

I don't know why I had such doubts about this one thing among all the other financial deals I was now associated with. Perhaps it was because Maria's apartment had seemed so personal to her that it struck me as wrong for us to be using it as a way of making a quick profit. I had wanted it to be a museum, now I was the one selling it off. The cost of the half share had been put at three hundred and eighty-five thousand dollars but with the lawyer's fees it added up to four hundred and twenty thousand dollars. I had also given Vasso a further one hundred thousand dollars for herself so that she had had a clear half million altogether. That, and the nearly eight hundred thousand dollars paid over to her for the Foundation between 1978 and 1980, accounted for the bulk of the inheritance.

In a way such enormous sums of money were meaningless to someone like me who had always been used to scraping and saving. It did not especially worry me that the money had all been paid over to Vasso: it was only right that I had done as Maria had wished and I didn't particularly want such wealth, it unnerved me after the years of poverty. But then again, the money hadn't really run out if there was this wealthy Arab waiting to buy the Paris apartment. It seemed like an endless flow of dollars and I was as ever quite satisfied that Vasso should be out there dealing with it all.

Again I was summoned to Geneva and once again I sat in a vault, this time in the Discount Bank. The shares were brought from the deposit box and Vasso and Meneghini's lawyer completed the formalities. On instructions, I signed for that huge sum and the lawyer pushed the shares over to me where they lay before me on the table. It was strange to think that Mother and I now owned Maria's home, a place she had never invited us to visit, where indeed she had made it very clear she never wanted to see us. The lawyer left and I sat there alone with Vasso again.

'Good,' she said. 'You did very well.'

Something in her voice, a tone of self-congratulation, irritated me. I looked at her with the same intensity she had with me.

'I don't think we should sell Maria's apartment,' I said, surprised that I had got the words out.

Her eyebrows shot to the top of her forehead. 'And why not?'

'I think we should set up a museum. The Foundation could be there.'

It was a wonderful idea and I was pleased it had come up on the spur of the moment.

'Don't worry about that,' she said firmly. 'I've sorted everything out.'

I started to rake in the shares fanned out before me but before I could gather them all in she leaned across the table and yanked them from my hands.

'I'll take these,' she said, her voice deathly cold. 'I'll put them somewhere safe. We'll keep them in the Discount Bank.'

I shrank back in my chair petrified, unable to so much as protest as she pulled the papers into a pile, lifted and bounced them straight, then stuffed them into an ordinary plastic shopping bag she had brought.

I made the sign of the cross three times in the Orthodox manner: the sign against danger.

'Come along,' she said. 'It's time for you to be getting back.'

I tried to explain all this to Mother when I returned but she said I was probably getting upset over nothing. It was better that Vasso should look after these matters. What did I know about such things? She was right, of course, I did know nothing about business. We now had enough to live on, so there seemed no point in getting ourselves involved in these details. Soon after my return to Athens we completed the purchase of our apartments and had no time for anything but the business of moving. Of course with Mother's health as it was, it fell to me to arrange both places: getting our furniture out of store and buying the endless things we needed to make the rooms comfortable. At the same time Mother had to have her meals and be kept happy. If I was out shopping too long she would complain that I was deserting her. Only if one of her relations or friends called was I free to do as I pleased, otherwise she expected me to be there to amuse her. I began to regret leaving the hotel where I had had some time to myself. After all the excitement and foreign travel my life was gradually sinking back into its old routine; the long empty days mainly devoted to fending off Mother's carping displeasure.

'You're late. Where have you been all morning? I needed a cup of coffee. You know, Jackie, you need to smarten up a bit. You should try to be more like your sister; she had style.'

On and on it went, alternating with periods of deep gloom as she sat at her window mourning her lost daughter, mouthing the sad little poems she had created in her honour.

I never complained. Never asked her to leave me in peace. I pitied her; she had thrown everything into her dreams for Maria and had been rewarded with nothing but misery. How could I add to it by crossing her?

My only friend was Irene, my old fellow music student who would call to see me from time to time. It helped to listen to her recount the difficulties of life on a small pension; at least there was someone else who had problems. It made me feel a lot less isolated. One day I heard that the third floor in our building was to be sold. It was a better apartment than mine and I suggested to Mother that we should buy it. It then occurred to me that we could keep the fifth floor as an investment and maybe let Irene and her husband live there without paying rent to me. That would be a great help to them as they had great difficulty finding the rent where they were. It would also be good company for me, someone to talk with apart from Mother. Inevitably Mother had doubts about the idea, no doubt suspecting that the presence of Irene would distract me from what she considered my full-time rôle of taking care of her, but I suppose she also suspected that if she pushed me too far things might backfire.

Irene was delighted, of course, and she and her husband were soon installed and helping me set up my new place. Just being two floors from Mother made a world of difference; it felt less like living together and more as if I had a truly independent existence. I gave the canaries their own room just as I always had in the past and they sang more sweetly than ever.

Of course now that everything was nearly settled we heard less and less from Vasso. She occasionally phoned to say that things were going well but never bothered us with details. Evidently she had set up a Foundation but where and what it was and what it was going to do was never forthcoming. I continued to send her money until the end of 1980, but there was no sign of any activity, though if pressed she always had a ready excuse. On one occasion I asked her if I could have the shares in the apartment transferred from the Discount Bank in Geneva to my own bank but her answer astonished me. She said that as the Discount Bank was run by Jews there was a real risk that it might be bombed by Arab terrorists so she had already transferred the shares to her notary in Paris and I should stop worrying about them.

In truth, the whole of 1980 was yet another of my empty years. Although we now had a little money, it was as if I had returned to that vacuum I had occupied after the death of Milton. Day succeeded day without anything to cause as much as a ripple on the placid waters of my existence. Even Mother's constant complaints about my shortcomings came to seem no more than the rumble of the traffic in the distant streets. Life was suspended. I rose, the housekeeper would come, I would do my chores, shower and make up, take the lift to Mother's apartment for lunch, return for my siesta, go up again for dinner, descend to sleep. The only hiccup in this flat existence was the rare call from Vasso. After a while it became clear that the rich Arab had fallen through and that the apartment was not going to be sold. Secretly, I thought this best. It was a solid investment, by then the last of the inheritance, and I was aware that it was all that was left to us. Better it just remain as it was for a while.

Early in 1981 we read in the papers that Meneghini had died. I felt sorry, I had rather liked his old-style courtesy and had always believed Maria might never have got where she did without him. Despite everything he had really loved her and now that he was gone it meant that only Mother and I remained of those who had been close to her. The thought made me sad.

Vasso telephoned to ask if we had heard about Meneghini's death. She knew an incredible amount about his affairs and said that he had left everything to his maid Roverselli. It was sad that Maria's servants were not included. Bruna had retired to her village in Italy with the money we had given her and Ferruccio had gone to work for Christina Onassis, a curious finale to that story. But I would have liked them to have been remembered again.

213

When I said this to Vasso she got quite angry and said I was too soft.

Well, I thought, if all else goes wrong at least we have the apartment, but when I asked her about it she shattered all my illusions.

'There's a problem with the place,' she said. 'The French government has sent a tax bill for the last five years and it's you who will have to settle it.'

I protested that that was impossible, no one had ever mentioned such a thing but she told me that I knew nothing about these things and that we'd have to sell the apartment to settle the outstanding debt. For once I refused to accept that such a thing could be true, at which point she abruptly told me that a notary would come to Athens to explain it all. Of course, when he came he made it all seem so inevitable. Yes, there was a tax bill and yes, I would have to pay it. The sum he mentioned was indeed enormous, nearly the value of the apartment, so he said. I again demanded to know how such a thing could have happened but his explanations were beyond me. There would be something left over, he said reassuringly, only a little but something nevertheless. What could I say? The man was an expert, he had to be right.

In any case I had graver worries nearer home.

Despite her avowed dislike of him, something about Meneghini's death upset Mother. He was, after all, her son-in-law and I suppose his demise made her more aware of her own age and infirmity. As usual she took out her distress on me, her nagging rising to an unbearable peak. A few weeks after the news of the death I went up to her apartment a little late and as I opened the door I overheard her complaining to one of her friends about my shortcomings as a daughter – always uncaring, seldom coming to see her. If only Maria were alive, then everything would have been well, she claimed.

God knows why I let such stupidity bother me; I suppose I must have been exhausted. Whatever the reason, as soon as her guest had left, all my pent-up frustration burst out.

'What do you say these things for?' I demanded. 'Of course neither of us wanted Maria to be dead but she is and we should just be a little thankful that we now have a comfortable life. So why do you complain so much? Why do you nag me all the time? It's your nature, isn't it?'

214

That did it. She was instantly transformed into the same hell-cat Maria had been. 'My nature?' she shrieked. 'What do you mean talking to your mother like that?'

But for once I wasn't going to be cowed. 'Be careful, Mother,' I warned her. 'God sees everything and He dislikes ingratitude. God has given you the chance to live peacefully now, so there is no need to nag. Just what is it you want? Tell me.'

'I want you here.'

'It's impossible,' I protested. 'I can't be here all the time. Heaven knows I'm here enough.'

'You're a bad daughter,' she shrieked. 'You abandon your mother.'

That was too much. 'Be careful,' I warned her. 'Your sister died miserably ill – be careful God doesn't punish you in the same way.'

She fell silent for the first time. I had never ever spoken to her like that before.

'I'm sorry,' I said firmly, 'but I think your ingratitude will be repaid. Goodbye, I'm going down.'

The next day Irene hurried in to see me.

'What's going on?' she asked. 'I've just been to see your mother. She's in a terrible state, she says you cursed her.'

I explained that I'd merely fought back for once and that I wasn't going to apologise. It was about time I tried to put an end to the misery she was making of my life.

I went to see her that evening and she tried to control her tongue but I could see it was a superhuman effort on her part and I doubted it would last long.

Ten days later I awoke in the night to feel that horrible sinking in the stomach that tells us Athens is on the verge of an earthquake. There was a sudden sickening ripple and the clock on my wall fell to the ground and smashed. I went up to see if Mother was all right and found her sprawled on the ground at the entrance to the bathroom. She was in a terrible state.

'I can't move,' she said in a barely audible whisper. 'I can't move my legs.'

I tried to lift her but she was too heavy. It was like the episode with Milton all over again. Suddenly there was a ring at the door. One of the electricians who'd been doing some work for us had come to see if we needed help. He helped me get her into a chair, and I got a doctor but we already knew that she was in a bad way and were not surprised when he told us she had had a stroke. We got her settled in the bedroom and I tried to make her comfortable.

When they had all gone she looked at me ruefully. 'You cursed me,' she said, her voice quiet and pathetic.

When I finally returned to my apartment to sleep, I saw the smashed clock on the floor, its hands frozen at the moment when she must have fallen to the ground and I shivered at the thought.

If I had cursed her, the result brought no relief to me. Mother was now a helpless invalid and needed more care than before. At first I struggled to nurse her myself but I soon realised it was an impossible task and I hired two professional helpers so that she could have someone near her day and night. Nevertheless I was now expected to be with her as much as possible; she even obliged me to take breakfast with her so that my mornings were no longer free. And, of course, as soon as the first shock of her stroke had passed that old burning energy rose again and drove her forward. To her credit, she refused to accept her condition. While she wailed and complained bitterly, begging the Almighty to give her back her health and strength, she nevertheless resisted any idea that what had happened was irreparable. She made me find her a masseuse who tried to pummel some life back into her legs and feet. Though nothing worked she never stopped hoping. The force inside that woman was extraordinary and there was no difficulty in seeing where Maria had got all her manic powers from. And of course there was the inevitable obverse to the coin, the incessant whining and complaining, always directed at me. Having had my one moment of revolt there was nothing left for me to say. She could never change now and so I said nothing. For a year and a half she lay there and struggled against the inevitable. Anyone who came to the apartment always said how much they admired her courage, though they were spared the moods of bitter depression that were inflicted on me when we were alone.

With the two nurses to pay for, our income was now under considerable strain and my only hope was something from the proceeds from the sale of the apartment in Paris. By any reckoning this should have brought over a million dollars. Even with the tax bill that should have left a sum sufficient to take care of our needs for ever. I wrote to Vasso asking what was happening but got no reply. I telephoned again and again. Eventually she revealed that the sale was going ahead and that I had nothing to worry about.

After months of telephoning and insisting on having the money she eventually sent a cheque – eighty thousand dollars. That was all! I stared at the piece of paper in disbelief. That beautiful apartment in the heart of the most fashionable district in Paris had come down to a mere eighty thousand dollars.

By then Mother was beyond caring. In the spring of 1982 her health declined to a point where we could no longer take care of her at home. She was moved to a clinic where she could have constant attention and my old life with Milton returned as I spent my days trudging to and fro between my apartment and Mother's bedside. For four months she lay there, that incredible life force gradually seeping away. Near the end a little remorse seems to have crept in and one of the doctors told me that she had asked whether he knew anyone who might be a suitable husband for me.

'Someone to take care of Jackie when I'm gone.'

I felt like laughing when I heard. She who had done everything to ensure I would be always available finally wanted to marry me off. I told the doctor not to bother, I would manage on my own.

Still, she was not going to be deprived of the right to orchestrate her own departure. At the beginning of August she announced that she would 'leave' on the 18th or 20th and sure enough on the 18th she sank into a coma. I continued to sit with her and on the 20th I went with Irene and Aristedes for the morning session. At midday, Irene suggested we go home for some lunch. Mother had not spoken for three days and there was little point in our being there. I went with them to their apartment but during the meal a nurse rang to say that Mother had passed away. I thanked her for calling then went down to my apartment and sat with the canaries. They sensed my mood and didn't sing.

PART THREE
Myself

CHAPTER NINE
1982–1988

The silence was the best thing. The calm of my own apartment with only the canaries to break the peace of my days. Did I mind being alone? No, not after the years with Mother. Now all I wanted was to be free to do nothing. After all, I had had enough practice in being content with little. I was used to having just enough to pay the rent and feed myself. I possessed only a couple of skirts and blouses, three pairs of shoes and a winter coat. They were all I needed. I knew that now that I had Mother's part of Maria's fortune I could have changed all that. Why not go to Kolonaki to the fashionable shops and buy a new wardrobe? Why not have a luxurious holiday, maybe make friends, go out and about? No, it was too late for such things. Just thinking of them made me tired. I tried to imagine living in a grand apartment like Maria's with cupboards stuffed with unused clothes, with coats and shoes one had never worn. But the idea merely made me smile to myself. What could I possibly want with so much baggage, I who had reduced my life to a sparse minimum? No, this was not the time to suddenly transform myself into another creature. Perhaps Mary and I weren't so different after all – she had had all those things then hadn't wanted them. Despite all the cupboards overflowing with silks and satins she had withdrawn into herself just as I had.

Not that I was completely isolated. There were those who would call to see me, relatives, people I knew. They always seemed to have such troubles. Life was so expensive they told me, it was difficult bringing up a family on so little money. I listened and sympathised. I who had had such problems all my life could hardly be other than sympathetic. And if some of the money would help them then why not? I hardly needed it after all. I had gone on helping Irene and Aristedes by letting them live free in the upstairs apartment and there were many others now who seemed to need assistance. Effi, the daughter of mother's sister Pepitsa was a frequent visitor. She had such troubles, her husband Nikos had lost his job as an accountant with a metalwork company and they could barely get by on their savings. They owned their apartment but had got into debt. Athens was getting more and more expensive yet what could they do?

Their main problem was space – they needed a larger house for the three children. So I decided to help them by paying off the debt and giving them three million seven hundred thousand drachmas to build a larger apartment above the one they had. I then gave them another three million drachmas to make them financially independent. It seemed such a little thing to give them the money to buy their own place and help them furnish it. Then there was a niece Vassiliki on my father's side who had almost the same problem. I gave her a furnished apartment.

Why did I give so much away? If I had not been kept so isolated, first by Milton, later by Mother, I might have acted differently. But it seemed so simple. I had money I did not wish to use, others needed it so why not help? I gave my maid Popi a new large apartment which I furnished and I gave her two million drachmas. I gave three million to Guido, the son of my cousin Mirka by her first husband, an Italian. Then there was Heleni Maurogeni, a friend of Irene, to whom I gave two million.

Perhaps deep down I just wanted to be rid of it, so that I could say to myself, 'Look, you have not profited from your sister's success. Let others have it if they need it.'

The bulk of the money still went to the Foundation and that seemed to me as it should be. The problem was that I never heard of anything it was doing and on the rare occasions when Vasso now called me there were only excuses and complicated reasons why this and that still needed to be done. But I told myself it was what Mary had wanted and that I should not regret that most of the fortune had gone in that way.

My one self-indulgence was my music. Free at last of any pressure I decided I really did want to sing again. Ambition? Perhaps there was a little of that lingering somewhere deep inside me. I who had had nothing, who had done nothing, all because others had kept me that way, I had had my dreams. Of course when I read about Mary's success, of course when I saw her picture in magazines, when I watched her accepting the ecstatic applause of thousands at Epidaurus, of course I had said to myself that could have been me. Is that so surprising?

There is no need for a voice to age. If your general health is good then the voice can be in good form. It's not the throat so much as a strong diaphragm. All those daily exercises since my New York modelling days had ensured that there was no slackness as far as my muscles were concerned. A voice can wear out if it is overused or strained and indeed that was probably the case with Mary. But I had certainly not done that. After that last concert, before I abandoned all hope of a singing career to nurse Milton, I had barely used my voice at all. Now I began to practise again. Just a little at first to build up my vocal strength, but then more as I realised that it was still there like a thin seam of gold in a rock. I began to get quite excited. What if I could sing again? Why shouldn't I have one last chance to do something, to be me? Without Mary there was no one to say I was merely using her name to build myself up. I could stand or fall by myself now. I went to the drawer where I kept the poster for my concert and looked at the photograph that had been taken especially for the programme. Could I do it again? Could I practise and practise to the point where I could stand up in front of a crowded concert hall and sing all evening – a second Callas, the only Callas? Ah well, it was my dream and everyone is entitled to that. But could I?

I found a new music teacher, Professor Antonio Kalaitzakis. He would call two or three times a week to set my voice exercises and correct any faults. At that early stage it was all very technical, one doesn't just burst into song straight off. But I looked forward to these sessions as the high spots of my week. Alone, I would run up and down my scales testing myself. It was good to feel my voice gaining strength again, to know that I could project and to sense the higher register firming up. Gradually I began to get out my music and to relearn the arias I'd sung for my concert. Sometimes halfway through a piece I'd suddenly stop, memories of that night rushing back, overwhelming me with sadness at what might have been. I had a voice, why had I not . . .

But it was pointless to think like that. Could I do it now? Professor Kalaitzakis was encouraging, the voice was there, the diaphragm strong. He was such a sympathetic man. After I'd finished practising we'd talk a little. He'd had a tragic life; he had been destined for a brilliant career as a tenor but had caught a chill in his throat when quite young and this had permanently damaged his voice. Now he had to get by teaching others. Naturally I told him I would be happy to help him and over time I gave him two million drachmas to enable him and his family to live more comfortably.

It seemed good to be able to do things like that. I especially wanted to help Maria Theodoropoulou who had been our hairdresser in the days when Mother and I had lived in the Park Hotel. When Mother was sick and bedridden, Maria had come to the apartment to do her hair and one day after Mother's death when I was feeling particularly lonely Maria asked me if I would like to come to her apartment to meet her family. When I arrived I was shocked to discover that she lived in a two-room flat with her mother, sister and the sister's two children. The sister's home had been destroyed in the earthquake and they were all forced to cram into Maria's place and there was no money to do anything about it. It made me very sad to see a family suffer like that and I knew at once that I had to help. I gave her enough to get a decent furnished apartment and to be independent. We both hoped that she might be able to find a husband now that she had a dowry but that didn't work out. In the end I helped almost all the people who did anything for me – two million drachmas to my dressmaker Sosso Kroustali and the same amount to Stefos Giossos, the man who made my curtains and upholstery.

One morning, early in 1983, I was just closing the piano lid after a particularly long but satisfying session on a new piece the professor had set for me when I heard what sounded at first like something scratching near the main door of the apartment. Puzzled, I went to see who was there but when I opened the door there was no one. I turned back and it was then that I saw a piece of folded notepaper that must have been pushed under the door. I bent down and picked it up. It would have been better if I had simply thrown it in the wastepaper basket unread. It was a letter of sorts, crudely written in scrawled capital letters; the language, too, was crude. The message however, was simple: wild allegations about a family I'd been helping. That was the substance of the missive, but the way it was expressed was very violent, the whole thing clearly motivated by jealousy and greed. I dropped the paper and went to sit down for a moment. This was something new in my experience and I wasn't sure how to handle it. I went upstairs to tell Irene and found Popi, my maid, there. She had gone to borrow something, I forget what. I told them about the letter and they were full of surprise and concern – who could have done such a thing? How terrible. They made me sit down again. Should I tell the police? They thought not, after all what could they do? Better to try to forget the whole thing. I went back downstairs and tried to shut out all thought of that vile paper by playing the piano but my heart wasn't in it.

I worried about it for days. I had not thought I was especially loved but equally I had never imagined I was hated. Someone out there was my enemy and the thought distressed me greatly. It made me realise just how isolated I was. Mother may have been destructive, even vile on occasions, but she had been there, another human being to talk things over with. Now no one. It made me think also of my family, my remaining cousins and their children. I felt closest to Mirka who had never asked for anything and I still kept in touch with Heleni, the daughter of my aunt in Florida with whom I'd spent such happy holidays as a child. Somehow that letter had made me realise that I could not go on living for ever. The thought that someone hated me made me think about death, my own death, for the first time. What would become of Mary's inheritance? I had already made a will leaving future income to Vasso for the use of the Foundation but there were also the apartments in Athens and other things I had inherited. I decided to make a will and found a notary. Then one of my relatives said her husband would drive me to the office and he insisted on accompanying me when I was shown into the office. I told the notary how I wanted to divide up my assets among my various relations and friends, something for each of them and he took it all down. When we got out to the car, my companion didn't seem best pleased and wanted to know why this one or that one was to get something. I was confused. Surely I'd done the right thing in giving them all a share? So why was the man so unhappy about it? How little I understood human nature.

Worse was to come. The man must have spread the word of what I had done, for soon there was an endless procession of supplicants, each protesting that he or she had greater claims than this one or that one to my money. Only my good cousin Mirka, the mother of Guido, stood up for me. Ten days after the signing of the will I was involved in a terrifying incident which did not help my frame of mind. I had been upstairs with Irene and Aristedes watching a late-night film, about a murder case. Irene said she would accompany me back

225

down the stairs to my door. I went ahead and as I turned on to my landing I saw someone trying to turn a key in my lock. Hearing our approach, the figure spun round – there was a stocking mask pulled over his face and he was holding a gun. We screamed and screamed, Aristedes came leaping down the stairs, nearly falling on the way. The terrifying figure blundered past us and disappeared.

We called the police but there was nothing they could do. There were no fingerprints and, apart from telling me to get a safer set of locks, little they could say. I knew someone had organised that apparition as a warning, but who it was I could not say. As I lay in bed that night with the bedroom door locked, I wished I had never got involved with Maria's money. There was a curse on it and I was its latest victim.

I fitted the new locks and put in an alarm, but now isolated in that sealed apartment my loneliness seemed complete. I no longer wished even to go upstairs to join Irene and Aristedes; I was cut off from the world.

One day Professor Kalaitzakis rang to say that he was not feeling well enough to visit me but would be delighted if I could go round to his place. I jumped at the chance to get out for a change, to get away from all those grasping people. I made an extra effort over my make-up and dress, determined to enjoy my little excursion.

When Mrs Kalaitzakis opened the door I could see a gentleman standing in the salon. He was handsome, smartly dressed in a suit and I wondered who he could be. Mrs Kalaitzakis made excuses for her husband, he would be there soon and would I mind waiting a little. She led me into the salon and introduced me to the other caller, a Dr Stathopoulos. He was, she explained, another pupil who'd dropped in on his way from work. She went to get coffee and I sat and talked with my fellow student. It was wonderful to be able to talk with someone about something other than money. I'd forgotten what it was like just to have an innocent conversation, especially with someone who shared my interest in music. He asked if he might wait while I practised and I agreed. Professor Kalaitzakis took me through my exercises then he suggested Dr Stathopoulos join us for a duet. He had a rich, powerful tenor voice and it was great fun to sing along with him, just letting the sounds pour forth.

'You sing very well together,' Kalaitzakis said. 'Perhaps you should have lessons together.'

Although we never arranged that, it did seem to happen that often when I went over to the house Andreas, as I soon learned to call him, would also be there. One day he asked if I would like to join him for supper afterwards and from then on we would often go for a meal or just a stroll among the crowds out for the evening parade.

One day after a particularly bad session of squabbling relatives I must have looked particularly depressed and when he asked me what was wrong the whole tale of woe came pouring out.

'But why do you put up with them?' he insisted. 'You don't have to.'

Of course he was right but what could I say? How could I explain what I thought about Mary and her money when I'd barely rationalised it for myself? Glad of a sympathetic ear I suddenly told him the whole story about Vasso and the fortune I had handed over to her. Even as I spoke I could sense his incredulity and in the telling I too began to see just how ludicrous the whole thing was.

Anyone else might have laughed at me, would certainly have told me what a stupid woman I'd been, would at least have thought I was simple-minded. Andreas merely looked at me and said, 'You're too good. You should have kept it for yourself.'

But I just shook my head. 'I couldn't,' I said. 'I really couldn't.'

Suddenly I didn't want to talk about it any more. I'd had enough of the Callas fortune and all the misery it brought. I wanted something else out of life, I wanted to be part of life.

'Tell me about yourself,' I said. It was just like the old days, letting the man do all the talking but this time I really wanted to know. 'Let's not talk about money, just tell me what you do, tell me all of it.'

And he did. He told me how he had a degree to teach internal medicine at the university though he had not done so, but he also had his own practice, partly private, partly within our national health service.

'Are you married?' I enquired.

He smiled ruefully. He had been but it had turned out badly. It was when he was a young intern and the woman had tricked him into marrying her, only to turn out selfish and unhelpful. The marriage had collapsed almost as soon as it began. He had divorced her and since then had lived alone, concentrating on his work and his music. There was no need to say anything, he knew I understood.

That weekend we drove out to Kiffissia where I had loved to go with Milton and walking again among the trees of that peaceful place I felt as if I had found again something that had been missing from my life. All the pent-up sadness came pouring out as I unfolded to Andreas the litany of what had happened to me, first with Milton and the years following his death, then since Maria's death and now in the year since Mother had died. He listened patiently and said that if he could do anything at all to help I had only to ask. From the beginning I liked his rather old-fashioned manner; his politeness was something I remembered from the past and was not often found today. I began to look forward more and more to our times together.

As that summer progressed and I took Andreas more and more into my confidence he began to encourage me to stand up for myself. I began to telephone Vasso insisting she explain what the Foundation was doing and to send me a full account of its finances.

With Andreas beside me I found the courage to go on insisting and for once Vasso did not try to browbeat me into giving up. Instead she was all wheedling sweetness, protesting her affection for me and assuring me I should have everything I requested. To sort it all out she would come to Athens to see me.

'I'd better come to the meeting,' Andreas said. 'That ought to surprise her.'

She arrived on November 4th and stayed at the Grande Bretagne, still the most expensive hotel in Athens. She came round that day and was indeed surprised to find Andreas there too.

'Ah,' she said. 'That explains a lot.'

With Andreas nodding his encouragement I asked her how things were with the Foundation.

'Would it be at all possible,' I asked, 'to see some accounts? After all, so much money has been handed over and nothing seems to have happened.' I only got it all out because Andreas was there.

She gave him a sharp look then immediately went on the offensive. What was I suggesting? Was I hinting that there was something wrong?

I shook my head. I just wanted the whole thing to stop. Why had I started this?

Andreas spoke up. He was very calm but very cold. He told her no one was suggesting anything. All that was wanted was an account of the money given, quite simple really.

Vasso calmed down. She became her old persuasive self. Of course, of course, how right he was, of course she would see to it. She hadn't done it because there had been so much else to do. Didn't I know how much she was doing for me? After all where would I have been if she hadn't stepped in after Maria's death?

What could I say? I always found it impossible to argue with her.

She then produced a piece of paper from her bag. 'There's another little problem,' she said. 'The Moral Right. I had the authority to use it from your mother, but now that she's dead . . .'

What did I know about all that? I looked at her, confused as ever.

'I need it again,' she explained. 'From you; you simply sign this. It's so useful when dealing with all the papers.'

I looked at Andreas but he too seemed unsure about what she was doing. More to get rid of her than anything, I signed.

When she'd gone Andreas praised my courage. 'She's a clever woman,' he said. 'I'm not sure you should have signed that paper but this is all new to me. I'll see if I can find out what she's actually doing.'

We went to Costoyannis Taverna, by then one of our favourite places and we tried to make sense of what had been happening.

'I'm not happy here,' I said. 'It's all too much for me. I have no friends except you, and Mirka. I don't think I can cope with it any more. I'd like to live somewhere else.'

He smiled. 'Where?' he asked.

'Oh, I don't know. Somewhere completely new. Like . . .' I thought for a moment. 'Like England,' I said. 'I'd like to live in London.'

'And so would I,' he said without hesitation. 'I've always wanted to go to London. For me it's the mecca, the mecca for medicine. I'd love to practise there.' He looked at me very hard. 'Do you really want to?' he asked.

'Yes.'

'There's one thing, though. As a doctor I could not be seen to be travelling with someone who was not my wife.'

It took me a moment to realise that he had proposed to me. I doubt I have ever been so pleasantly confused.

Alone in my apartment I tried to make sense of what was happening. I had wanted a life, wanted what anyone else would regard as a real existence but I had hardly thought this would be the route I would take. Andreas had not pressed me for an answer which, given my confusion, was just as well. He had said that he realised it was an enormous step for us both. He wanted above all, he said, to help me sort out the confusion my affairs had got into. It would be his privilege to protect me. It was a very tempting offer. I liked his company and I was so used to having someone take care of me. I could only look at what had happened since I had been on my own to realise that it was perhaps better for me to surrender the task to someone else. But I was also frightened of making the biggest mistake of all. I was so used to being alone, how could I cope with having another person close to me?

Andreas was very patient about the whole thing. He explained to me that after his unhappy experience he needed someone understanding with whom he could be happy and he said he was now sure that I was what he was looking for. The more I saw what a polite sincere person he was the closer I felt towards him and the more my doubts receded. I had always been alone. Milton had been the love of my youth. That love had not ended in marriage but who was to say it would have worked had it done so? I had seen enough to know that most people change after they wed and that made it hard for me to embark on this adventure. Used as I was to being alone how could I cope with having someone so close to me? But as time went on I was happy to let him take over more and more of the problems that had arisen over the inheritance. It was so good to know I could rely on someone. One day he was visiting when he remarked that I often seemed to wear the same clothes – it was so like myself and Bruna in Paris. I laughed and showed him my wardrobe with its handful of things but he didn't find it at all amusing. Instead he got very angry and said it was outrageous that I had so little when other people were living well on my money and with that he stormed out of the apartment only to return an hour later with a new dress for me. It was the first of a shower of gifts of new clothes. And again I rather liked it. All my life people had been picking my wardrobe for me and when I was free to do so myself I had simply given up trying. Now here was someone willing to do so again and I found it quite relaxing.

One day he came round as I was about to feed Milton, the last surviving canary. I took Andreas in to see him and he went up to the cage, making the usual noises to amuse the bird. Milton, however, went berserk, I have never seen such a jealous tantrum; he squawked around the cage in an uncontrollable fit.

'He's really jealous of you,' I laughed, and that night I agreed to marry him.

Shortly afterwards, Vasso telephoned to see how things were. I asked her how the Foundation was going and she started to complain that there wasn't sufficient money. But what about the seven hundred and ninety-two thousand dollars, I demanded, but she only snorted and said she knew nothing about such money.

'Have you any papers to prove you sent it?' she asked, then she laughed. 'Why don't you dig up Meneghini, maybe he can help you prove what you say.'

I was appalled. It was useless talking to her, nothing would make her admit what she had done.

With Andreas' help I tried to put the whole sorry business out of my mind for a time.

On December 16th we had a quiet wedding. I had already got to know his mother and father and his brother's family. They seemed so loving and supportive, light years away from my brood with their endless bickering and plotting. If they ever had any doubts about their son marrying an older woman they never once showed them.

I chose to be married in the Church of the Metamorphosis in my beloved Kiffissia. Although the area has now been absorbed in the incredible growth of Athens over the last few years there are still enough trees and green spaces to remind me of that country place I visited so often with Milton when I was young.

A few weeks later the second poison pen letter was pushed under the door. Andreas had moved into Mother's old apartment and I called him down before I opened it. He took it from me and read it first. It was predictably disgusting, a list of insults to Andreas, trying to poison my mind against him. It was pointless to ask who had done it. There were many who knew that Andreas had stopped me from being so gullible and naturally they hated him intensely.

'I want to leave at once,' I said. 'I can't stay here any longer.'

Andreas tried to persuade me that we shouldn't be too hasty, that to leave Athens was a major act and that perhaps we should visit London first to see if I liked it. But I wasn't in the mood for common sense.

'I just want to get out of here. I want to go.'

He agreed. I suppose the strain of all this enmity had blinded me to the fact that whereas I had only to pack my things and leave, Andreas had to give up his career. Selflessly he did so, resigning from his various posts, ending a lifetime's work with little hope of rebuilding it again. He would not be able to practise medicine in England until he had obtained a licence and for a middle-aged man to re-embark on medical studies in a foreign language was clearly a major task. However, he said he was happy to do so for my sake.

Before we left there was some old business to settle. Now that we had started making contact with people who really knew the full background we had learned that far from being a close friend of my sister Vasso had been a rather troublesome hanger-on. At first she had been considered something of a nuisance, for ever dropping in, trying to ingratiate herself. But gradually, as Maria had sunk into the deep lethargy of her final years, it had seemed easier to let the woman do things for her – odd jobs, errands. So, by degrees, Vasso had wheedled her way into Maria's affairs. By the end, when she died, Maria had no close friends near to her and it was left to Vasso to take over the direction of the funeral and thus of me. The rest I now knew.

On my lawyer's advice, I wrote to Vasso and pointed out that as I was now married I no longer needed her to handle my affairs and that she should realise that my will in her favour was now cancelled. Predictably this provoked another hasty visit, this time with some sort of maid in attendance. It was clear that the arthritis was getting worse and she obviously needed help. She arrived with two Swiss chocolates – our wedding present, she explained. Whether this was an insult or just plain meanness it was impossible to say. Either way we were in no mood for her tricks. Andreas insisted she render an account of the Foundation's finances and she again attempted to browbeat us, telling us that there were lawyers all over Europe handling these things and what could we know about such complicated matters. Better we should keep out of it.

But this time Andreas would not back down. Gradually it began to dawn on her that things were going to change, that at last something was going to be done about the money. She left, again promising to send us all the details. But this time we knew she wouldn't and that action would have to be taken.

In late April we despatched our luggage, closed the apartments and left for London. Andreas had found a flat in Porchester Terrace, Bayswater. We arrived in pouring rain. It seemed to stream down out of heavy dark grey skies. We had left Athens in the first days of spring, blue skies, wild flowers on the mountains. Andreas tried to cheer us both up by saying it would soon pass. The next day it rained again. It was impossible to go out in such weather. Even with our own rooms, I felt the presence of another person in that confined space more acutely than I'd imagined. I was so used to closing the door of my own apartment behind me and finding myself in my own world; now that had gone. It was hard to sleep. I could hear the wind and the rain on the panes. I woke early the next morning and went to the kitchen. Outside the street was utterly deserted, the rain fell in dark lines and rippled the puddles in the overflowing gutters and I realised I had made a terrible mistake. What had I done? I who had wanted so much to be free had now linked my life to that of someone else, someone I hardly knew. I had spent half a lifetime with Milton but had still lived apart from him. Now, after only a few months, here I was cooped up with Andreas in this tiny flat in a foreign city, trapped by freezing rain. I told myself I must have been mad.

Andreas was trying to fix up a post at a local hospital so he had reason to be out part of the day but I knew no one and had in any case no particular desire to get soaking wet by walking about. It was Paris all over again. I was truly my mother's daughter and the realisation appalled me. I ought to have had more sense than to let something like this happen. When Andreas got back that evening I told him it was no use.

'I have to go back,' I said. Though God knows what those words can have meant to him. He must have known me well enough to know I meant what I said so there he was, a man who had thrown away his career for nothing.

I told him I would understand if he wanted to stay, I knew he still dreamed of a medical career in London. I told him I would divide everything in half with him if he wanted a divorce.

What must the poor man have felt? Here we were only a few days into the great adventure that had totally transformed his life and here I was resolutely throwing it all up without any chance of discussion.

He was angry, and at first I assumed that that was his natural reaction to my hasty change of heart. But no, his real distress was that I had considered he might want to leave me. He insisted that no matter what, he wouldn't, he still wanted a wife who would love him sincerely.

I fell silent. Wasn't that part of what was on my mind? Wasn't it less to do with the miserable rain lashing against the windows and more to do with my own inability to accept someone near to me? There I was a little girl again in my room with the little Mary asleep in the next bed and the sounds of our parents' endless bickering echoing against the walls. There was my father slumped in his chair, his business in ruins while Mother kept on and on about how useless he was, about how he could never do anything right. And there was the remembered image of Father charming the ladies, twirling his moustache, betraying my mother. What was the point? Why share in all this unhappiness people hand each other? Better to stay safe and alone within one's own little space. I felt smothered, enclosed.

'You need time,' Andreas said. 'It's all been too much too soon. Give it time.'

He was so unhappy, what could I do but agree? If we were back in Athens it would be better, there was space for us both there and no need to feel enclosed as I did in London.

'We'll go back,' he said. 'As soon as I can arrange it.'

No one could have been more sympathetic nor have better understood the confused state I was in. After twenty-five cold, depressing days we were back in Greece. We took a holiday in Corfu while the apartments were set up again, a chance for us to try to take stock of both our lives. I realised that it was going to be hard for him to pick up the threads of his career and I began to wonder if there wasn't some kind of curse hanging over the Callas family that cast such a destructive pall over those caught up with us.

While he set about trying to build up his private consultancy again, Andreas found a new interest in the legal side of my affairs. It was increasingly clear that we were never going to get any satisfaction out of Vasso and that this would inevitably lead to judicial proceedings of some kind. The problem, as Andreas soon discovered, was that the whole messy business spanned several countries and thus several different legal systems. To sort it all out it was no use simply relying on any one lawyer, you needed to know for yourself what was being discussed. With time on his hands, Andreas now plunged into these strange waters. He would come down to see me – happy whenever he turned up something new, happy to be doing something useful for me. It was a way of sharing something. Vasso, from having been a menace, was rapidly becoming a shared hobby. After two days my lawyer got me to send her a formal letter revoking the Moral Right. This produced an immediate telephone call but this time it was Andreas who answered and who firmly pointed out that the time for talk was over. Because of the way she had behaved there was really nothing more to be said.

She must have realised that the game was nearly up but what else could she do but fight on? I wondered if she had started out meaning to rob me or whether she'd genuinely wanted to help at the beginning but had then been unable to resist the temptation to relieve two gullible women of their inheritance. Either way it was too late to pity her. Her next twist was to panic and try to claim that Andreas had insulted her. She attempted to sue us for defamation in the Greek courts but as there could not possibly be any proof of such an allegation it never even came to trial. She then did something so strange it could only be explained by her sheer desperation at how near she was to being exposed. She brought a civil action in Greece to claim that the Moral Right was hers and not mine. Neither Andreas nor I could imagine how she hoped to prove such a thing; the Moral Right is the automatic possession of the immediate family. What was she trying to do, we wondered? When the case came to court Vasso offered a photocopy of a typed letter with a copy of Mary's signature on the bottom. The letter, supposedly from Mary, made Vasso responsible for her inheritance. It was a palpable fraud, the signature having been cut from another letter and stuck down on the one typed by Vasso herself. In any case, if it was real where was the original and why had it taken her nine years to produce it?

In some ways it was a relief to realise that this woman who had so effectively dominated and used me was no cunning monster after all but a mere opportunist who was now desperately trying to save her skin. She needn't have bothered with such a silly trick, the court refused even to consider the document, ruling that it was in no way a Will of Maria's. They also ruled that, of course, I as the surviving sister was the only possible recipient of the Moral Right. Sadly, with her back to the wall, it was clear that we were going to have to fight all the way. At one point she had told the court that she had never received as much as a single drachma from me even though she knew that I had all the bank transfer documents for seven hundred and ninety-two thousand dollars that I had given her for the Foundation. By lying in this way she was clearly willing to heap perjury on top of theft in order to stave off the evil day.

With Andreas working nearly full-time on the research, the evidence now began to flood in. He next discovered that the Foundation had been set up in the town of Fribourg in Switzerland. As no letters were ever answered, he proposed we take a little holiday and see for ourselves. After much searching, we discovered that the great organisation intended to honour the name of the century's most illustrious soprano was only the name of a notary on a board outside an office, sandwiched between a cheap shoe shop and a hoarding advertising Löwenbrau beer. When I thought of the great cities associated with Maria's successes that should have been home to her Foundation – Milan, Rome, London, New York, Paris – and looked at that miserable sign, the full enormity of what Vasso had done finally sank in. Our next trip was to the South of France where Maître Bensusan, the lawyer who had handled the original agreement with Meneghini, had his summer home. When we told him the story of the missing parcels he was stunned. He had never been asked to pass on Vasso's letter to Meneghini asking where they were. It was obvious to us all why not. So now we knew that she had had most of my share of Mary's things, my sister's very clothes had gone to her. The next blow was to discover that there had never been any question of my having to pay a tax bill on the Paris apartment. Vasso must have sold the shares in the holding company for a fortune and all she had passed on to me was the ludicrous eighty thousand dollars.

'You must think I'm a fool,' I kept saying to Andreas.

But he wouldn't accept such a judgment. 'You're just too good,' he said. 'Too kind-hearted.'

Thank God somebody wasn't laughing at me. For it was that that hurt me most about Vasso. I had willingly given her a fortune in her own right from the sale of the diamonds and yet now I knew she must have laughed herself to sleep thinking about how easy it was to gull me out of the rest of the money as well. I sometimes wondered how she really felt. Was there ever remorse or only the fear of being caught? Had she ever really been my friend or was I just a ridiculous simpleton ready for conning?

The final bad joke was Andreas' discovery that we had been completely misled by our own lawyer way back at the very start of the whole thing. The Greek lawyer in Paris whom we'd gone to for advice in 1977 had apparently advised us badly. Under French law Maria's inheritance was subject to the laws of the land of her citizenship and Maria had renounced her American nationality to remain Greek when she hoped to marry Onassis. As a Greek Orthodox her marriage to Meneghini, a Catholic, was non-existent, let alone the fact that they had divorced in 1971. Maria's will had no force at all under Greek law; all the inheritance belonged to the family.

By 1986 Vasso must have realised that unless the Foundation did something there would be a scandal over the missing funds. As it was the ninth anniversary of Maria's death she organised a televised concert in which various famous singers were given awards for outstanding merit by the Foundation. It was a grotesque travesty of everything Maria, and later I, had hoped to achieve with the money. Why give to those who already had so much?

The idea had been to give assistance to young singers struggling to make a start but Vasso clearly wanted publicity and by offering big stars to television worldwide she got it with ease. She herself presided over the event though it was clear to those who saw her that she was unwell; the arthritis was beginning to take its toll, as no doubt was the strain of knowing that soon she would be exposed.

Watching Vasso's celebration on television I suddenly felt utterly weary. Had it really come to this? Was Mary's memory to be so badly served? I had wanted so much to do something good with the money. If I had simply spent it on myself I would have acknowledged to myself and to the world that I was nothing but the shadow of my sister. That I had refused to do. I had thought that by using the money to help other singers I would be building on what she achieved, not living off the harvest she had sown. But it had all been beyond me. Inexperienced in the ways of the world I was bound to rely on someone and my misfortune was that that someone turned out to be Vasso Devetzi.

Still, there were little things I could still try to do. The following year, 1987, was the tenth anniversary of Mary's death and there was a ceremony at the Athenaeun Cultural Centre in Athens. I gave a prize – this time for a genuine student of music just as Mary would have wished. My sister had many faults but she was never ungenerous to those struggling to make their way in her arduous profession. It is the gravest tragedy that her fortune could not have been spent as she intended. Andreas had now discovered that there was little chance of recovering the money; the wretched Vasso had invested it badly and lost it all.

Ah well, maybe it was meant to be so. By not leaving a will Mary had cast the money into the winds that it might land where it would, one great gust and it was gone. It was another way in which we were very similar, for although she liked to live in luxury she had no

237

interest in money as such; what she wanted was a rich man to take care of her so that she didn't have to worry about anything. Left alone she shopped in Woolworth's and refused to drive anywhere in order to save on petrol. Yes, how similar we turn out to have been at the end, but whereas she was left with no one to help her I at least have Andreas. Happily his medical practice is growing again, though with all he has had to learn in order to handle my affairs he could become an international lawyer one day.

I hope we have heard the end of the Callas fortune. There does seem to have been a curse on it as Vasso discovered. In that anniversary year, 1987, her illness finally caught up with her and she sank into a painful terminal condition, crippled with arthritis at last. She died that November. Her folly lived on after her for in her will she requested that the Greek government scatter her ashes on the Aegean near the spot where she had caused those of my sister to be blown back at her. Not surprisingly they demurred.

Now there is no one left to disturb my peace. I live quietly in my apartment, Andreas feels that I am protected and loved. Before I finish I would like to thank my Lord who never deserted me throughout a long and difficult life. Now he has given me a husband who tries in every way to see that I am happy. I feel confident and secure now that he is near me. And I have my true friends – my cousin Mirka and her family, for example, and my niece Vassiliki and my dear cousin Heleni in America who has happily been able to visit me at last. Sometimes Andreas and I stay near his parents' summer house at Nea Makri on the coast and we always take a little holiday in Kiffissia, as ever my favourite spot. Apart from that I have little desire for change or excitement of any kind.

But there are some things that need to be settled before the lamps are finally dimmed. Two years ago I got Andreas to use his influence as a doctor to have Mother disinterred so that I could rebury her with Father. We placed her underneath him so that she could know for eternity the rôle she ought better to have fulfilled during life. Strangely enough Andreas said that the body had hardly decomposed; it was as if she were waiting for the move.

What sadness my family has known. I often think of little Vassily whose life ended so abruptly. Had he lived Mother might never have turned her burning ambition on to Maria who might thus have grown up a normal, happy woman. She always told me she longed for children. 'Give me twins and I will be happy,' she said.

Fortunately I never wanted them. Perhaps Vassily's death was a sign that our line was to end. Maria gave up everything for her art and I was cheated of any chance to fulfil myself.

It is strange to realise that there was an earlier example of all this: when I finally received Mary's books I was intrigued to read the story of Maria Malibran, the soprano she so identified with. Perusing Malibran's life I was amazed to discover that she too had had a sister who had given up a career as a singer for the man she loved.

Still, I often say to myself, today you must start practising again then who knows what might happen? Everyone is entitled to dream.

I am not discontented. I alone of my extraordinary family have found a little peace now that I am no longer the sister, but just myself alone, the last Callas.

APPENDIX
The Performances of Maria Callas in Greece 1938–45

The full range of my sister's performances in Greece between 1938 and 1945 has never been fully documented outside Greece. Most biographies appear to have based their information on those productions my sister remembered or chose to confirm. The full list is in fact far more extensive than any of her biographies credit and I am grateful to Dr Polivios Marchand who let me use his excellent research into this period to stimulate my own recollections.

SECTION ONE

Performances during 1938–39 while studying under Maria Trivella at the National Conservatory.

Monday, April 11th, 1938
Parnassos Concert Hall
Recital with fellow students
Weber: *Der Freischütz*: aria
Gounod: *La reine de Saba*: aria
Psarouda: 'Two Nights': Greek song
Puccini: *Tosca*, duet with John Cambanis, a professional tenor, who
    was also a pupil of Trivella.
Pianist: Stefanos Valtetsiotis

Sunday, April 2nd, 1939
Location unknown

Mascagni: *Cavalleria Rusticana*
  Santuzza: Maria Callas
  Turiddu: V. Semeriotis
  Lucia: A. Copanou
  Alfio: C. Atheneos
  Lola: P. Euthemiadou

Monday, May 22nd, 1939
Parnassos Concert Hall
Offenbach: *Les Contes d'Hoffmann*: 'Belle nuit, ô nuit d'amour', duet
  with A. Bourdacou
Weber: *Oberon*: aria
Verdi: *Aida*: 'Ritorna Vincitor'
Psarouda: 'I Will Not Forget You': Greek song
Verdi: *Aida*: 'O, terra, addio', duet with the tenor Zanni Campani
Pianist: Stefanos Valtetsiotis

Tuesday, May 23rd, 1939
Parnassos Concert Hall
Weber: *Oberon*: aria
Massenet: *Thaïs*: 'Air du Miroir'

Sunday, June 25th, 1939
Location unknown
Verdi: *Un Ballo in Maschera*: rôle of Amelia (act 3)
Mascagni: *Cavalleria Rusticana*: rôle of Santuzza (scene 2)
Pianist: Elli Necolaidou

SECTION TWO

Performances during 1938–39 while studying under Elvira de
Hidalgo at the Athens Conservatory

Friday, February 23rd, 1940
Odeon Concert Hall
Bellini: *Norma*: 'Mira, o Norma', duet with Arda Mandikian
Pianist: Gerassimos Coundouris

Sunday, June 16th, 1940
Odeon Concert Hall
Puccini: *Suor Angelica*
　　Suor Angelica: Maria Callas

SECTION THREE

Performances during 1940–45 while under contract to the Lyric
Theatre

Tuesday, January 21st, 1941
Palace Theatre
Franz von Suppé: *Boccaccio*
　　Beatrice: Maria Callas

Thursday, July 3rd, 1941
Park Summer Theatre
Franz von Suppé: *Boccaccio*
　　Beatrice: Maria Callas

August 27th, 1942
Summer Theatre, Klauthmonos Square
Puccini: *Tosca*
　　Floria Tosca: Maria Callas
　　Cavaradossi: A. Dellendas
　　Scarpia: S. Calogeras

September 8th, 1942
Summer Theatre, Klauthmonos Square
Puccini: *Tosca*
　　Floria Tosca: Maria Callas
　　Cavaradossi: L. Couroussopoulos
　　Scarpia: T. Xirellis

October 1942
Palace Theatre, Salonika
Concert of Rossini arias for Italian troops

Friday, February 19th, 1943
Location unknown
M. Calomeri: *Ho Protomastoras*
  Maria Callas in chorus during intermezzo between first and
  second acts.

Sunday, February 28th, 1943
Sporting Cinema, Nea Smerni, Athens
Benefit concert
Music unknown

Thursday, April 22nd, 1943
Casa d'Italia
Giovanni Battista Pergolesi: *Stabat Mater*, with Arda Mandikian
  (mezzo)
Conductor: G. Lycoudis

Saturday, July 17th, 1943
Summer Theatre, Klauthmonos Square
Puccini: *Tosca*
  Floria Tosca: Maria Callas
  Cavaradossi: A. Dellendas
  Scarpia: T. Xirellis

Wednesday, July 21st, 1943
Costa Moussouri Summer Theatre
Maria Callas solo recital of arias:
Handel: *Atalanta*: 'Care Selve'
Rossini: *La Cenerentola*
Cilea: *Adriana Lecouvrer*
Verdi: *Il Trovatore*
Lavda: 'They Marry My Love': Greek song
Pianist: A. Paredis

August 1943
White Tower Theatre, Salonika
Concert of music by Schubert and Brahms for the Italian troops

Sunday, September 26th, 1943
Olympia Theatre
Benefit concert
Beethoven: *Fidelio*: aria
Massenet: *Thaïs*: aria
Verdi: *Aida*: 'Ritorna vincitor'
Mozart: 'Et Incarnatus Est'
Turina: 'Canciones español'
Lavda: 'They Marry My Love': Greek song
Pianist: Costas Cydoniatis

Sunday, December 12th, 1943
Cotopouli-Rex Theatre
Benefit concert
Beethoven: *Fidelio*
Rossini: *Semiramide*
Verdi: *Il Trovatore*
Turina: 'Canciones español'
Pianist: L. Androutsopoulos

Saturday, April 22nd, 1944
Olympia Theatre
d'Albert: *Tiefland*
   Martha: Maria Callas

Saturday, May 21st, 1944
Olympia Theatre
Mascagni: *Cavalleria Rusticana*
   Santuzza: Maria Callas
   Turiddu: A. Dellendas
   Alfio: T. Tsoubris
   Lola: M. Courahani

Sunday, May 22nd, 1944
Olympia Theatre
Benefit concert with other artistes
Bellini: *Norma*: aria

July, 1944
Olympia Theatre
M. Calomeri: *Ho Protomastoras*
  Smaragda: Maria Callas

Monday, August 14th, 1944
Herodes Atticus Theatre
Beethoven: *Fidelio*
  Leonore: Maria Callas
  Florestan: A. Dellendas
  Pizarro: E. Magliveras
  Marcelline: Z. Vlachopoulou

October 1944
Salonika
Concert for troops
Music unknown

Wednesday, March 14th, 1945
Olympia Theatre
d'Albert: *Tiefland*
  Martha: Maria Callas

Tuesday, March 20th, 1945
Olympia Theatre
Musical afternoon for British troops
Anonymous: 'Willow, Willow'
Landon Ronald: 'Love, I Have Won You'
Ralph Vaughan Williams: 'On Wenlock Edge'
Conductor: Totis Caralevanos

Friday, August 3rd, 1945
Cotopouli-Rex Theatre
Farewell recital
Arias from:
Mozart: *Don Giovanni*
Rossini: *Semiramide*
Verdi: *Aida*
Verdi: *Il Trovatore*
Weber: *Oberon*

Spanish folk songs
Greek folk songs
Pianist: Alice Lycoudi

Wednesday, September 5th, 1945
Summer Theatre, Alexandras Avenue
Millöcker: *Der Bettelstudent*
   Laura: Maria Callas
Maria Callas did not complete the run of this opera, having left for
America on September 14th, 1945

PICTURE
ACKNOWLEDGMENTS

All the photographs are from a private collection with the exception of page 6 above right, Popperfoto and pages 7 above and 8 above, Hulton Picture Company (Keystone Collection).